1973

Soldiers without Enemies

≫ LARRY L. FABIAN ≪

Soldiers without Enemies

PREPARING THE UNITED NATIONS FOR PEACEKEEPING

THE BROOKINGS INSTITUTION
Washington, D.C.

THE BROOKINGS INSTITUTION is an independent organization devoted to nonpartisan research, education, and publication in economics, government, foreign policy, and the social sciences generally. Its principal purposes are to aid in the development of sound public policies and to promote public understanding of issues of national importance.

The Institution was founded on December 8, 1927, to merge the activities of the Institute for Government Research, founded in 1916, the Institute of Economics, founded in 1922, and the Robert Brookings Graduate School of Economics and Government, founded in 1924.

The general administration of the Institution is the responsibility of a Board of Trustees charged with maintaining the independence of the staff and fostering the most favorable conditions for creative research and education. The immediate direction of the policies, program, and staff of the Institution is vested in the President, assisted by an advisory committee of the officers and staff.

In publishing a study, the Institution presents it as a competent treatment of a subject worthy of public consideration. The interpretations and conclusions in such publications are those of the author or authors and do not necessarily reflect the views of the other staff members, officers, or trustees of the Brookings Institution.

Foreword

SELECT AT RANDOM any standard litany of proposals aimed at the goal of "a stronger, more effective United Nations," and almost without exception it will somewhere proclaim a need to bolster the organization's peacekeeping capabilities. This book explores the problems and prospects of doing so. The author analyzes why international peacekeeping institutions still remain underdeveloped, even after the 1970 observance of the UN's entry into a second quarter century. He explains how some improvised building of peacekeeping institutions has been possible despite persistent and often intense political controversy over the UN's responsibilities as a peacekeeper, and he speculates about what must happen if substantially improved peacekeeping mechanisms are to emerge and expand in the years ahead.

This study was conducted as part of the Brookings Foreign Policy Studies Program, under the direction of Henry Owen. The author had the benefit of the views of an advisory committee, which convened at various stages in the planning and execution of the project. Members of the committee were Robert E. Asher of Brookings; Lincoln P. Bloomfield of the Massachusetts Institute of Technology; Arthur M. Cox, formerly of Brookings; Ambassador Seymour M. Finger of the United States Mission to the United Nations; Colonel Bengt Hultgren of the Swedish Mission to the United Nations; Elmore Jackson of the United Nations Association of the United States of America; James E. Knott, formerly of the International Information Center for Peace-

Keeping Operations; Ernest W. Lefever of Brookings; Vice Admiral John M. Lee, formerly of the United States Mission to the United Nations; Karl Mathiasen III, formerly of Brookings; and Nathan Pelcovits of the Department of State.

The author also wishes to thank, for their helpful comments and suggestions, Edward K. Hamilton, formerly of Brookings; Richard N. Gardner, Louis Henkin, David A. Kay, and Ruth B. Russell, all of Columbia University; John W. Holmes of the Canadian Institute of International Affairs; and Anne Winslow of the Carnegie Endowment for International Peace. The author is indebted to Daniel Adams, who served briefly but valuably as his research assistant, and to Merle G. Fabian, whose professional skills as a bibliographer were indispensable in the preparation of the book's extensive documentary citations. The book was edited by Elizabeth H. Cross, and indexed by Helen B. Eisenhart.

As in all Brookings studies, the interpretations and conclusions are solely the author's and should not be attributed to those whom he consulted or to the Brookings Institution, its trustees, officers, or staff.

KERMIT GORDON
President

November 1970
Washington, D.C.

Contents

Soldiers without Enemies

GLOSSARY

ONUC	United Nations Congo Operation (*Opération des Nations Unies au Congo*)
UNCI	United Nations Commission for Indonesia
UNCIP	United Nations Commission for India and Pakistan
UNCIVPOL	United Nations Civilian Police (Cyprus)
UNEF	United Nations Emergency Force (Middle East)
UNFICYP	United Nations Force in Cyprus
UNIPOM	United Nations India-Pakistan Observation Mission
UNMOGIP	United Nations Military Observer Group in India and Pakistan
UNOGIL	United Nations Observer Group in Lebanon
UNSCOB	United Nations Special Commission on the Balkans
UNSF	United Nations Security Force (West New Guinea or West Irian)
UNTEA	United Nations Temporary Executive Authority (West Irian)
UNTSO	United Nations Truce Supervision Organization (Middle East)
UNYOM	United Nations Yemen Observation Mission

ONE

From Collective Security
to Peacekeeping

THE United Nations was born into a world soon to be transformed fundamentally and irreversibly. Nowhere has the impact been greater than on the organization's career as a peace preserver. Not that declared purposes ever changed. "To maintain international peace and security," as the Charter puts it, has been no less energizing a goal for the UN during postwar years than it was for the constitution makers gathered at San Francisco in the early summer of 1945, a few months before the atomic bomb devastated Hiroshima. What did change were the assumptions about how this mandate could be translated into action.

To read the Charter is to glimpse the kind of future the drafters of that document were making provision for, even though many were not optimistic about its likelihood. Great powers, their wartime unity sufficiently preserved, were to be the foundation of a new collective security system. They jointly were to guide it from the Security Council; they were to guarantee it with armed forces, principally their own, placed at the Council's disposal; they were to guard their own interests from unwanted UN action by their veto power, without which none of the Big Five would have joined the UN. Potential aggressors were to be deterred or, if this failed, were to be punished by the combined military might of the international community.

But it was a community in name only. The Charter framework, aimed as it was at preventing another war like the last one, rapidly lost its relevance in the cold war between nuclear and ideological adversaries, each able to immobilize the Security Council, each at the head of rival military blocs in a divided Europe, and each determined to wage the cold war on a worldwide scale. Furthermore, one of the postwar great powers, the Peking government, remained excluded from and stridently hostile toward the organization that had condemned it for its inter- vention in the Korean conflict. For a brief period, the United States successfully enlisted as an ally in its containment strategy a United Nations whose early majorities were regarded as fully dependable by Washington. Thus the Korean war was fought under a UN umbrella. Membership rolls of the UN, however, expanded after the mid-1950s, and the new entries proved reluctant to have the organization aligned with either half of a bipolar world. In these circumstances no system of global collective security was a realistic prospect. If the UN were to help its members order their relations peacefully, the Charter version of peace preservation would have to be consigned to another day. The organization would have to trim its aspirations and modify its self- conception as an instrument of international security.

These things were done, gradually and imperfectly, but in ways that radically shifted the emphases of 1945. The metamorphosis has been accurately summarized in this single paragraph:

> Perhaps the most significant development in the thinking of scholars and statesmen about international organization in the postwar period has been their gradual emancipation from the collective security fixation, their breaking out of the intel- lectual rut in which it was taken for granted that the suppression of aggression was so crucial a function of general international organizations that if this function could not be exercised, the only issue worth thinking about was how to make its exercise possible. Dag Hammarskjold gave dramatic and forceful expression to the new and less constricted approach to international organization when he put the question of how the United Nations could contribute directly to keeping the peace when it could not enforce the peace and answered the question by formulating the theory of preventive diplomacy, now generally known as peacekeeping.[1]

This change has not been a wholesale one. Escaping from a "fixation" about collective security need not mean discarding it altogether as an area of concern. A reminder of its possible importance is provided by the nuclear nonproliferation treaty that entered into force in 1970. The three Security Council signatories, the United States, the United Kingdom, and the Soviet Union, pledged themselves to protective action through the Council on behalf of any nonnuclear state victimized by the threat or actual use of nuclear weapons—a guarantee on which nuclear have-nots insisted during negotiation of the treaty and one which could conceivably entail a joint response to aggression that would in some ways resemble classic models of collective security.[2] Despite this contingency, priorities for a UN role in peace maintenance have been reordered, and peacekeeping has come to occupy the place of greater prominence.

Here, too, evolution has been very gradual. While Dag Hammarskjöld exerted enormous influence both in refining concepts about peacekeeping and in applying them as no one before him had done, the idea of peacekeeping really preceded him. Even before he was given responsibility in 1956 for interposing the UN's first large force between Egypt and Israel following the Suez war, the UN had begun experimenting—as the League of Nations had done—with the peacekeeping alternative to collective security. It required no finding that anyone was guilty of aggression, no application of armed force by the UN against a delinquent state, and no enforcement of political settlements on disputants not voluntarily accepting them. Hammarskjöld and the experience predating his UN stewardship together generated "consensual" peacekeeping.

This casts the UN in the role of an impartial intermediary in local wars or tense situations that threaten stability. With the consent of the parties directly involved, UN peacekeepers employ measures short of armed force to damp down local violence, to reduce risks of escalation and outside military intervention, and to ensure an atmosphere as conducive as possible to constructive negotiations. In a dozen such situations since 1946, where vital interests of the superpowers were not directly engaged, the UN has performed these politically impartial, essentially noncoercive peacekeeping chores. Each case has added impetus to the redirection of UN doctrine habitually associated with the name Hammarskjöld.

Not only has the organization provided concrete assistance in specific crises, it also has tried to do whatever it could to increase its capabilities for responding effectively to future ones. This attentiveness to longer-range requirements, though widely considered an important part of the

UN's vocation as a peacekeeper, has produced meager results. Erratically, often energetically, but with little lasting success, efforts have been made over the years to build peacekeeping institutions durable enough to outlive individual crises and adaptable enough to anticipate diverse types of peacekeeping assignments. These objectives call for a network of technical arrangements and diplomatic understandings—at the UN, and within or among member governments—that will enable the UN to muster the requisite human and material resources for future peacekeeping. They call for something the UN still lacks, namely, a comprehensive system of preparedness for peacekeeping.

This notion of a preparedness system needs to be broadly viewed. It means more than merely an assortment of well-conceived technical designs, although it does include a substantial technical dimension. For example, UN members must be ready to supply peacekeeping manpower—sometimes a taxing succession of large military units, sometimes only smaller contingents of officers or specialists. The secretariat must be ready to mobilize international civil servants able to provide political management for peacekeeping operations. Logistical and other material support must also be available. But these ingredients, these aspects of resource organization, are only the dependent half of the UN's preparedness agenda. The controlling half is almost wholly nontechnical, for preparedness is above all the handmaiden of politics. A comprehensive preparedness system can be constructed only when there is a working diplomatic consensus behind it. The search for this consensus is the second dimension of preparedness. Available today in some abundance are all manner of blueprints for permanent or semipermanent UN forces, schemata for centralized military planning at the secretariat, curricula for international training in peacekeeping skills, suggestions for easing the UN's logistical burdens, and ideas for using new technologies such as surveillance and monitoring devices in the service of UN peacekeeping objectives. Most of these are gathering dust on shelves around the world, not necessarily because they lack intrinsic merit—some are quite sensible—but because they are not judged solely (or even largely) on their reasonableness or technical sufficiency. Instead they are measured ultimately against the powerful UN members' political preferences, against their fundamental views about what kind of peacekeeping responsibilities the UN ought to have, and against their attitudes on how any system of UN preparedness should be politically controlled.

These two dimensions—the diplomacy of preparedness and the resource commitments on which a preparedness system must depend—dominate this book. They are examined from both a historical and a contemporary standpoint, and the emphasis is on preparedness for peacekeeping rather than on the actual peacekeeping operations. The aim is not to resift once again the performance records of successive peacekeeping missions or the lessons to be learned from them. Theorists and practitioners have by now written authoritatively on these topics, yet far less attention has been given to efforts to fashion basic peacekeeping institutions.

The intellectual conversion from collective security preoccupations to peacekeeping ones is the core phenomenon around which this book is organized. As this change came into sharper relief and as new concepts about the peacekeeping function acquired greater acceptance, there was evidence of a profound reorientation in thinking about UN preparedness. A comprehensive measure of the international organization as a peacekeeper is incomplete unless it explores the complementarity of these trends. The chapters that follow deal, in this sense only, with both peacekeeping and preparedness. For as peacekeeping became progressively more closely identified with politically impartial and essentially noncoercive UN behavior in conflict management, it became increasingly clear that the military or quasi-military institutions needed to perform these tasks were going to be qualitatively different from the ones envisaged in the Charter.

In the sphere of resource organization, the differences between preparedness for collective security and preparedness for peacekeeping are conspicuous. Collective security armies, for instance, were to be largely Big Five armies, a proviso not written explicitly into the Charter, but imprinted there—in one writer's metaphor—"in invisible ink."[3] These permanent members of the Security Council were to be the mainstays of UN striking forces because they were thought to possess the political and military weight to enforce the UN's collective will rather than because they displayed political impartiality and lack of interest in outcomes of local quarrels. But the latter are often the crucial badges of a peacekeeper. They are also the grounds on which the permanent members have been excluded from participating in most peacekeeping missions. This ineligibility has led to one of the most important of all developments in UN preparedness activities: the emergence of a grouping of relatively like-minded, dependable peacekeeping nations from among the middle and smaller powers at the UN. Impartial behavior requires impartial agents, and on them have fallen the major burdens of providing peacekeeping soldiers and services. Their interest in this role has been stimulated by the fact that peacekeeping involves impartial, noncoercive services, not the sanctions type of warmaking the Charter's collective security obligations would have entailed.

In the diplomacy of preparedness, the differences have been just as fundamental. To prepare the UN for its collective security responsibilities, the Big Five were to have reached a sufficient political consensus on the detailed structure and functioning of the Council's military arm, particularly their own contributions to it. After their failure to do so led to stalemated negotiations in the early years of the UN, they remained in a basic standoff about whether and how to create any military institutions at all to act on behalf of the UN, either for collective security or for peacekeeping. Instead of their agreement being the basis for institutional growth, their disagreement guaranteed persistent stagnation. If the impasse were to be broken others would have to take the diplomatic lead. A secretary-general, an interested middle power, or a temporary coalition of especially concerned peacekeeping nations tried occasionally to find ways of maneuvering around the deadlock. But they never got very far: preparedness institutions could not be substantially strengthened without consensus among the major powers, especially the superpowers, as a minimum permissive condition.

That the superpowers have been the decisive protagonists throughout the history of UN preparedness diplomacy is another phenomenon emphasized at numerous junctures in this book. Much has already been written about the causes and the consequences of the progressive "de-Americanization" of the UN. A now-familiar line of reasoning underscores the effects of the General Assembly's membership explosion. Washington's once-favorite avenue for nullifying the force of Soviet vetoes in the Council rapidly lost its pro-Western "automatic majorities." After having vigorously championed use of the Assembly, the United States came to view it with some apprehension. For a time during the 1960s, official warning bells sounded the theme of a so-called apportionment problem. Disparities between "real" power and voting power, went the argument, had reached alarming proportions, threatening to open the way to unrepresentative, potentially irresponsible Assembly actions. While these assertions did raise a genuine issue of how to balance power and responsibility in the UN, they occasionally were used somewhat self-servingly. (Neither superpower has been able to resist the strong temptation to support "majoritarianism" for sympathetic majorities only; in any event the Assembly has been malapportioned right from the very beginning, because in the early years it was weighted in Washington's favor by a bloc of "over-represented" Latin American votes almost always available to the West on vital issues.[4]) What is worth stressing here, however, is that this kind of argument tended to obscure another apportionment problem: the one between the United States and the Soviet Union.

Seen in retrospect, the evolution of superpower relations at the United Nations is traceable through the gradual reapportionment of their power in the organization's deliberative bodies and their influence over its policies. This larger pattern has altered balances in several respects. Paradoxically, both superpowers now often find themselves part of a new minority in the UN on matters that divide members along North-South rather than East-West lines. Both, for example, are often on the receiving end of demands from an insistent "many" for larger transfers of wealth to the Third World poor or for special concessions in big-power arms-control arrangements that touch interests of the less powerful. On a wide range of other concerns, the old two-way distribution has shifted. One superpower has been losing its customary political predominance and has been having to work harder to exert leverage that it once took for granted. The other has been breaking out of its strictly defensive position and has succeeded in making itself a force to contend with in the organization rather than one whose irritating obstructiveness had somehow to be sidestepped. In the course of these changes the United States has lost its assumed majority—in a political not simply a voting sense—while the Soviet Union has enlarged its role far beyond that of leader of a permanent minority.[5]

This overall process has influenced nearly everything to do with preparedness institutions and diplomacy. As the United Nations aged, American views on the subject of the organization's military prepared-ness ceased to prevail. Even though the superpowers' interests con-verged sufficiently on a number of occasions to permit UN peace-keeping forces to be improvised and launched on an ad hoc basis, the Russians almost routinely resisted Western moves to persuade the organization to create significant, longer-range preparedness capabilities. Doctrinal objections played a part, in that any fundamental reforms would, in the Soviet view, have given the UN some of the trappings of power that only sovereign states were entitled to—recall Soviet Foreign Minister Andrei Vishinsky's contemptuous remark of twenty years ago that a secretary-general does not need military expertise to run mimeograph machines.[6] Later, in the second half of the 1950s, another preparedness proposal was rejected, this time in language that clarified a more immediate, perhaps more compelling reason for Soviet objections: new UN capabilities would be placed "in effect into the hands of the United States and its partners in NATO and would be used for causes having nothing in common with the objectives of the United Nations."[7]

In large measure Soviet opposition was responsible for the inability of the United States and other strong proponents of peacekeeping to improve UN preparedness in the ambitious directions they desired. In the post-Stalin era, and particularly after *Sputnik*, the Russians insisted on an equal voice in UN affairs they considered critical. Only on these conditions would they negotiate in UN bodies dealing with outer space and disarmament questions; even more appropriate, they felt, were direct talks on these issues between the Big Two. The same motives led to the Soviet troika proposals, which were aimed at restructuring not only the UN secretariat but also a number of spe-cialized agencies to permit greater Russian influence. The logic of these demands extended to all the major aspects of preparedness for peace-keeping. The 1960s were to demonstrate that this logic was fully compatible with the superpowers' growing willingness to consider their mutual interests served by the kind of UN peacekeeping they jointly approved—for example, when violence erupted in Cyprus in 1964 and on the India-Pakistan border the following year. Moreover, they came to realize that their reach within the UN, however pervasive, was finite. Just as the bulk of the membership turned down the troika gambit, so too they refused to support the campaign led by the United States in the mid-sixties to strip the Soviet Union of its Assembly vote as a penalty for being in arrears on peacekeeping dues. Subsequently, when negotiations about preparedness were started in a special committee of the Assembly, both superpowers were full and coequal participants. That they were discussing these matters together at all was in itself novel in UN annals. More important, the controlling ground rules for this dialogue carried an unmistakable message: if there is to be more peacekeeping, and better preparedness for it, terms must be worked out that are acceptable to both of the main players.

This study attempts to provide a basic political history of preparedness for UN peacekeeping, to isolate the factors most instrumental in shaping preparedness institutions and diplomacy, and to suggest some desiderata for analysts and policy makers thinking about the future of UN preparedness.

Chapter 2 addresses a preliminary question: "What is it that is being prepared for?" If it is correct to say that preparedness is given a distinctive identity by the version of peace maintenance for which it is intended, then it seems helpful at the outset to sketch briefly the essentials of the idea of peacekeeping that has displaced collective security as the UN's main motif and to introduce the categories of technical requirements that it generates. The basis for links between peacekeeping and preparedness rests largely on the impartial and non-coercive features of peacekeeping measures. These two principles lead to various consequences that are explored in subsequent chapters: certain special kinds of operational skills are most desirable, certain countries tend to be the most politically acceptable as peacekeepers and therefore the most enthusiastic about national preparedness programs such as the creation of UN standby forces, certain preparedness tasks fall most readily upon the secretary-general and other international civil servants from the secretariat, and certain approaches to preparedness diplomacy have proved to be more productive than others.

Chapters 3 and 4 inquire into the antecedents of Hammarskjöld's departure from the conventional wisdom about collective security. Twentieth-century international organization up to the time of the UN's second secretary-general is sprinkled with predecessors of peacekeeping. To some extent pre-League experience is also relevant. Yet it was the League's sparse record of peacekeeping that gave the first hints of what an adequate preparedness system would have to include. And it was during the UN's first decade, when the requirements for peacekeeping were becoming clearer in outline, that the rudiments of such a system became a subject of active concern on the part of the secretariat and some member states. The nature of present-day preparedness diplomacy, the status of preparedness, and projections into the future are almost incomprehensible unless sufficient account is taken of the residues from these early years at the UN. In them occurred the initial, unsuccessful attempts to equip the UN with military capabilities. In them is rooted much of the mistrust that still characterizes superpower dealings on preparedness matters and that still prompts Soviet suspicion of any significant preparedness activities by the secretariat. In them are revealed the severe limitations—which were to reappear frequently, if in different guises, during later years—of a general international organization's capacity to create military institutions when its principal members hold incompatible preferences about what courses the organization should pursue to achieve peace and security.

Chapters 5 and 6 examine in considerable detail the national preparedness programs that were inaugurated as a direct consequence of Hammarskjöld's reaiming of UN concerns toward peacekeeping. Well aware that this shift created a requirement for companion institutions to support it, the secretary-general set about articulating fresh preparedness proposals and encouraging their implementation. His target audiences, indeed his tacit allies, were those middle powers who, being high on the list of potential peacekeepers, formed a sort of preparedness constituency within the UN. Most preparedness results were, to a large degree, the outcome of a determined dialogue between Hammarskjöld and this constituency. To begin with, the efforts of these states drew much of their initial momentum from his singular style of leadership, which he displayed here as elsewhere to move the UN in constructive directions despite an imperfect or even a plainly inadequate political consensus inside the organization. This constituency also contained states that were strongly self-motivated to be responsive to the secretary-general's suggestions, for they regarded their own national interests as well served by an active involvement in peacekeeping and preparedness. It reinforced or blended well with their own foreign policy and defense objectives, their world views, and their general attitudes toward participation in international organization. Their national preparedness programs—designed to facilitate rapid and effective dispatch of men and material assistance to future UN peacekeeping operations—started to take hold in the late 1950s and early 1960s, first in Canada, then in the Nordic countries, and eventually in a handful of others as well. The development of these programs since their inception and the catalog of their successes and failures provide the raw materials for a virtual guidebook to national preparedness planning in years to come. They help to illuminate not only the internal problems and choices facing national establishments committed to preparedness programs but also the connections between the broader environment of preparedness diplomacy and what happens in national contexts.

Chapters 7 and 8, respectively, attempt to answer two broad questions about the overall state of preparedness for UN peacekeeping. First, What determines the kind, scope, and quality of the preparedness system at any given time? Second, What are the prospects for the foreseeable future? Both lines of inquiry call for an appreciation of diplomatic and technical dimensions; both are enhanced by a sense of those events and turning points in UN preparedness history that most directly condition contemporary attitudes about the subject; both require a close look at the details of diplomatic bargaining over preparedness in the 1960s, at the special interests of the secretary-general and the secretariat, and at the concerns of the military practitioners. There is a dynamic interaction among all these actors, and the competing demands that result are responsible for shaping the general contours of preparedness. On the basis of these analyses, an effort is made here to devise a medium-range strategy for UN preparedness, one that synthesizes the principal thinking and experience into a number of guiding propositions that ought to inform future preparedness objectives. Finally, from this strategy is drawn a series of specific policy implications for the UN and its members, suggesting one possible avenue for setting in motion desirable changes in the system of preparedness for peacekeeping.

TWO

Preparedness for United Nations Peacekeeping: The Setting

THAT "the quality of its courts of law and its armies gives the most minute insight into the essence of an empire"[1] was Goethe's way of saying what today's sociologists understand with increasing refinement: military institutions are characteristic offspring of the society that breeds them. This interdependence is timeless, no more evident now than when armies were first levied, no more operative in Western than in non-Western cultures, or in industrialized than in modernizing countries. The interplay is most easily discerned during historical periods of profound social and political upheaval. From early imperial Rome to the later Eastern empire, from the beginnings of the Middle Ages to their terminal shading into incipient nationalism, from postfeudal modernity to the French Revolution—all were transitions associated with enormous changes in military forms and doctrine.

International military institutions are not exempt. If societal roots have shaped military institutions in contemporary nation-states, they have decisively determined the military configuration of this century's two experiments with global organization. Neither the League of Nations nor the United Nations ever possessed the multinational armies permitted by their constitutions. Their architects constructed not permanent military capabilities but permanent incongruities between what the organizations were expected to do to preserve peace and the military resources available to them for this purpose. Twice international society could not and would not tolerate any significant military power in the hands of world agencies; twice the chasm was unbridgeable between the political milieu and the international military arrays that were supposed to function within it and on its behalf.

President Woodrow Wilson's self-typed first draft of what eventually became the League Covenant anticipated that members might have to resist, with their combined armed might, violations of the peace and of the objectives of the League.[2] His prescriptions to this end were weakened during negotiations prior to and at Versailles, so the Covenant, consonant with its partly pacifist intellectual underpinnings, threatened wrongdoers mainly with economic rather than military sanctions—a priority that was thought justified by the relative success of Allied economic warfare during World War I. Yet the European victors and a United States soon to abandon the fledgling organization did empower the League Council to recommend what military resources members might contribute ad hoc to any specific collective action.

Like its progenitor, the UN bore many marks of an American president's thinking. By 1942, at an embryonic stage in the planning, Franklin D. Roosevelt conceived of a peacetime concert of the Big Four, whom he saw as the world's "four policemen" acting through the new organization.[3] Out of San Francisco came a charter that theoretically gave its Security Council the means to mobilize forces that the League never had, and gave it the authority to order mandatory use of these resources. When this far more ambitious collective security structure was rapidly disfigured beyond recognition by the emergent cold war, the great power policemen, dominating the Council and protected by their vetoes, were simply confirming that they saw each other as community lawbreakers rather than as coguarantors of a stable world peace.

Although they were unable to raise the armies anticipated by their founders, both organizations could call upon their members to supply other types of military forces for the purpose of carrying out the peacekeeping tasks that in practice were coming to overshadow traditional collective security concerns. But not until after the mid-1950s did the UN's peacekeeping responsibilities become demanding enough to warrant widespread attention to the lack of readiness for future contingencies. Only then did statesmen begin to appreciate sufficiently how great the political and technical obstacles to the creation of an effective system of preparedness for peacekeeping would be. Within the space of several years they saw how difficult it would be to provide a controversy-ridden UN with military resources, and they saw how firmly the idea of international military institutions would be resisted in a world of sovereigns accustomed to discounting them as Pollyannaish, useless, or perhaps even downright dangerous.

Peacekeeping: An Overview

Diplomatic lexicons bulge with overused, ill-defined words. One of them is "peacekeeping," a term now so notoriously distended and imprecise that the phrase "preparedness for peacekeeping" will invariably convey too much. For rhetorical purposes the word is very often treated as virtually open-ended and is used with a literalism that defies clarity: any policy or behavior avowedly intended to keep someone's version of peace is labeled "peacekeeping." So apologists and disinterested observers alike can freely, almost casually, classify under a peacekeeping rubric such disparate phenomena as European military intervention in former colonies, the North Atlantic Treaty Organization (NATO) deterrent, Soviet intervention in Hungary or Czechoslovakia, the prospects held out by African states for regional military measures against South Africa, the 1965 American intervention in the Dominican Republic, and the Vietnam war, as well as the conventional UN missions in Cyprus, the Middle East, Kashmir, and elsewhere. Also, voiced occasionally in the United States during recent years is the wistful refrain that future, more effective UN peacekeeping capabilities could somehow "take over" or "substitute" for U.S. military "peacekeeping" if only the UN possessed the requisite military forces and political will. This syndrome predates the new isolationism spawned by Vietnam, although it has certainly been heard more often as war frustrations have grown. It rests on an assumption, often unstated, that, despite qualitatively different political objectives and methods, UN peacekeeping is really only a kind of unilateral intervention on a large scale, a cheaper, domestically more palatable route for achieving similar ends.[4] Rhetorical distortions like these evoke a skepticism akin to Alice's commonsense response to Humpty Dumpty's linguistic tyranny: "The question is," she objected, "whether you *can* make words mean so many things."

You cannot, of course—not without distorting the concept of peacekeeping to a point where it means everything and nothing. To give "preparedness for peacekeeping" a coherent and manageable identity, the phrase is used throughout this book to denote preparedness for a particular type of international activity: UN political-military control of local conflict by politically impartial, essentially noncoercive methods. This definition highlights the two aspects of peacekeeping that are most relevant to an understanding of preparedness as a subject of inquiry. Many more elaborate definitions of peacekeeping have been devised for other special purposes by scholars, diplomatic experts, and military analysts. Differences in their approaches often hinge on important particulars; at other times they are mere quibbles. Yet there seems to be wide agreement that peacekeeping institutions and skills are distinguishable by these two integral qualities, political impartiality and noncoerciveness. Moreover, this conforms to how peacekeeping professionals, civilian and military, perceive their roles. These two qualities are not absolutes. Impartial intent can have partial effects, and noncoercive methods sometimes are tinged with coercion. These are not pure models of the peacekeeping art, not rigorous, black-and-white categories of action, and not easily definable in the abstract. But they do identify the general patterns of peacekeeping policies and behavior; they embody the norms that peacekeepers are guided by; they are the underlying sources of peacekeepers' strength and influence; and they determine in major ways the nature of the preparedness arrangements required for peacekeeping.

A contemporary definition of local conflict control was given a few years ago in a study by a Massachusetts Institute of Technology team:

> By "control" we mean the prevention, moderation, or termination of organized violence at the intranational and international level. By "local" we mean the small interstate wars, the bitter civil wars, the proxy conflicts behind which the super-

powers hide, and the insurgencies and guerrilla warfare in the backwaters of the developing world—in short the wars that *do* get fought in this era rather than the big one most planned for and feared, but mercifully not fought. . . . What we mean by "conflict" is a dispute that is being or is likely to be dealt with by predominantly military means.[5]

In the hypothetical arsenal of conflict control measures, UN peace-keeping is but a single option. It operates, however, on an assumption rarely applicable to other control methods with military overtones—that the controllers can help maintain local order only if they enjoy a fairly high level of willing cooperation from the disputants who are the potential sources of disorder.

Stated another way, every UN peacekeeping operation has had to assume a large element of self-deterrence by the disputants. This is not to say that the activity of peacekeepers "really makes no difference," but rather to point out that the various intermediary services they perform are intended ultimately to reinforce this self-deterrence and to strengthen the interest of the local parties in avoiding violence or other destabilizing moves.

Pursuit of these objectives has taken a rich variety of forms and has registered different degrees of success in the dozen or so missions fielded by the UN in the past twenty-five years and now customarily referred to as peacekeeping. As early as the 1940s peacekeeping maps were dotted at Greece, on the borders of the new state of Israel, in Indonesia, and in Kashmir. The next decade added Gaza and Sinai in Egypt, and then Lebanon. The 1960s added the Congo, West Irian (West New Guinea), Yemen, Cyprus, the India–Pakistan boundaries, and again the Middle East.[6] Cease-fires have been monitored, borders patrolled, troop disengagements supervised, truces guaranteed, hostile armies insulated at safe distances, internal security maintained, and essential governmental functions preserved with the assistance of peace-keeping presences. Circumstances and political or operational requirements have dictated great diversity in the detailed organization of these missions and in the specific mixture of techniques they have used.

Some of the smaller, so-called observer missions have performed largely symbolic, sometimes only face-saving services; or they have engaged in what, relatively speaking, are functionally simple assignments, such as investigation, reporting, verification, and other informa-tion-handling chores. Occasionally, local mediation and other third-party assistance is given. In this category of missions—a few of the more recent examples being the observers dispatched to India and Pakistan after the 1965 border war and to the Suez Canal cease-fire lines in 1967—the self-deterrence ingredient is naturally paramount. Observers wield little concrete power beyond their ability to expose violations of agreements and other instances of misbehavior. Yet this is not a trivial function; UN experience is filled with cases that show how important it can be for one disputant to have reliable evidence from an impartial source that his adversary is obeying the rules of their understanding. Potential exposure can itself be a deterrent in some cases, and the availability of a trusted third party on the scene often contributes to the expeditious resolution of minor flare-ups.

Many of these functions, plus a host of others, are a standard part of the UN's larger, more complex operations, such as the Congo or Cyprus. Here the parties must still display a substantial amount of voluntary restraint if peacekeepers are to be effective, but the peace-keepers play a far more active part in inducing this restraint. Larger military formations can be deployed to assist in the maintenance of law and order, military presences of various kinds are injected at critical points of possible military confrontation between parties, key facilities or geographic locations that are in dispute can be controlled by UN soldiers, and permanent patrolling and dispersion of UN per-sonnel can check crises before they expand. In Cyprus, for example, these kinds of services palpably contribute to a reduction of low-level, potentially disruptive violence. On a day-to-day basis and in countless ways, UN peacekeepers on the island have often made the crucial difference between calm and chaos, greater and lesser bloodshed, rising and receding tensions.

In both the observer and the larger missions, military personnel have generally predominated as peacekeepers, although all UN operations have to some extent required the involvement of civilians in one political capacity or another as well as in a variety of administrative jobs. Most of the peacekeeping civilians in political slots have been drawn from the secretariat or specially recruited from outside as international civil servants under the direction of the secretary-general. For the earlier observer missions launched in the 1940s, the UN usually had on the local scene some kind of political commission composed of civilian delegates from member states, and these bodies undertook investigations, negotiations, and various mediatory responsibilities. Yet at one or another time in their histories, all such commissions required a military arm composed of teams of officers acting in observer capacities: to appraise a military situation, to interpret its implications, to identify military equipment, to perform under operating conditions so rigorous as to be inhospitable to anything but properly prepared military formations, to appreciate potential military threats to order, and to deal on a continuing basis with military officials of the disputants. And in the UN's major operations, which were mandated to restore and maintain order in the wake of local hostilities, or to prevent their occurrence, the UN response inevitably had to include substantial military components. But even in heavily "militarized" arenas such as the Congo or more recently Cyprus, the UN has used not just infantry and other conventional military units but also operational specialists in various paramilitary or nonmilitary categories.[7]

United Nations peacekeeping is a process involving multiple, layered responsibilities. Peacekeeping forces at sites of local confrontations are widely publicized, which tends to draw attention from the critically important supplementary conflict controls needed to back them up. A successful deterrent system engages not only the peacekeepers who are on the scene but also the dovetailing restraining efforts of other influential actors—a key government with leverage or a group of interested states, perhaps a regional organization, and most probably the Security Council or the General Assembly. Sometimes the personal diplomacy of the secretary-general is needed. Because solid multidimensional support was available, the Cyprus operation could be launched in the spring of 1964 and sustained through major flare-ups that summer and again in late 1967. Because such support was lacking, the UN forces in Egypt were in effect left alone in May 1967 to carry a burden they were never meant to carry, to meet a threat they had neither the power nor the authority to meet—so the system collapsed.

Overpraise of UN peacekeepers misses the mark as badly as over-criticism. They generally do not deserve all the garlands bestowed when unwanted violence is forestalled or all the opprobrium directed at them when peacekeeping fails.

If peacekeepers are able to rechannel a dispute into nonviolent, non-military courses, if they are able to bring about what UN jargon calls a cessation of hostilities, they will have accomplished their principal assignment. An experienced UN military officer in describing peace-keeping as an antiescalation device pinpoints its basic purpose. It may be a valid observation that the presence of peacekeepers sometimes reduces the willingness of parties to get at the roots of problems and settle underlying differences, but it is quite another matter to infer from this that peacekeepers must bear the blame for the absence of political accommodation. Pejorative metaphors abound—that peacekeeping serves only as "a Band-Aid operation," that it merely perpetuates so many "festering sores" around the world, that it is a palliative rather than a cure. The implication is that peacekeepers fail unless they can reach behind the immediate confrontation to remove the causes as well as the symptoms of violence and tension, to deal with remote as well as proximate causes, to adjust the parties' ends as well as their means.

Certainly every effort must be made to ameliorate conditions that generate violence and to encourage peaceful political settlements. But it is misguided, and probably overly optimistic, to set these high standards for judging whether or not to inject a peacekeeping mission or whether or not one has performed effectively over time. Most con-flicts that reach or might reach a military phase are not neatly, con-clusively soluble—by anyone. Aptly, someone observed that the reason so many UN "emergency" forces tend to become semipermanent is because there are so many semipermanent emergencies. Dean Acheson's celebrated remark during the 1965 India-Pakistan war that the highest diplomacy in such situations would be to cordon off the local con-testants and let them fight it out has a distinctly cavalier ring. Modern international violence is neither predictable in its course nor necessarily constructive in its results; nor would letting local hostilities unfold "naturally" to some military conclusion guarantee longer-run stability any more than would an uneasy stalemate. Rarely do local circum-stances justify the assumption that statesmen must be more ambitious

in the middle of a crisis than to put a lid on it if one is handy; or that
it is wiser, more just, more compassionate, or more expedient to refuse
to interpose peacekeepers or to withdraw them in the hope of forcing
the parties to come to terms. In all, then, there are multiple responsibilities for fundamental peacemaking just as there are for peacekeeping
itself. A United Nations military mission simply sitting on top of an
unresolved, simmering dispute may be testimony not to its own shortcomings but to broader imperfections over which the peacekeepers
have little control.

Peacekeeping as Political Impartiality

Impartiality is difficult to find and hard to sustain for a long time under
conditions of stress. But it is the sine qua non for whatever effectiveness,
authority, and leverage peacekeepers have, and perhaps more than
anything else it makes peacekeeping a distinctive kind of conflict control activity, one that has worked where partisan control methods
would have failed. The impartiality of UN peacekeepers means that
they can be invited in by the disputants in the first place, and because
of it they are able to perform control services with which the parties
would not trust each other and which would not be accepted from
other outside controllers not considered impartial.

Impartiality is a composite and intricate quality, a blend of objective
credentials and purposes as well as subjective perceptions. In a conflict
control situation this means that peacekeepers' policies, attitudes, and
demeanor must not be intended to further the interests of any con-
testant in the dispute, nor must they seem to. Regardless of how
impartially motivated the peacekeepers are or of how consistently they
conform to impartial standards of behavior, unless the disputants
genuinely believe the peacekeeping system to be nonpartisan it will be
worthless as an intermediary. Thus a dilemma is inherent in every UN
mission: an effective peacekeeping mechanism inevitably affects the
balance of interests among the parties, the local scale is tipped in favor
of one side, and this redistribution in turn tends to reduce the willingness of the disadvantaged party to continue good-faith cooperation

with the UN. Peacekeepers cannot escape the dilemma; they can only try to compensate by creating as many incentives as possible for all parties to settle their differences and by constantly demonstrating adherence to international policies.

To be impartial is not to be devoid of all interests or preferences. It is really a special bias in its own right. "In this sense the impartiality of the international decision-maker is not the absence of partiality, but rather a partiality to the values and mores of the international" community. "Where he differs from the parties, and the only unique quality he brings to a dispute, is that *his* subjectivity is *not that of a disputant*. His detachment gives him an opportunity to make a subjective determination on the basis of the greatest possible openness, sensitivity, and receptivity."8 This international bias manifests itself in peacekeeping policies that favor order over disorder, negotiation among contending parties over their noncontact, third-party supervision of local agreements over unilateral verification by the disputants themselves.

Application of politically impartial controls represents a sharp break from the theoretical implications of that cornerstone doctrine of twentieth-century international organization—collective security. The two concepts posit totally incompatible operating principles. Collective security has been defined and redefined, yet always faithfully to the underlying purpose, that mystique of mutual universal protection for which Plato offered philosophic justification in the *Republic*: the bonds of ideal communal unity among the extended family of the ruling guardian class were to be preserved, first, by reciprocal respect, but if this failed, by fear of collective action on the part of those who would uphold the existing order. Similarly, potential wrongdoers were meant to be restrained by the knowledge that modern collective security institutions could and would marshal overwhelming international armed force against them. This guarantee "purports to provide security *for* all states, *by* the action of all states, *against* all states which might challenge the existing order by the arbitrary unleashing of their power."9 In other words, collective security was to operate undiscriminatingly but not impartially, explicitly against one party rather than on behalf of all disputants. It was to be an adversary, punitive process, not an impartial, cooperative one, and its activation was to depend on identification of a declared common enemy, while peacekeeping presences are built on the premise that none exists.

Between peacekeepers and disputants exists a functional relationship analogous to a quasi partnership, conceived for limited purposes and based on equally limited common ends. Peacekeepers are agents not only of the international community but also, in a sense, of the parties themselves. This is the mutuality signified by the now-orthodox description of peacekeeping as "consensual," requiring the formal acquiescence of the parties from beginning to end. It is even embodied in the equivalent of written contractual understandings in which the UN and its host condition for the proposed mission.[10]

The reality, however, is not as sociable as these legal texts might at first imply. Very often, consent is a product of pressures, sometimes extremely intense, brought to bear on parties in an emergency situation. Disputants are seldom equally disposed to accept UN intervention, which may appear to be merely the least unattractive course of action for one side or the other. External sources may help to "engineer" consent, through the urgings of an ally, the pressures or even the threats of a strategically influential great power, or perhaps a strongly manifested UN consensus. Local military or diplomatic factors also generate their own logic for each side, and usually there are differently balanced preferences toward involvement by outside parties, impartial or otherwise. Thus when the UN does become a consensual peace-keeper, the partnership may well be reluctantly entered into, unsatis-factorily ambiguous about terms, fragile in execution, and uncertain in durability. Though these strains make it no less a joint venture, it is nevertheless an immensely difficult, complex undertaking. The basic contractual agreement, which defines what the peacekeepers can and cannot do, has to be hammered out, not always amicably, in the middle of a crisis. Both peacekeepers and hosts want as much freedom of action as possible, but neither will grant it. The result is an agreement vague to a fault, which, while it may appear balanced in print, invari-ably favors the host. In practice the peacekeepers must continually try to protect both the peace and their own prerogatives.

Operationally a dynamic tension is set up, a precarious balance based on neither fully good nor fully bad faith but on a kind of gray faith.

The peacekeeping system can function effectively only if the disputants show at least a modicum of cooperation by voluntarily respecting a certain threshold of compliance. Yet at the same time, if they think the risks and gains worth it, they will not be averse to cheating, to hedging a bit, to violating the spirit if not the letter of the arrangement. Complete good faith would eliminate any need for peacekeepers; its opposite would render them powerless. In the middle, gray area, the parties must remain convinced that their ends can be achieved at least cost by preserving the integrity of the peacekeeping mechanism, and the peacekeepers have to exercise what latitude they have to increase the level of compliance and to decrease possibilities for accidental disruption and low-level breakdowns.

Demands for political impartiality dictate not only the postulates of peacekeeping policies but also who the peacekeepers may be. While the secretary-general is the final arbiter of selections, he is obliged to weigh an often cumbersome assortment of opinions from member states with legitimate political concerns about the composition of each new mission. Crossed off the list of possible suppliers at the outset are usually two categories of states for whom impartiality is assumed to be unlikely: the great powers on the Security Council and all states having direct interest in the dispute. Although these rules are now generally followed, a notable exception that contravenes both has been British participation in the Cyprus force, permitted largely because British troops were already performing order-maintenance functions when the UN arrived on the island and because their numbers could be reduced as the UN presence expanded. Both categories of members, however, owing to their special positions, are frequently consulted during negotiations about force composition. Host states naturally exercise the greatest sway over selection, not nominally a veto but nearly so in practice. They have turned down candidates on reasonable grounds as well as on many capricious ones—a hostile vote in the UN, a prime minister's unsympathetic remarks, an old policy viewed unfavorably, and the like. Archbishop Makarios, president of Cyprus, is said to have refused an offer from the Netherlands because of its colonial background and to have excluded any black African contributors. In tandem with objections communicated to the secretary-general by the

British and the Americans, he reportedly also declined to accept any communist troops after a unit had been offered by Czechoslovakia.*

Few states are natural, automatic choices as peacekeepers, and each circumstance tends to add a few of its own criteria for acceptability. Yet time after time the bargaining has narrowed the range of candidates predictably. Regularly during its peacekeeping career the UN has drawn on the same small reservoir of volunteers. By almost every yardstick the prominent national suppliers of military personnel have always been Canada and the small states of northern Europe. The rank ordering of participation-frequencies in all twelve peacekeeping missions is Sweden (ten), Canada (nine), Denmark (eight), seven apiece for Norway, Ireland, and Finland, and six apiece for the Netherlands, New Zealand, Italy, and India. Only three—Denmark, Sweden, and Canada—provided key units to all three of the largest operations, Egypt, the Congo, and Cyprus. When just observer missions are tallied, the top-ranking still are Sweden (six), the Netherlands (five), and four apiece for Denmark, Ireland, Norway, France, and Belgium, the last two mainly because of steady involvement in the earliest UN observer corps during the late 1940s.[11]

That so much responsibility for peacekeeping has been absorbed by this tiny fraction of the UN membership says something about how strong the commitment to the peacekeeping idea is in most of these countries. But perhaps it says even more about how stable the ingredients of impartiality are and how constant a reputation for political aloofness can be. As in the Orwellian barnyard, some states *are* more impartial than others. In spite of the subjective, contingent judgments required each time candidates are selected, northern Europeans and Canadians have repeatedly exhibited enough of the trademarks of impartiality—absence of significant political or economic interests in Third World areas of conflict, lack of prejudicial colonial or imperial histories, identification in and outside the UN with active, independent

---

* With the exception of Yugoslavia, no communist countries have ever participated in UN peacekeeping operations. Czechoslovakia and Romania volunteered units during the Suez crisis—which under the circumstances had no chance of being accepted. In 1965 Czechoslovakia, Romania, Poland, and Hungary showed some interest in sending observers to the new India-Pakistan border mission; after the host states agreed, they were invited to participate by U Thant but in the end declined to take part.

internationalism. Along with this nonpartisanship, these states regularly give their firm political support to UN peacekeeping and possess the requisite military expertise to qualify as participants.

Judgments about impartiality, or about its lack, continue to affect personnel and composition policies even after missions are established. States have been removed when their impartiality has been seriously challenged by a host, and conversely, new participants have been added when it has been necessary to broaden the membership base to assure greater impartiality. On occasion impartiality has been intentionally breached by members of national contingents, and while an incident may not be grave enough to warrant repatriation of the entire unit, it may compel a redeployment, as once happened to a Cyprus contingent whose members were caught smuggling contraband to one of the parties. Host assessments of possible partisanship among peacekeepers have sometimes reached preposterous extremes. One of the stranger incidents took place in the mid-1960s when the personal histories of some individual Canadian officers were turned to their disadvantage while on observer duty on the India-Pakistan borders and in Kashmir. They were discovered to have served a quarter of a century earlier, during World War II, with either the British army in India or the preindependence Indian army. After complaints were made, the Canadian government brought them home, explaining that there had been no explicit charges of favoritism and that the withdrawal was merely intended to avoid future pretexts for claims that their backgrounds were tainting their impartiality.

This case illustrates a generally valid point: the need for impartiality makes peacekeepers extraordinarily vulnerable to both real and trumped-up charges of bias. Parties seem able to draw on an inexhaustible supply of stratagems for getting what they want. They try to vitiate the professed impartiality of the UN by doing everything from playing one nationality against another to manufacturing evidence of misbehavior. Even when this sort of scheming is not involved, evaluations of impartiality have a way of making convenient solutions to problems harder than they should be or downright unacceptable politically. Thus the UN's need for collecting military intelligence— which it does and has to do in peacekeeping theaters—becomes a standard bugaboo and is carried out more clumsily than peacekeeping intelligence ("information") officers would like. These same pressures operated in another direction during the 1956 Suez crisis, when the Canal had to be somehow unblocked. British and French salvage vessels were nearby, but Nasser insisted on clearance by impartial agents under UN control. Accommodating him with a special seven-nation fleet, Hammarskjöld and his staff accomplished one of the most spectacular technical feats ever connected with a peacekeeping mission.[12]

Despite the difficulties encountered in structuring and managing peacekeeping operations as consistently as possible with a criterion of impartiality, this UN pattern of impartially composed, commanded, and controlled peacekeepers does avoid many of the built-in obstacles and frustrations of what might be termed a "quasi-representational" or a "geometric balance" approach to questions of membership on observation commissions. Both approaches have been used outside the UN peacekeeping context—to supervise the Korean armistice of 1953 and the Indochina settlements of 1954.[13] In each case, though there were substantial differences in details of organization and modes of operation, observation and supervisory functions were carried out by a combination of joint commissions made up of the belligerents only and multinational commissions made up of outside states chosen directly by the belligerents and balanced in neat numerical ratios. In the Korean situation the second body consisted of Sweden and Switzerland plus Poland and Czechoslovakia, and its powerlessness was continually documented by 2–2 votes, which amounted to vetoes by the communist half. Communist negotiators at Geneva were pleased enough with this arrangement to propose that it be used a second time, with some modifications, to supervise the Indochina accords. The Western allies refused, largely because of the Korean mechanism's failure; and after long haggling over new formulas—mostly involving ingenious contrivances of five-nation or three-nation mixtures of partisans and neutrals preferred by each side—everyone was willing to settle on the infamous troika solution, constructing a rough balance with a Western country (Canada), a neutral one (India), and a communist one (Poland). On most important issues, unanimity was required, and the effect was to create another system not much more flexible than the

Korean one. Conditions and factors other than membership do indeed determine the overall ability of any peacekeeping effort to achieve its objectives, but it is also undeniable that some membership criteria tend to reinforce the impartiality and independence of peacekeeping mechanisms while others tend merely to harness the peacekeepers to the immediate interests of the disputants. This is a difference between impartial peacekeeping that attempts to be sufficiently responsive to the parties and peacekeeping that can only mirror their disagreements.

Peacekeeping as Noncoercion

A UN general officer once drew this comparison: "Peacekeeping is to war-making what acting is to ballet—the environment is similar but the techniques are very different."[14] For the soldier-turned-peacekeeper, the contrasts are vivid, although the problems of adjusting to them are frequently overrated by those who hold too stereotyped a view of the military profession, who see its members as devoted to combat and driven by heroic fantasies. Nevertheless, even while peacekeeping is not a wholly alien experience for soldiers, it is an unfamiliar one. Peacekeeping perhaps least resembles war because of its premium on noncoercion. Peacekeepers dress like soldiers, organize like soldiers, live like soldiers, and are equipped like soldiers, but in terms of traditional images of fighting men, they behave in a thoroughly unsoldierly way. They have no deadly foe to destroy or be destroyed by. They fight very little and use their weapons rarely. They prefer compromise to conquest. They substitute persuasion and prevention for punishment, and they apply tact and patience instead of firepower. To invert Robert Murphy's phrase, they are warriors among diplomats.

For UN peacekeepers, noncoercion is a norm, a policy intended to be controlling in the absence of sufficient cause for departing from it. They have relied on coercion, including armed force, in the past, and doubtless they will do so in the future when necessary. Their formal authority to employ force has always comprised self-defense, which has been progressively defined with greater permissiveness, giving them more leeway for so-called active self-defense.[15] Beyond this peacekeepers have been allowed to use minimum force as a last resort in carrying out whatever tasks have been assigned to them. United Nations commanders in Cyprus, for example, are so instructed. Furthermore, both they and their predecessors in the Congo were routinely empowered to use force to uphold practical arrangements agreed on by the parties.[16] On the whole, less can be learned about the peacekeeping art from the extent of such formal authority than from the sparseness of its actual use. The stuff of peacekeeping is not a capacity to coerce but an ability to induce compliance with as little coercion as possible.

Perhaps in the end the most persuasive rationale for this emphasis is not the theoretical imperative—that habitual use of armed force would make peacekeepers synonymous with collective enforcers, acting neither impartially nor consensually—but rather the utilitarian, pragmatic one—it plainly works best. Under the political and military conditions usually prevailing in peacekeeping theaters, a policy of less rather than more coercion assures the UN the most leverage with disputants and maximal opportunity for modifying their behavior. Restrictions on the use of force are logical, inescapable corollaries to impartiality and consent, because above a certain point in the scale of coercion, a point that moves with circumstances, the parties will no longer cooperate voluntarily. The intermediary will then have changed from collaborator to adversary.

These constraints are not well understood. All too frequently, simplistic pictures are painted of UN commanders shackled by the restrictions, straining against them, demoralized, and resentful of what they consider a lack of sufficient coercive capability and an absence of blanket permission to use freely even what little they possess. Expert commentators, civilian and military, translate these images into recommendations for more and better-armed peacekeepers, able to demonstrate indisputable military superiority over local contestants and with the sanction of superiors to use it against recalcitrants. True enough, a few senior military men with UN experience and a few civilians who accept their judgment believe this to be the essentially correct thrust of peacekeeping strategy. But many other peacekeeping practitioners see things quite differently; they are convinced that greater coercion not only is usually unnecessary but in fact may often decrease the UN's real leverage. One senior commander, after extensive UN service, has said in a private retrospective report: "The use of force is no panacea for the difficulties and frustrations which are likely to surround a peacekeeping mission. *In the Cyprus operation it is difficult to find a single instance in which UNFICYP could have done a better job had it possessed and employed the power to use more force.* [Rather] it can be argued that had force been used against either of the contesting communities UNFICYP's status and reputation would not be as good as it is today, nor would the force have been as effective." (Emphasis supplied.) Another officer who has exercised top command responsibilities writes, without reference to any particular mission, that "the provision of extensive powers to use force is not necessarily an advantage; it can in fact be very much the reverse, for a UN Force possessing such powers will find itself pressed by each disputing party to use force against the other. In these circumstances it is fatally easy for UN Forces to be maneuvered into acting, or seeming to act, [on behalf of] one or the other of the disputing parties. By contrast, a UN Force with . . . ability to use force only in self-defence [and to protect interparty agreements] may well be in a much stronger position."[17]

A companion notion about peacekeeping is equally simplistic. This one fabricates a dichotomy between pure coercion and pure noncoercion. It says that peacekeepers are effective *either* because their supposed moral authority as symbols of international public opinion is respected fully by disputants *or* because they have at their disposal a preponderance of military power so decisive that the parties are left with no real choice but to do what the UN wants. It also says that the only two kinds of peacekeepers are those who supposedly can do little without punitive powers and those who supposedly can do everything with them. To some degree this polarization is a spin-off from arguments about broad peacekeeping strategy: obviously if one wants to argue generally for greater coercive powers it better suits one's purpose to portray the choice as between tough, omnipotent peacekeepers and servile, spineless ones. This is the ploy of advocates of militarily superior UN forces as alternatives to the "nonsense about blue helmets or blue berets being enough."[18] A red herring at best. No one in a responsible position is saying that they are enough, despite the images evoked by rhetoric over the years that peacekeepers are "moral plate-glass windows," symbolic stand-ins for all UN members, and the like.

Armed coercion and utter passivity are not alternatives. They are extremes, between which is an assortment of tactics that peacekeepers can use to exert influence and real deterrence. United Nations commanders are under orders always to rely if possible on peaceful rather than forceful methods for securing compliance, always to use minimum force when force is needed, and always to use armed force with the greatest of care.[19] Instructions to open fire have been rare, controlled, and judicious. Lesser measures are standard fare for peacekeepers, measures that, while not coercive in the strict sense of disputants being forcefully compelled to act in a certain way, do involve applications of leverage that makes them behave with more restraint than they might otherwise show.

Thus UN commanders' orders to use means other than weapons to impose the UN's will may entail riot- and movement-control procedures, interpositionary and area-control tactics, and a variety of military patrols, presences, and monitors. Small-scale diplomacy by the military peacekeepers, in the form of local negotiations, mediation, and problem-solving with military authorities of the parties, is also required.[20] And as in Cyprus, the performance of additional—and extraordinarily successful—tension-reducing services not usually associated with military commands but operating in this case as integral parts of the force may be called for.

One such service is the employment of UN civilian police recruited as individuals from supplier countries and performing many tasks distinctly separate from those of the military peacekeepers. Both groups, however, are tightly synchronized, the UN military generally dealing with their local counterparts and the UN civilian police with theirs. In circumstances much like those thirty years earlier when the League dispatched international civilian policemen to the Saar alongside military peacekeepers (see Chapter 3), the UN needed policemen in Cyprus because civil war had factionalized Cypriot police into hostile intercommunal partisans with great power on the island. The Cypriot police accepted other policemen as intermediaries more readily than they would have soldiers; and the commonality of police work helped the UN policemen understand the problems and the methods of persuading their local confreres to act with restraint. Although they have no formal law enforcement powers, the UN policemen try to keep tabs on all local police activities that might generate political violence. They act as investigators, reporters, observers, negotiators, go-betweens, and even as consciences for the locals. They are the military peacekeepers' liaison with police from both communities. They do their own patrolling and checkpointing, sometimes jointly with Cyprus police; they maintain representatives at local police stations; and they perform services that require special police investigative skills in connection with political crimes.

They work closely with another novel element of the Cyprus UN mission, a separate branch of the military headquarters that deals exclusively with local-level relief and economic matters that are potential causes of disorder. Just as local police actions tended to heat up the dispute, intercommunal economic dealings too served as a constant source of tension, for which the UN peacekeepers had to develop an organizational response. Through a complex islandwide network of military economic officers and staffs, the UN force deals with refugee relief, transportation and distribution of economic goods or services, and medical, agricultural, and educational problems. This can engage the UN in anything from arbitrating a local dispute over water or land rights to providing military protection during harvests.

All in all, this military and quasi-military system for deterring low-level violence is always active, always searching out ways to exploit whatever shared interests the disputants have in stability, and always taking advantage of the UN's position as the only mutually trusted third party available. Peacekeepers manage to coax, cajole, demand, motivate, urge, persuade, and sometimes simply browbeat the contestants into line. They need not resign themselves to inaction when confronted with shifting, contrary whims of the parties. Nor, however, need they aspire to full military control over conflict situations.[21] Instead, peacekeepers must make strength of their comparative weakness and combine diplomatic methods with military ones in order to produce influence that neither alone could bring to bear.

Preparedness: Some Basics

Preparedness for UN peacekeeping is today a loose system, really little more than a collage of voluntary, informal arrangements within and among a handful of UN member states, as well as some centralized capabilities inside the secretariat in New York. Together they must mobilize the necessary resources for peacekeeping by fashioning a triple-barreled capability for manpower, managers, and matériel sufficient to maintain ongoing missions and to anticipate new ones.

The key component of preparedness has perhaps been that core group of national suppliers willing and able to provide the UN with military and civilian police personnel on a more or less regular basis, the group having the highest frequency rates of participation in peacekeeping operations. Some of these have made unilateral, conditional offers to the UN, indicating that they would undertake various advance measures within their military establishments to prepare for participation in future UN operations supported politically by the supplier government, and to develop a rapid-response readiness for emergency call-up. Canada, Sweden, Norway, Denmark, Finland, the Netherlands, Austria, the United Kingdom, Italy, Iran, and New Zealand have all done so, mostly during the 1960s. These offers have commonly been described as standby forces, but the description is a misnomer. From country to country radically uneven progress has been made in implementing these standby programs, and widely different meanings are attached to the standby concept. Some units are fully organized, standing by, and ready to go on short notice. Others are on standby in the sense that they can be put together over a comparatively longer period. Work on many of these complicated programs remains at one or another stage of partial completion. Some have never gotten beyond the printed page of the initial offer; some remain on drawing boards; some have proved unworkable in important respects. Although much has been learned from these planning efforts, much remains to be done before an effective aggregate of national standby forces is available to the UN. Additional member states that ought to be considered potential peacekeeping suppliers, even though they have not made formal

offers and have not 'taken advance steps that they call standby preparations, are Ireland, Yugoslavia, India, and Brazil. Each has made
relatively recent, major contributions to UN operations and has accumulated national experience that could be relied on in the future.

The second preparedness component, a managerial capability within
the secretariat, is the source of executive direction and administrative
backup for peacekeepers. International civil servants, working at field
headquarters as well as in New York, touch virtually every aspect of
peacekeeping missions from inception to termination. On the political
side the secretary-general and his immediate staff are responsible for
transforming a usually fuzzy mandate from the Security Council or the
General Assembly into operating directives for peacekeepers. Fundamental mission policies must be set, constantly interpreted, adjusted,
and explained to UN members, disputants, and field commanders.
Administratively the secretariat bureaucracy must gear up to provide
support services not available through national military channels, to
handle all financial matters, to coordinate overall procurement and
supply functions, and to establish the necessary administrative links to
supplier countries. At this stage of the secretariat's evolution, these
functions have to be performed with meager resources—small staffs,
cramped budgets, the scantiest of military advice in the secretariat, and
only minimal planning beyond the needs of current operations.

Matériel support, the third preparedness component, involves several
primary actors—national suppliers, whose units always contain some
integrated logistical potential, the secretariat, whose responsibility
varies from mission to mission, and member states with national
capabilities sophisticated enough to provide major military hardware.
Altogether it comprises everything from paper clips to strategic transport, from foods to complex communications systems. Multinationality
involves countless possible variations in support requirements—different
dietary scales, vehicle patterns, weapons, and so on. All multilateral
military formations, no matter what their aegis, must tolerate inherent
logistical complications and inefficiencies. Some that plague the UN
are in the "inevitable" category, but most are products of unique
strictures confronting UN political administrators. The organization
has none of the logistical advantages that might compensate for the

diversities involved. It maintains no substantial logistical depots; it has limited common procedures; it operates under severely restrictive purchasing practices and financial regulations; and the skimpy pre-planning that is done for future contingencies must be done blind, without knowing for certain who the national participants will be in any new operation.

Interdependence among these three components is close, and inter-connections are numerous. Some preparedness problems can be dealt with adequately by any one of the three. For others, action in one is required before related progress can occur in another. Progress in one component can often relieve pressure in another, or it can serve to stimulate complementary forward movement. Thus the components have not evolved simultaneously, equally, or according to preconceived schedules. Each has been the object of separate initiatives; each has required that different kinds of political or technical obstacles be over-come.

Governments, like men, pay great attention to service institutions when they are most sorely needed, then afterwards lapse into apathy. So it has been with the preparedness system. "While it seems to be agreed," U Thant said in 1967, "that the United Nations must have some capacity to act effectively in time of danger, it has not so far been possible to agree on methods by which that capacity would be increased and made more reliable."[22] It is not just a question of a marginal short-coming here and another there or even just a matter of being able to rekindle interest in preparedness after emergencies have passed. It is, rather, that the state of UN preparedness is deficient in all respects. The system moves jerkily from crisis to crisis. Although each new challenge does give new momentum to preparedness, leaving it somewhat better off than it was before—the UN today is immensely more seasoned about preparedness than it was when the Suez operation was pasted together in 1956—the net results nevertheless are still substandard, still too riddled with uncertainties, still too dependent on scattered good-will and concentrated good luck.

Temporary armies, assembled with great difficulty, lacking perma-nent skills and accumulated experience, without central discipline, their components unaccustomed to acting in concert, their leaders in want of a clear hierarchy of command and control, their storehouses filled with miscellaneous assortments of equipment, their systems for provisioning inadequate, their continuity preserved only by reliance on mercenaries—these are trademarks that critic and friend alike often attribute to UN peacekeepers. Each of these descriptive phrases is directly lifted not from studies of UN missions but from a classic treatise on armies and warfare in the Middle Ages.[23] It is no exaggeration to say that the UN is forced, by the absence of international political community, to mobilize armies on medieval principles of organization for the performance of modern tasks in modern settings. The decentralization, the impermanence, the improvisation, and the unprofessionalism are all singularly ill adapted to the jobs occasionally thrust upon the UN by member states who suddenly, often reluctantly, find themselves left with nothing else to do but dump a problem, as the British say, in the lap of Aunt Sally.

The underdevelopment of UN military institutions has already been competently documented through performance evaluations of UN peacekeeping missions, particularly of the largest ones—Egypt, the Congo, and Cyprus.[24] Certain features internal to the preparedness system are no less instructive in revealing just how feudal the organizational patterns are and how much out of harmony with reasonable expectations of military readiness.

Take, as a single example, joint training. By the late 1960s, between 200,000 and 250,000 soldiers from fifty-one countries had seen some UN service. All peacekeeping missions had revealed something about the difficulties of combining heterogeneous national elements under UN command, and all taught something about the advantages of specially orienting national units and officers to the peculiarities of peacekeeping. Yet not until 1965 did *any* combined UN-related training occur across national boundaries—this in Scandinavia, and limited to training of individual officers, not full units. There is today still no joint multinational training of military peacekeepers under UN auspices.

In both concept and execution, this Nordic-centered activity says as much as anything can about the state of UN preparedness throughout the 1960s. The first session of this regional training, which has since been expanded considerably (see Chapter 5), brought together some seventy students from the four Nordic military establishments for courses in UN observer duties, which were later broadened to include preparation for assignments as UN staff officers in larger missions. The first remarkable thing about this venture is that it enjoys no UN cachet whatever, no explicit support or formal blessing from any UN source. Resolutions of the Council and Assembly have never once mentioned it or, for that matter, even a need for such training. No official UN document authored by the secretary-general gives the slightest hint that this training even exists. No UN secretariat personnel have ever attended the course in any capacity, and not one penny of UN money is used to defray expenses. Even though the initial sessions of the schooling convened eighteen years after the first national soldiers put on UN armbands, an instructor at the course has at hand no UN-approved interpretations of past missions, no orderly international archives from which lessons can be drawn, no official training doctrines promulgated by New York, no training aids from the secretariat, and no UN military staff to provide advice and assistance.

Corresponding irregularities permeate the entire preparedness system. Sometimes more glaring, sometimes less, they are to a large extent common by-products of the widespread mistrust impeding institutional-ization of peacekeeping arrangements at the UN. Defects in the struc-ture of contemporary preparedness stem from political rather than technical causes. Without question, there is vastly more preparedness know-how than there is diplomatic consensus to apply it. Pivotal member states, chiefly but not exclusively the superpowers, harbor dissimilar, often incompatible convictions about how peacekeeping missions should be conducted and prepared for. Preparedness proposals are often inextricably tangled up with disagreements over the proper peacekeeping authority of the secretary-general, the relative distribu-tion of powers between the Council and the Assembly, and the respec-tive competence of alternative sections of the UN bureaucracy. Thus peacekeeping practitioners must face not only heavy doses of simple policy-making inertia but also the prospect of having preparedness measures squeezed inefficiently into ad hoc, voluntary channels where political confrontations can be avoided but where the problems are not dealt with satisfactorily.

Preparedness diplomacy is a product not only of UN members' current policy objectives but also of their historical perceptions and misperceptions. In many respects, the past weighs even more heavily than the present in determining whether, on preparedness matters, the UN shows its cooperative, constructive face or its dissentious, dilatory one.

THREE

The League and Before

THAT peacekeeping and preparedness must have had approximately the same birthdate is self-evident, yet just when it was is not so certain. Modern peacekeeping's genesis is obscure, and attempts to retrace it are unsatisfying. One of the stock historical interpretations running through contemporary analyses of peacekeeping is that United Nations forces in Egypt, the Congo, or Cyprus are simply one more variant of international policing institutions, or ideas about them, that not only predate Western multistate relations but are as ancient as war itself. This proposition assumes an essentially linear historical evolution spanning several millennia. It claims, in effect, that peacekeeping forces are but one offshoot of the collective security armies that have been proposed or used ever since political collectivities have sought mutual security, whether Greek city-states, medieval principalities, or modern nations. This depiction is intended to convey an appealing sense of historical continuity. It encourages a search for prototypes deep in antiquity, as far back as the fifth century B.C. when members of Greece's Delian League jointly contributed military resources for protection against Persia and for policing the Aegean Sea.[1]

More frequently, however, another suggested genealogy is drawn within a shorter historical perspective, beginning near the end of the Middle Ages, typically a time frame bounded by the past six or seven centuries. One major peacekeeping study, for example, illustratively singles out Dante, the Duc de Sully, William Penn, the Abbé de Saint-Pierre, and Jean Jacques Rousseau, concluding that from their universal government or collective-security-cum-world-army blueprints "would inevitably emerge the concept" of smaller, limited-purpose peace-keeping forces, because "the idea of a large world army and the idea of a small police force" for peacekeeping "are fundamentally linked."[2]

Antecedents and Irrelevance

Hypotheses in this genre amount, at the very most, to superficial historical analogies, all unable to survive critical evaluation. They see "inevitable" consequences where there is only chance, and they un-cover "fundamental" links where there are only accidental, insignifi-cant parallels. They end up postulating essential similarities among all the international military forces ever conceived, discarded, or deployed. They attribute historical continuity to events and ideas that merely succeed one another in time.

With the sharp verdict that "people often study history less for what they might learn than for what they want to prove," a contemporary British historian has demolished the notion that most of these early models were forerunners of twentieth-century collective security structures.[3] With consistent persuasiveness he demonstrates that the collective sanctions machinery written into the League of Nations Covenant and the UN Charter owe no real conceptual debts to peace planners between the thirteenth and seventeenth centuries—from Dante to Sully—most of whom were less concerned with peace than with the organization of political power in Europe, with concerted military action against the Turks or Russians, or with other immediate objec-tives that took war for granted as a necessary means. There were exceptions even before 1700, in transitional publicists like Emeric Crucé, Hugo Grotius, and, to some extent, Sully, whose writings began to show more concern for peace itself than for political goals that might have required peace to be broken. In this same vein were later essayists such as Penn, John Bellers, Saint-Pierre, and Rousseau, each of whom broke radically in this respect with traditions preceding them.

These conclusions should be taken still one step farther: if the causal connections are tenuous between these pre-twentieth-century models and collective security experiments, they are nonexistent between them and politically impartial, noncoercive peacekeeping institutions.

The vintage peace plans were all aimed at preserving someone's version of peace and order against known or probable common enemies, and these ends could never have been pursued with non-coercion or impartiality. Early in the Middle Ages the Church arrayed its princes in the Crusades to impose the Truce of God, and the pope or his agents employed all manner of spiritual, economic, and military sanctions against deviants. As an emergent secularism eroded the Church's temporal power, civil authority was championed as preserver of stability. Dante's antipapist advocacy of universal monarchy was modeled on the Roman Empire; and Pierre Dubois, a contemporary of Dante's, drew up a plan for a confederation of European sovereigns under French political control, an association that would not only regulate political relations on the Continent but would also reconquer and colonize the Holy Land. The coercive purpose explicit here was implicit in Dante.

After two centuries of relatively obscure proposals for European leagues or quasi federations designed to stabilize Europe or to wage war against the Turks, the early 1600s saw the elaboration of the celebrated "Grand Design" of Sully, a former French minister whose plan would have established French hegemony in Europe at the expense of Austria and Spain and would have laid the groundwork for war against both Turks and Russians as well as for extra-European colonization. During the same century the Thirty Years War prompted another flurry of peace schemes, including those of Penn and Saint-Pierre. Theoretically their proposed associations were to be set up and sustained by force of arms if necessary, though the authors did not believe that coercion would ever be required. Saint-Pierre, for instance, insisted that his European Society be omnipotent and all-inclusive. Anyone threatening war, disobeying the society's regulations, or other-

wise contravening its collective judgment was to "be declared an
enemy to the Society, and it shall make war upon him." Its wrath
would be felt by any ruler who refused to join. The society would
"make war upon him 'til he enter into it, or 'til he be entirely dis-
possessed." Saint-Pierre's plan moved Frederick the Great to write to
Voltaire: "The thing is most practicable; for its success all that is
lacking is the consent of Europe and a few similar trifles."[4]

The termination of the Napoleonic Wars and the Congress of Vienna
in 1815 provided the victors with an opportunity to construct an
imperfect version of European peace enforcement. Within the frameworks of the Quadruple Alliance, the Concert of Europe, and the
Congress System, the great powers sought first to deter renewed
French aggression and then to suppress internal revolutions threatening the status quo, which was vital to Continental sovereigns. By the
century's end major war had been averted, though military interventions by stronger against weaker states and a sprinkling of small
wars pockmarked this veneer of general peace. Throughout, there
were no international armies. The substitute anticipated by the statesmen at Vienna—combined great power military action—never materialized, for it took only a decade to discover that there were not
enough policies in common to support systematic military collaboration. Only as the Hague period closed out the century with a distinct
internationalist emphasis did interest revive in some form of international peace-enforcing army. From private and public sources,
reams of proposals were circulated widely among turn-of-the-century
peace groups. But it was not until the urgency following a world war
that such ideas influenced policies, as Woodrow Wilson, in the losing
political struggle synonymous with his presidency, set out to construct
a collective security system and convince his country of its rightness.
The question of forming and using an international army within that
system confronted Wilson with one of the trickiest obstacles in his
campaign on behalf of the League. He had to persuade his constituents
that the League would have real coercive power, economic and military, while simultaneously convincing them that, contrary to what his
political opponents were saying, American membership would not
commit U.S. armed forces to sanctions in far-off lands under foreign

command. "Wilson had set out to sell the League of Nations to the American public, and having identified the feature which aroused greatest buyers' resistance, he shrewdly played it down."[5]

Impartiality, the source of legitimacy and effectiveness for peace-keepers, had no place whatsoever in the functioning of either the early peace models or the more recent collective security experiments. Indeed, both could have worked only if virtually the entire, organized international community accepted responsibility for acting against a common enemy. Impartiality would have been a hindrance to common policies. Unless the adversary was *everyone's* adversary, or nearly so, punitive action by the community would have been without credibility as a threat and ineffectual in execution.

Peace-enforcement plans, in sum, paved the way for peacekeeping institutions only by their repeated, abysmal failure. The intellectual underpinnings of these institutions are rooted in third-party mediatory diplomacy. Peacekeeping is only one contemporary embellishment. Though the ideas behind it are as old as the arts of negotiation, its practice has been in evidence only since the beginning of the nineteenth century, and then only in faintly identifiable shape.

The nineteenth-century and early twentieth-century joint international projects that probably ought to be considered adumbrations of peacekeeping include supervisory measures in the fields of navigation and sanitation. These displayed the rudiments of methods used later by peacekeepers. To implement, mostly peacefully, agreed solutions for controlling cholera and the plague and for monitoring international rivers and harbors, interested European governments formed on-the-spot commissions empowered to use local officials and police as supplemental supervisory agents. Sanitary police were engaged in Constantinople, Alexandria, and Tangier; navigation police in the Danzig and Memel harbors. Other activities of historical importance were the special international administrations set up by Europeans in Cracow, Crete, Shanghai, and Tangier.[6] Far more complex and comprehensive than the supervisory operations, these administrations were part intervention, part occupation by Continental powers, part protection of foreign material interests, part order-keeping in controversial territories. European motives arose from competition, mutual jealousies, and mistrust, all of which debarred any single government from appropriating these pieces of real estate. Internationalization and sharing of responsibility were the only acceptable expedients; a reciprocal check-and-balance system resulted. These governments jointly wished to avoid conflict over critical areas, and they were forced to settle for methods far less blatant than their straightforward military interventions in Latin America and on the fringes of Europe. They were willing, most notably in Tangier and Shanghai, to employ combinations of local gendarmerie, imported police officers, and reserve military units to effect combined control.

League Experience: Vilna and the Saar

All of these administrations were narrowly functional precedents. Politically, they lacked the essential quality of impartiality. The taproot of modern peacekeeping did not take hold until the League sent an international force to supervise a plebiscite in the Saar in 1935. This was a decisive step beyond the previous century's internationalization arrangements, whose shortcomings were widely recognized during the League period. One expert perceptively predicted, before its establishment, the kind of operation the Saar force was to become. He argued that if future international police were "really employed in the service of justice" countries would "not see anything unnatural" in them. National composition would be a "vital" determinant. If "neutral states" performed needed services "with strict impartiality," their effect would be "more calming." This requirement, he said, had been "too little considered" in the past, and earlier forces had not been "truly international."[7] The eventual performance of the Saar mission amply justified the judgment, voiced many years later, that impartiality was the "secret of its success."[8]

Heavily industrialized and politically important, the Saar territory was the object of a difficult compromise designed by Wilson at the Versailles Peace Conference. It was to be governed from 1920 to 1935 by a League commission, and at the end of this interval, its inhabitants would vote either to renew international rule or to be assimilated by

France or Germany. Hitler's accession in 1933 seemed to change the consequences of the choices available to the overwhelmingly Catholic Saarlanders, whose natural preferences as Germans were diminished by the prospect of threats to their religion under Nazi rule. In the brief but volatile initial period of Nazi terror and propaganda, and to avoid the outbreak of serious internal disorder during an agitated electoral campaign, the League in January 1934 began drawing up plans for the plebiscite after France and Germany had consented to an international presence. Hitler realized that further alienation of the Saarlanders would only undermine his own interests by increasing their ambivalence about rejoining Germany, and eventually he moderated somewhat his excessively threatening stance. Even the Saar's Catholic hierarchy came around to supporting a pro-German vote. In January 1935, 90 percent of the electorate indicated a desire to become part of Germany, and the transfer was completed in less than two months.

A staff of German-speaking civilians had to be recruited to manage a complicated system of vote supervision. Ultimately these included Swiss, Swedes, Dutch, Irish, Norwegians, Spaniards, Italians, and other nationalities. Measures had to be taken to assure security and to guarantee voters as peaceful an environment as possible. Under the command of a British major general (the head of the Saar Commission of the League was also British), military contingents totaling 3,200 troops from Great Britain, the Netherlands, Sweden, and Italy took on this assignment. Here the League undertook its first and only major peacekeeping operation.

The outlines of this "unprecedented and successful experiment"[9] were not entirely novel. Preparedness for peacekeeping in the Saar had begun, in a sense, fifteen years earlier. In anticipation of a plebiscite in Vilna, a territory contested by Poland and Lithuania, the League planned in 1920 a supervisory force drawn from nine countries not associated with the dispute. Had the plebiscite not been canceled because of disagreements between the parties, it would have been monitored by soldiers from France, Belgium, Denmark, Greece, Norway, Spain, and three other states that were later to serve in the Saar—Britain, the Netherlands, and Sweden. While responsibility today for putting together a new UN force would fall primarily on the secretary-general's staff, this was not the case during the League years. At no time did a comparable role in managing field missions devolve upon the League secretary-general. The first, Sir Eric Drummond, had in 1920 been in office only a year. He drafted some of the formal communications for the League Council, including requests to members for peacekeeping units, and he may have been active diplomatically behind the scenes, but executive and planning tasks fell to specifically appointed national agents of the Council. The French dominated the entire preparedness process for Vilna, just as the British were to do later for the Saar operation. The leading actors were all French. The Council met in Paris; its president was Léon Bourgeois; a five-man military commission appointed earlier by the Council to verify a Vilna cease-fire was led by a French colonel who was deeply engaged in the diplomacy of the dispute and was scheduled to be force commander; the French general staff under Marshal Foch took charge of all logistical arrangements for the proposed mission.

Making their debut five decades ago during the Vilna episode were a remarkably large number of the political factors and operational difficulties that have been all too familiar to peacekeeping managers ever since then. The politics of impartiality operated in various guises. The Lithuanians, and by extension their Russian supporters, had grave reservations about the pervasiveness of the French—and justifiably so as both official policy and public opinion in France were frankly sympathetic to Poland. Possible suppliers of Vilna contingents seem to have shared this concern. Belgium, for instance, offered its troops only on the condition that the force be genuinely impartial and international in character, an assurance now sought as a matter of course by UN suppliers. In an obviously conscious effort to balance the force's political makeup, the League Council, one month after issuing a general membershipwide request for volunteers, specifically tendered new invitations to the Danish, Swedish, Norwegian, and Dutch governments, each a respected neutral.

Today in many supplier states decisions to contribute personnel for UN peacekeeping or to earmark units in advance require parliamentary consent at one stage or another. In Scandinavia and the Netherlands parliamentary influence over national preparedness decisions began

with Vilna. In some cases offers were made fully dependent on subsequent parliamentary approval. This was then a greater constraint
than it is now. Particularly in Scandinavia, the League was by no means
as readily accepted as the UN is these days, more or less in an act of
political faith.[10] As diplomatic stalemate dragged on over the conduct
of the plebiscite, some of the countries holding troops in readiness
began to worry about whether their men would have to stay in Vilna
longer than originally planned and whether the Soviet government's
growing hostility to the entire enterprise would lead to a war in which
these suppliers did not want to be involved. Also heralded then were
two other features of contemporary Scandinavian peacekeeping practice: they raised exclusively volunteer units for Vilna duty, and because
this involved proportionally higher extraordinary costs than countries
using regular army personnel, the Scandinavians presented the League,
as they do the UN, with comparatively high bills for services rendered.

Finally, some now-standard technical problems cropped up. Most
were attributable to the League's general unpreparedness for any field
operations. The confusion when the five-man cease-fire commission
was dispatched is apparent from this description: "both the Council
and the Secretariat showed their inexperience. No names were ready,
no preparations made. The . . . members of the Council nominated one
officer each—a process which not only involved loss of time but resulted in a commission whose members knew nothing about the
League, and were prevented by difficulties of language from forming
any direct judgment on the local situation, or even understanding one
another."[11] Efficiency reports on a few UN operations would contain
distressingly similar observations. It is curious that in all these years
solving logistical problems in peacekeeping has come full circle. What
the French did for the Vilna force closely resembles the technical support
roles of the Canadians in the United Nations Emergency Force (UNEF)
and the British in the United Nations Force in Cyprus (UNFICYP).[12]
All kinds of experimentation with logistical systems have been tried in
UN operations, and gradually it has become clear that many of the
glaring problems are best dealt with on a so-called core-nation basis.
This approach allocates logistical responsibilities to the individual contributors most capable of handling them on behalf of all suppliers.

Or if possible, one country assumes primary responsibility for overall force logistics, as can be done in Cyprus because of the convenience of existing British base facilities. By the time Foch's planning for Vilna was completed, logistical forward bases had been converted, supply systems established, transportation scheduled for all contingents, medical facilities organized for routine services and for possible complications in this typhus-infected area, and billeting arranged in the territory. The complications were relatively few in the planning phase, with some notable exceptions: the Greek contingent had to be refused because it could not be transported or supplied, comparatively distant as Greece was; and neutral Switzerland was unwilling to grant the League overland transit rights for international contingents, although Austria and Czechoslovakia assented to this request.

Like its successor in the Saar, the Vilna force was designed as a noncoercive instrument and—to borrow a phrase popularized in the UN era—"as a peace force, not a fighting force." The League Council instructed it "simply to perform police duties." The word "peace-keeping" was not yet in vogue, but the Council's intent was plain enough. Once the mission was in place it was authorized to leave if the plebiscite was not held, and in the event of "fighting occurring in the plebiscite area" the Council indicated "that the military force shall be withdrawn." Other orders gave the commander authority to take "necessary measures," presumably for self-defense, "in case of emergency."[13] The Saar mission a decade and a half later was a replica of this untested blueprint.

Peacekeepers were given a far-reaching assignment in the Saar, dictated by its unusual political landscape. The Saar had no local government, so the League commission was legally host to the peacekeeping force, whose mandate, therefore, was as sweeping as the commission's, under whose authority it was "entrusted with the maintenance of order in the territory before, during, and after the plebiscite."[14] The force discharged this function smoothly and reportedly without having to fire a shot.

In retrospect, the special significance of the Saar experiment is three-fold. It pioneered the use of international civilian police in peacekeeping (in addition to civilian voting supervisors), a technique that was tried even before the four-nation military force was established. The operation was consent-based and politically impartial, the first of its kind. And finally, it generated fresh technical and tactical insights, many of which were later recorded by the British commander of the Saar force, Major General Brind, in a fascinating report never distributed widely and now of interest to historians only.[15]

The use of internationally recruited civilian police in the Saar was at once a major advance on nineteenth-century practice and a forerunner of the UN's use of regular civilian policemen in Cyprus. In both cases their use was prompted by similar conditions. Internal political divisions polarized local police ranks, and law enforcement could be neither fair nor divorced from partisan loyalties. Instead, two police corps served two competing versions of community order. Cypriot policemen, during their forced identity crisis in 1964, saw themselves not merely as Cypriots but as Turkish Cypriots or Greek Cypriots. Maltreatment by police across communal lines was rampant, and law and order became partisan weapons rather than standards for the public good. Agents of impartial justice were no more. In the conduct of the Saar plebiscite, pro-French and pro-German inclinations produced acute dichotomies in much the same way. The British chairman of the League Commission for the Saar, the tough, able Geoffrey Knox, reported that the Saar constables "find it difficult to free themselves from the influences of their families and friends, or even to refrain from taking sides in political strife. Moreover, they are nearly all former German soldiers and it is to be feared that this early training creates in many of them a conflict of conscience that will render difficult the strictly impartial performance of the duties which will be assigned to them at the time of the plebiscite."[16] Thus in both the Saar and Cyprus, the populace had been thoroughly accustomed to modern, efficient police services, but in times of crisis both displayed gaps in internal policing machinery that could be filled only by outside sources having no vested interests in local political outcomes.

Subsequent written accounts have largely ignored this civilian police feature of the Saar operation. Doubtless this is because the police were involved only in what might be called the first phase of the affair. The second was the more dramatic, and its several thousand League troops completely obscured the initial, modest civilian police presence. The earlier period began with the League planning at the opening of 1934 and lasted until autumn of the same year, when the dispute nearly spiraled out of control. Phase two began then and terminated with the dispatch of the international military peacekeepers. During these months fears of a Nazi putsch in the Saar grew, the French responded by threatening to intervene unilaterally, and a war loomed that no one really wanted. Threat and counterthreat, plot and counterplot, included at one point an attempt to assassinate the head of the international civilian police corps. The contending parties were saved from themselves by the availability of League intermediaries who could provide security in the territory during the preelection period.[17]

Before phase two Knox would have been satisfied to keep all armed troops out of the Saar and to rely for peacekeeping on international civilian police.[18] In June 1934 he secured from the League Council the authority to recruit, for plebiscite supervision, police from outside the territory. A trial effort to find enough police supervisors among local Saarlanders failed when Knox declared ineligible any individual belonging "to any group which had already taken up a definite attitude in favour of one or other of the plebiscite alternatives." This was thought to be "an essential minimum for the formation of an impartial police force." Knox then told the Council that order could be maintained only if he had immediate recourse to outside recruits, which he said "might be chosen, in the first place, in the countries Members of the League of Nations where the German language is used."[19] In practice, it appears that the geographical sources for police had to be broadened beyond this if adequate numbers of men were to be enlisted. The Council arranged in September to pay for the police and instructed the secretary-general to inform all member states of Knox's request and to urge on the Council's behalf that they fully support the recruitment program. Knox set a target of 2,000 international police, twice the number in the national Saar force. To hope to recruit this many over a period of a few months was probably wildly optimistic; it was impossible with the advent of the next phase. At any rate, by the end of November Knox had completed an officer cadre headed by an Englishman and staffed by British, Norwegian, and Czechoslovakian nationals. When recruiting ceased at about the time planning for the military peacekeepers began, some one hundred constables and twenty officers had been selected. This differed from procedures during the previous century's international administrations, which placed European foreigners in top command positions but left local police intact and unsupplemented. These international policemen stayed on duty throughout the life of the Saar military force and apparently helped occasionally to alert League troops to possible disorder.[20]

The consensual, impartial character of the Saar force was widely in evidence. When governments offered troops to the League Council, they made "their decision conditional on the acceptance of the proposal by France and Germany."[21] Consent came orally from France and reluctantly but in writing from Germany—even though Hitler had already pulled out of the League. In Council debates distinctions were made, if not always neatly, between French military intervention—which, even assuming a Franco-German war would not have resulted, hardly could have been construed as impartial and based on German consent—and some substitute military presence—which Britain's Anthony Eden, speaking to the Council, proposed should be deployed with the consent of France and Germany but should not contain troops from either country.[22] Eden also said that London would supply, under these circumstances, "a suitable proportion" of such a force. As one of its architects, Eden lobbied for the Saar operation at the League, within his own government, and against the tide of British isolationist press opposition to the use of His Majesty's soldiers. (He thereby staged one of the supreme ironies in peacekeeping history: this prime mover in the League's first large-scale peacekeeping experiment blundered, twenty years later, into the Suez fiasco, making himself both the "victim" and the cause of the UN's first major peacekeeping venture.) Impartial intent at the top, in Geneva, was duplicated in the organization and demeanor of the mission. When the contingents arrived, their orders from Brind read: "The Saarforce has been expressly composed of troops drawn from countries which have no direct interest in the result of the Saar Plebiscite. All ranks will maintain a strictly neutral attitude in their dealings with the inhabitants."[23]

The Saar experience solidly fixed the doctrine of the interdependence of impartiality, consent, and noncoercion. Regardless of the breadth of its formal mandate, the force's political identity and purpose rigidly circumscribed the methods it could apply. The limits were obvious to everyone concerned. Shooting Saarlanders to enforce local order was out of the question, for their cooperation was no less essential than that of Germany and France.[24] The force therefore had to adopt a specific policy on the use of coercion, one that could be quickly understood and practiced by all participating troops and that could be clarified in advance to the parties. British doctrine was a natural choice as the source of guidelines. The commander was told that his men would have duties "analogous to those of military units if employed on 'duties in aid of the civil power' in Great Britain."[25] Translated into troop orders this meant use of minimum force, emphasis on corrective rather than punitive measures, cooperation with local authorities, reliance on indigenous security forces whenever possible, high-visibility patrolling, and carefully graduated procedures for crowd and movement control. Aid-to-civil-power techniques have since been incorporated into UN peacekeeping tactics. In fact if not in name, this has been an important framework for peacekeeping training. Canadians have used aid-to-civil-power pamphlets in UN drills. In actual missions, military units with this training background have been asked to pass it on to others—India has done this on occasion, as has Nigeria. Indeed, in tactical terms, UN operations have in some ways been indistinguishable from classic British internal security structures.[26]

In recruiting the Saar force, the League discovered that one cost of impartiality is the possibility that potential donors will come forward only if other states thought to be impartial do the same. The Dutch were willing to offer a Saar contingent only if and when the Swedes did.[27] Sweden acted the same way thirty years later, offering to go to Cyprus only with other neutrals—the presence of Austria and Finland eventually eased Sweden's worry about being politically compromised in a force mainly composed of North Atlantic Treaty Organization (NATO) members. Also seen in the Saar case were the difficulties confronting statutorily neutral countries that must judge the constitutionality of sending their soldiers into international service. At that time the Swiss Federal Council decided against participation in the Saar on constitutional grounds. Today, in a UN context, Austria has had to adjust its basic law to permit taking part in peacekeeping, and Switzerland, though not a member of the UN, has begun to grapple with possible constitutional implications of a future peacekeeping role.

Finally, Brind's postmortems on the Saar experiment cataloged troublesome operational problems that were to become standard. Foresightedly, he drew up a list of future preparedness priorities that included reliable intelligence, local language capabilities and interpreters, secure communications, public relations and information services, financial standards acceptable to all national participants, adequate central preplanning and advance party reconnaissance, local political and military liaison—in short, a list easily recognizable to UN peacekeeping planners today.[28]

Preparedness in Transition: The League to the United Nations

These modest peacekeeping legacies apparently were of little interest to the war-weary, impatient, but hopeful delegates assembled at San Francisco in 1945, who regarded their mandate in far more ambitious dimensions: theirs was the staggering task of forging a new world order, a new system for peace. They erected the century's second scaffolding for collective security; when it collapsed imaginative statesmen started over again where the Saar peacekeepers left off.

Peacekeeping institutions in the League and the United Nations have been stunted by the same types of defects, the same underdeveloped bonds of transnational political community, the same reluctance of sovereign powers to change decentralized patterns of international authority, the same refusals to assign broader prerogatives to supranational actors. If there has been this thematic continuity, however, there also have been enormous disparities in the levels of concrete achievements. League practices made the merest beginning in the peacekeeping art. Perhaps the most important omission was the League's inability—to be fair, perhaps its lack of opportunity—to mold genuinely international structures at peacekeeping field missions. Today, reproducing the internal organization of the Saar force in a UN operation would be unthinkable. The Saar contingents were under central but not integrated command. Brind's official title was "supreme commander," and he exercised effective and apparently unchallenged control over all national components. Yet none of the participating countries were even represented at central force headquarters, which was staffed almost entirely by British personnel, the exception being English-speaking liaison officers from each contingent.[29] Brind, furthermore, received guidance from and reported directly to the British government in an unconcealed manner that would swiftly end the career of a UN peacekeeping commander, whose scrupulous avoidance of such national links is now considered essential if the UN is to be regarded as an impartial agent not advancing parochial national policies.

Not only was Brind's latitude presumably acceptable to the parties concerned, but it was also consistent with the League's doctrinal and political foundations. Heavy dependence on national resources and even national decision making was a necessary by-product of the prevailing conception of the League secretariat. Its civil servant administrators were generally expected to limit their direct involvement in operational activities and to rely instead on willing member governments for administrative implementation.[30] An active responsibility for managing peacekeeping field missions—which later became characteristic of the UN secretariat—was accordingly precluded. Moreover, the League secretariat never really began to develop the unified international control over field operations that its successor started to acquire in the late 1940s. The contrasts are especially sharp between the roles played by the great powers in each era. The UN fashioned peacekeeping institutions that minimized the direct presence of the permanent members of the Security Council, while the League could not have engaged in peacekeeping without giving the great powers of the day central responsibilities—witness the French in the Vilna planning and the British in the Saar case. In one sense these two countries *were* the League, though they entertained very different visions of what would be a desirable peace-and-security role for the organization. They were conspicuous in more than just the peacekeeping theaters. For example, each gave the League a secretary-general and between them they occupied most of the important staff positions in the secretariat.

Thus, while the League's civil servants did manage to evolve an esprit de corps, a sense of international loyalty (which was gravely challenged by fascist members), and limited forms of influence over member states, the secretariat and the secretaries-general adhered closely to a passive, secondary image. Technical and financial capabilities were minuscule—annual League budgets averaged $5.4 million. The secretariat never accumulated the political weight or the competence needed to supplant the national agents on which it had to rely. The second secretary-general, Joseph Avenol of France, had no greater part in the Saar than Drummond had played in the Vilna case. The record does not show that Avenol influenced selection of peacekeeping participants or the design of basic policies of the Saar force. Rather, these responsibilities fell to the League Council, the Saar Commission, and the national suppliers. Brind in his report does not once even mention the secretary-general.

Also missing during the League period was an appreciation, or at least an articulated one, of ways that the Saar type of peacekeeping forces might be helpful in conflict situations other than plebiscites. Perhaps this was because plebiscite problems were numerous during these years as a result of territorial adjustments in postwar treaties, and there was a good deal of preoccupation with their supervision. But even then the League was often not considered useful. After the Vilna negotiations aborted, a half-dozen major plebiscites were controlled by Allied commissions that were anything but impartial. Following the Saar success, such little speculation as there was seemed not to go beyond that precedent—particularly in assuming that peacekeeping was somehow dependent on the existence of a formal international governing structure like the Saar Commission. Brind himself, for example, appears to have considered it necessary that the League have authority to impose martial law on troubled locales, though he acknowledged the difficulties that this would present to national contributors whose soldiers might then be considered occupation armies.[31] The proposition that fairly large peacekeeping forces could help maintain order even without prior internationalization, if considered at all, was generally rejected, usually because of host-state apprehension that anyone's foreign troops, including the League's, would infringe national sovereignty.[32]

Notable advances were made, however, in League experience with smaller, observer-type military commissions functioning in non-plebiscite situations. This peacekeeping variant was first used in early stages of the Vilna dispute, and again in Albania in 1921. In other League cases, national military attachés served as observer arms of civilian commissions, as during a Greek–Bulgarian crisis in 1925. The League's temporary, limited-purpose administration of Leticia in 1933 presaged the UN's administration of West Irian in 1962, both involving peacekeeping and the provision of public services on a small scale.[33] These were ancestors of later practices. A genealogy would connect the League investigative commissions to the UN's initial observer operations in its first decade and would relate the Saar force directly to UNEF.

League peacekeeping left no residue of national or regional preparedness programs similar to those later designed by potential suppliers for the UN. Experience after 1945 was to reveal that member states' interest in preparedness tends to follow the contours of the international organization's career as a peacekeeper, peaking when it seems to be vital and active, waning at other times. On the whole, the interwar years generated little demand or motivation for the earmarking of troops for League call-up, for exchange and coordination among possible contributors, or for advance planning and readiness. Fifteen years separated a Vilna force that never materialized and a Saar operation that might have generated some enduring interest had it not come at the nadir of the League's influence. The League's observer corps, because of their modest size, their usually brief duration, or their reliance on national military personnel from nearby embassies, likewise prompted little continuing attention to preparedness matters. Nevertheless, the organization had stumbled onto a new technique for conflict control, one that was to be regenerated in a later, more receptive environment containing measurably maturer international organization. Yet UN peacekeeping and preparedness are not copies of League versions. They are mutations, and their evolution is still in its infancy.

FOUR

Beyond San Francisco:
The Early Years

PREPAREDNESS for peacekeeping deserves a special place in the aggregate of United Nations accomplishments because it is the only preparedness system to materialize, even imperfectly, since 1945. Quite another kind of system had been laid out in Chapter VII of the Charter, aimed at what could be called preparedness for collective enforcement.* Though it remained a dead issue for many years, it attracted fresh interest in the 1960s. With growing frequency, proposals are heard for a retailoring of the dormant Charter system to fit the requirements of modern, consensual peacekeeping. (These proposals are examined in Chapters 7 and 8.) Precisely how this might be done has not yet been made clear, but because at least a part of the original superstructure presumably would remain intact, surveying these institutions, their demise, and their relation to early peacekeeping preparedness is worthwhile.

---

* This typology is borrowed from Ruth B. Russell, *The United Nations and United States Security Policy* (Brookings, 1968), Chaps. 5 and 6. In distinctions that clear a lot of semantic fog and commend themselves to general usage, she separates "peacekeeping" from "collective enforcement," the latter covering the original Charter system, the Soviet and American general disarmament plans of the 1960s, the Uniting for Peace Resolution of 1950, Soviet proposals for Chapter VII measures during the 1956 Suez crisis, and more recent moves to enforce political change in southern Africa.

Preparedness for Collective Enforcement

The first of two enforcement preparedness schemes, the Article 43 system, was an integral part of Chapter VII. When it quickly became defunct, an effort to put something in its place resulted in the Uniting for Peace Resolution, adopted by the General Assembly in 1950. Both were collective security variants, both provided for substantial preparedness, and both were historical curiosities by the UN's tenth birthday.

THE ARTICLE 43 SYSTEM

With a few brief paragraphs, the framers of the Charter had hoped to remedy the egregious defects of the League of Nations security machinery. The Article 43 system reflected a Big Five agreement to agree on how the Security Council would be given an effective military arm—a set of teeth, as it was called, for the new and stronger UN. Article 43 asks all member states to

> undertake to make available to the Security Council, on its call and in accordance with a special agreement or agreements, armed forces, assistance, and facilities, including rights of passage, necessary for the purpose of maintaining international peace and security.

These agreements were supposed to

> govern the numbers and types of forces, their degree of readiness and general location, and the nature of the facilities and assistance to be provided.

A Military Staff Committee, authorized by Article 47 and representing the Big Five Chiefs of Staff, was to be responsible "for the strategic direction of any armed forces" available to the Council, and was

> to advise and assist the Security Council on all questions relating to the Security Council's military requirements for the maintenance of international peace and security, the employment and command of forces placed at its disposal, the regulation of armaments, and possible disarmament.

The committee's first assignment from the Council was its last. For nearly fifteen months, it examined Article 43 "from a military point of view," as the Council cryptically directed.[1] A report on its findings merely unveiled to the public vast areas of mistrust and disagreement among the five permanent members. Though agreeing on the common assumption that they themselves would supply the bulk of the projected Article 43 call-up units, they could reach no accord on the most elementary issues concerning force structure and composition. Never again did the committee deliberate substantive matters, though it still exists, as Trygve Lie wrote, "as a symbol of disappointed hopes which are not dead, but have been put aside for a better day."[2]

Article 43 was the fruition of ideas fervidly espoused by the French throughout the early twentieth century. Léon Bourgeois believed perhaps more strongly than any other League architect that the new international organization needed a well-planned, standing military capability. The French wanted at the League's disposal contingents supplied by members, to be kept at strengths fixed by the League, deployed around the world, and supervised by a permanent general staff.[3] Anglo-American resistance killed these proposals, and the League languished without credible military power, its Council able only to recommend "what effective military, naval, or air force the Members of the League shall severally contribute to the armed forces" used for collective security purposes.[4]

The League's imperfections dismayed all internationalists and caused considerable apprehension in those European countries, especially France, that thought their security vis-à-vis Germany dependent on either disarmament or broad international guarantees. Disarmament progress was nil, and the British were not eager to increase Continental commitments, so France gropingly sought a strengthened League. In the main, this policy failed, although passing comfort was taken from ambiguous plans like the Geneva Protocol of 1924. Drafted and recommended that year by the League Assembly, the Protocol would have bound its signatories to compulsory arbitration, increased the powers of the League Council, and urged new disarmament efforts.[5] France had hoped for more. Without success it had recently pressed the League for foolproof triggers to activate the Covenant's sanctions provisions. But France lukewarmly accepted the Protocol, in part because its terms reemphasized the permanence of the 1919 peace settlement and territorial arrangements—the continuation of which was regarded by France as a bedrock national interest.

A newly elected British Conservative government was by no means the only League member to have doubts about the wisdom of the Protocol. A number of smaller states shared them. But Britain's rejection was decisive in dooming the Protocol and, with it, a single provision that anticipated the substance of Article 43. This would have entitled the League Council "to receive undertakings from States determining in advance the military, naval, and air forces which they would be able to bring into action immediately to ensure the fulfillment of the obligations in regard to sanctions" recommended by the League.[6] After the Disarmament Conference of 1932, where French initiatives again failed to produce an international legion for the League, the idea dropped out of official sight until the four-power sessions at Dumbarton Oaks in 1944 produced a tentative version of what later became Article 43.

The subsequent impasse in the Military Staff Committee deprived the UN of its army, which one U.S. participant at the time hoped would be "a mobile force able to strike quickly at long range and to bring to bear, upon any given point in the world where trouble may occur, the maximum armed force in the minimum time."[7] Without a preliminary consensus in the committee, the Council was unable to proceed at all. Experience then, in a collective enforcement setting, gave rise to an axiom that has never lost its validity: the ability to agree on preparedness for international forces is tied inextricably to national political judgments about their purposes. Just as there were in 1946 no purely military perspectives on Article 43, there have been none since on preparedness for peacekeeping. Before organizing such a force and giving it a real capacity to act, governments want adequate assurance that it will neither be used against their interests nor be controlled by countries threatening those interests. Soviet and American representatives on the Military Staff Committee had no reciprocal assurances. The concrete negotiating packages presented by each side were basically incompatible. No common conclusions could be reached about the overall size of Chapter VII forces, the relative size of their own national contributions, the desirable ratios of air, naval, and infantry units, and other fundamentals. These were not merely different technical military evaluations. Each adversary suspected the motives behind the other's proposed force. Each was convinced that the other could not "be trusted to give military aid to the United Nations without indulging in the pursuit of ulterior objectives."[8]

The deadlocked Article 43 negotiators, however, made one important choice. They agreed that UN forces should be composed of units ordinarily part of national military establishments but subject to call-up for international service.[9] There was really no contest on this point in the committee, for the respective governments had each accepted this approach at Dumbarton Oaks. But during the League years two other alternatives had received some exposure, and both are still mentioned as possibly appropriate models for peacekeeping forces. One would be a self-contained international army under exclusively international control—a centralization of authority that was firmly resisted during the 1940s in American official circles and by influential private citizens. The other approach would be a hybrid—a small internationalized nucleus that could be supplemented by national contingents of the Article 43 type.[10]

The agreed call-up system of the United Nations enjoyed some procedural advantages over that of its predecessor. The League also was supposed to rely on national units, but without any prearrangements—it was simply expected that unspecified contingents could be offered completely ad hoc when the time came. When the Security Council proved unable to enter into Article 43 contractual relations with potential suppliers, a third system evolved. Still used for peacekeeping purposes, it simply consists of an advance unilateral offer by a country to the UN secretary-general, with no formal agreements signed or implied.

The last had not been heard of Article 43. During negotiations about possible enforcement of the UN partition plan in Palestine, Secretary-General Lie and his advisers seemed to believe that the Big Five might jointly be able to deploy forces of the Article 43 type despite the failure of the Military Staff Committee only a year and a half before.[11] In 1950 the secretary-general raised the question again when he circulated his widely publicized twenty-five-year peace plan. Intended to be a coexistence agenda for the Russians and the Americans, with whom he discussed the plan before making it public, the list of measures included renewed Article 43 negotiations leading to some compromise agreement on an "interim accord for a small force sufficient to prevent or stop localized outbreaks"—essentially the same kind of force that he had tried to inject into Palestine.[12]

UNITING FOR PEACE

Attention subsequently shifted away from Article 43, because in the wake of the Korean war came the Uniting for Peace Resolution, a Chapter VII substitute that shifted collective security thinking into new, if no more productive, channels. In the background of the resolution were two crucial stimuli. The failure of the Military Staff Committee had left the United Nations without a system for mobilizing military resources; and in August 1950, the Soviet Union returned to its seat on the Security Council after its six-month boycott (over the exclusion of the Peking government), which had made it possible for the Council to respond rapidly in June to North Korean aggression without encountering a Soviet veto. On the assumption that the Russians might well not be so obligingly absent next time, the United States sponsored the resolution, which the Assembly adopted in November over the negative votes of the Soviet bloc. It presented some not entirely new procedures by which collective security measures could be recommended by the General Assembly, where the Soviet veto could of course be avoided.

In addition, the lengthy resolution urged three readiness steps that soon came to dominate thinking about preparedness. All members were to maintain within their military establishments "armed forces elements so trained, organized and equipped that they could promptly be made available" to the UN. National programs were to be reported, without prior negotiations, to a Collective Measures Committee. And the secretary-general was to appoint a special panel of military experts to give "technical advice" to countries offering units.[13] Essentially this structure paralleled the Article 43 system and was to take its place.[14]

To drafters of the resolution, the Korean experience had underlined a need not only for rapid decisions by UN political organs and for better military preparedness but also for some kind of early-warning device that could alert the UN to dangerous situations or report the facts from the scene in case of aggression. By coincidence a small, temporary UN commission that had been in Korea at the time of the attack from the north was able to perform this valuable function for the Security Council. So the Uniting for Peace Resolution also established, for such fact-finding and reporting purposes, a Peace Observation Commission of fourteen member governments. Technically still in existence, this commission drifted into limbo in the early 1950s after a brief, somewhat confused career.[15]

Misconceptions flourish about the relation between the resolution's military provisions and later peacekeeping. It is easy to overlook what the United Nations was in 1950. Searching for a collective security role when international politics were dominated by superpower confrontation, the organization nearly always found itself sharing American world views of how the cold war should be fought, a reflection not only of the international security preferences of most members at that time but also of the vigorous U.S. efforts to incorporate the UN into its anticommunist strategies.

For the United States, the organization was an increment to its containment equipment. American power, levers of persuasion, and the UN membership structure coalesced to isolate, expose, and outmaneuver the Soviet Union and its satellites. Western successes can be only partially measured by the multitude of Assembly resolutions that were passed over objections of a Soviet-bloc minority and by the frequency of Soviet vetoes in the Council. Defensiveness and unrelenting hostility hardened Russian attitudes, and UN-Soviet relations entered, "during 1949–1950, the period of complete deterioration" when the Soviet Union "seemed to be on the verge of pulling out."[16] The Acheson Plan, as the Uniting for Peace Resolution came to be known, was a stepchild as well as a casualty of these years.[17] Though not carrying mandatory legal weight, the new procedures could be employed for the same ends as Article 43 but with a critical difference: Article 43 assumed Soviet cooperation, while Uniting for Peace was designed to operate after Soviet noncooperation had been documented by its veto in the Council. By clear implication the resolution could engage the UN against Soviet interests. So

> in terms of the *kind* of international security pursued, the Uniting for Peace Resolution . . . is more closely related to the North Atlantic Treaty Organization than to the collective security of Chapter VII of the Charter; it represents a stage in the alignment of United Nations members in hostile military camps. It 'divides for war' even as it 'unites for peace'.[18]

Resting on top of the preparedness clauses of the resolution, then, was ideological baggage so heavy that it was impossible to separate the preparedness system of 1950 from the East-West divisions that helped to create it. Sixty countries were UN members at the time. Only four—Norway, Denmark, Greece, and Thailand, three of them North Atlantic Treaty Organization (NATO) members—made even conditional offers to set aside armed forces. Moreover, during the three years the Collective Measures Committee actively studied problems of future enforcement under the resolution, most of the half-hearted interest that was expressed came from partners in one or another Western defense alliance. The close association with regional pacts is plain in written communications received by the committee.[19] Many simply state that national units already on NATO duty might be available for UN collective action, implying that no special units were needed. In the cases of Denmark and Norway, any newly formed UN units were also to be on call for NATO or would be used only after consultation with the alliance. The United States deliberately encouraged this connection in its "effort to establish the thesis that forces contributed to such arrangements were in fact contributions to the total forces available to the United Nations," an interpretation explicitly accepted by the Collective Measures Committee and the General Assembly.[20] As the feeble pattern of these responses emerged, Jawaharlal Nehru's characterization of the resolution as a conversion of "the United Nations into a larger edition of the Atlantic Pact"[21] acquired pinpoint accuracy. With similar reasoning, other nonaligned countries like Indonesia and Burma had nothing to do with the Acheson Plan. For many potential suppliers, the desire for ideological noncommitment was coupled with fear of involvement in great-power wars.[22]

This concern was appreciated, too, by the secretariat. An official in the executive office of the secretary-general acknowledged that the resolution could be used "in any case of aggression whether committed by or with the support of a big power." "The responses of Member states to the invitation to earmark voluntarily specific forces to the United Nations," he added, "have been conditioned to a considerable extent by this consideration."[23]

The Collective Measures Committee's development of working principles was intended to serve two purposes: the completion of collective enforcement contingency planning never done by the Military Staff Committee, and the assimilation of recent lessons to lay groundwork, it was said, for "future Koreas."[24] The committee began the first and only broad assessment of UN enforcement capabilities, covering political, economic, and military dimensions. Relevant secretariat departments were engaged in research and planning, outside experts were consulted, and sanctions experiences predating the UN were reviewed.

Lie's own proposals to the committee were obviously influenced by the Korean precedent. In effect he resurrected an idea he had toyed with early in the war, when it was obvious that most states would not have military resources large enough to send major combat units. So he urged them to volunteer, instead, individuals who would make up a heterogeneous international brigade. In later revising this approach for the committee, he proposed that part-time individual volunteers join combat and technical units that were trained and held in readiness within national military establishments and capable of being integrated rapidly with the bigger field forces presumably forthcoming under Uniting for Peace. His plan was quietly shelved, as he realized its impracticalities and yielded "to the dual pressures" of "disinterest of Members, and the doubts of his Secretariat colleagues most closely concerned."[25]

The resolution's political milieu and underlying motives help to explain not only the unenthusiastic immediate response but also the later tendency to treat its military provisions as unrelated to peacekeeping. The reasons for this are not always appreciated. One commentator thought it remarkable that a basic statement of Scandinavian peacekeeping policy did not even mention the resolution as a historic milestone, instead taking the United Nations Emergency Force (UNEF) as a "starting point."26 It is of course not remarkable at all. Neither Hammarskjöld nor Thant customarily referred to Uniting for Peace as a seminal event. And rightly, for the better part of tactical wisdom has been to assume that this implied association would be prejudicial to peacekeeping's image of impartiality.

Preparedness for Peacekeeping

Discussion about enforcement preparedness limped along until 1954, when the Collective Measures Committee closed its doors for good. By then, hopes for an effective collective security system had receded entirely, and the UN was moving through a period of transition from an organization regarded as a weapon in the cold war to one that might help moderate its effects in arenas of local conflict. Hammarskjöld had been chosen secretary-general early in 1953 after the surprisingly timed resignation of his beleaguered predecessor, who had been under continual attack from Moscow for his active part in Korean war decisions, and whose personal effectiveness in relations with the Soviet Union had broken down completely. The year 1955 brought a Soviet-American package deal that conferred UN membership on a profusion of impatient candidates whose entry into the organization had long been prevented because each of the superpowers had excluded the other's nominees. From their new Assembly seats these novice members watched the Security Council devote ominous lengths of time to the growing hostilities in the Middle East. There, on Israel's tense borders, the UN was soon to be thrust into a kind of peacekeeping that owed much to the inventiveness and leadership of the second secretary-general. Throughout his tenure, his own concepts of peacekeeping as preventive diplomacy were to depend heavily on the active political support of a rapidly expanding, more heterogeneous membership eager to avoid the dreary battles of the past over collective security machinery.

Yet even before this, while the failures of collective security planning were becoming more and more glaring, the UN had begun to inject itself into conflicts in ways short of collective enforcement, foreshadowing the dispatch in 1956 of the UNEF to Egypt. United Nations military personnel had earlier been sent out with a frequency surprising for so new and untested an organization. The cases came in rapid succession: Greece, Palestine, Indonesia, and Kashmir, all between 1946 and 1949. Peacekeeping was not yet a term in use, and such consistency of description as these missions received was simply to label them agents of "peaceful settlement." This designation served to distinguish them from Chapter VII sanctions and identify them generally with diplomatic rather than military arts.

They were all observer operations. Three were responsible for monitoring agreed cease-fires and performing related services—the United Nations Truce Supervision Organization (UNTSO) in Palestine, the United Nations Commission for Indonesia (UNCI) in Indonesia, and the United Nations Military Observer Group in India and Pakistan (UNMOGIP) in Kashmir. The United Nations Special Committee on the Balkans (UNSCOB) in Greece was a fact-finding mission to ascertain whether Greece's communist neighbors were infiltrating her northern borders. All acted with the consent of the host state or the parties to cease-fires, and all reported to a UN political organ or a subsidiary body.[27] The UN initiated its preparedness career during the course of supporting these four missions in the field. The organization did not look over its shoulder at the League, nor did it consciously try to fashion coherent institutions for the future. What happened, as one secretariat official has said, was an evolution "almost by accident."[28]

Methods and solutions were usually dictated less by concern for enduring precedent than by political imperative or technical expedience. Experimentation and pragmatism were the rules at the secretariat and in the field. Attempts by Lie and others, however, to wrap congeries of ad hoc approaches in doctrine and to convert them into long-range plans with a UN imprimatur fared very badly. Then, as now, doctrine lagged far behind practice.

EARLY IMPROVISATIONS

Incidental differences were many among the early missions. Variety in operating conditions and demands affected the number of observers and their equipment, deployment, and tactics.[29] But several factors shaped the special characters of the four missions: their composition, American and Soviet attitudes toward them, the U.S. role in materially supporting them, and the secretariat's progressively greater managerial responsibilities for them.

Slowly but perceptibly, political impartiality gained acceptance as an essential criterion for determining the composition of missions. This was most evident in the two that outlived the UN's first decade, UNTSO and UNMOGIP. But impartiality has always been a relative concept, and it had different connotations in those years, especially in that it did not preclude a level of direct American participation that now would be thought taboo.

One measure of this trend was an erosion of the assumption that members of field missions were to be representatives of states seated on the Security Council. The initial formula used in the Greek case restricting participation to the eleven members of the Council is the antithesis of Hammarskjöld's deliberate exclusion of the permanent members from operational roles in peacekeeping. The UNSCOB system was never used again; it was followed by the practice of permitting participation only by states with consular representation in areas of observer operations—the basis for selection in UNCI, and in UNTSO until its expansion in 1954. And UNMOGIP departed sharply from its predecessors. Invitations to participate in it were tendered to all UN members, specially recruited national personnel were used instead of men already attached to diplomatic agencies on the scene, and composition was decided in consultation with host states.[30]

Control of mission personnel gradually shifted away from supplier states and toward the United Nations. Except for UNMOGIP, the early observers were either instructed—that is, openly receiving orders from their governments and presumably reporting to them—or the formal lines of their responsibility were ambiguous. The shift began as early as 1948, but it was slow, it was paced differently by the various suppliers, and it meant comparatively little at informal levels where national controls were strongest. Formal rules to the contrary were technically in force: an UNSCOB Handbook for Observers was strict about their obligation to maintain "complete impartiality" and the "utmost discretion." They were ordered to serve UN interests and to accept instructions from no one but UN superiors.[31]

These injunctions were not fully implemented immediately in UNSCOB or elsewhere. There was some compliance with the prescribed standards, but probably neither more nor less than that of the U.S. government and its observers on UN duty. During congressional testimony in 1949, top-ranking officials of the State and Defense departments said that American officers then in all four missions were under the "administrative" authority of the United Nations but had always been under the "operational" command of the United States. The legislators were told that the United States had "not thus far instituted any channel of command, which would bring a foreign commander in between our military personnel and the National Military Establishment here in Washington." In the future "our observers will be able to report directly to the United States Government."[32]

Without exception, the early operations accorded politically with U.S. interests and were dependent technically on U.S. logistical and other assistance. The Soviet Union was consistently and effectively excluded from any active involvement. This asymmetry explains why Lie's later proposals for institutionalization provoked violent Soviet objections and why the Russians have long harbored suspicions that peacekeeping is and always has been at bottom a Western machination. This attitude is not simply a product of the Congo operation, the Korean war, or the general isolation of the communist minority in the UN throughout the cold war. It reaches back to the very beginnings of what is now called peacekeeping.

In view of the anticommunist purposes of UNSCOB, Soviet hostility was automatic. A preliminary UN investigation in Greece produced a report that was vetoed by the Russians. The United States sidestepped this obstruction, took the issue to the Assembly, and thereafter UNSCOB operated with its two communist slots boycotted under protest. In UNTSO and UNCI, it was not self-exclusion but adroit Western maneuvering that squeezed out the Soviet Union. This was the motive for the rule that observers would be chosen only from states with local diplomatic representation: the Russians had none in either location, so pro-Western composition was assured. This was basic U.S. policy. Washington generally felt that it was "especially important to prevent the sending of Soviet military personnel to troubled areas under United Nations auspices. By working through subsidiary organs on which the Soviet Union was not represented, and by leaving to those organs the responsibility for recruiting needed personnel, it was possible to exclude the Soviet Union altogether."[33]

The Russians were infuriated by this tactic, and once engaged the United States in a rare verbal skirmish over the composition question.[34] When hostilities broke out in Palestine during May 1948, the Security Council called for a truce and ordered UN political representatives already there to be given the necessary military observers, but without saying how they should be chosen or where they should come from. Count Folke Bernadotte, whose career as UN mediator was ended by an assassin later the same year, was able with this ambiguity to secure observers directly from the United States, France, and Belgium, and a small number of officers from his own country, Sweden.

Each had previously been given UN fact-finding responsibilities because, as the United States argued, they already maintained consuls in the area who could quickly relay information. On hearing of Bernadotte's move, the Russians accused him of exceeding his authority but did not mention that earlier, after the Council's truce resolution, Bernadotte had approached Soviet diplomats in Cairo about arranging for Soviet observers in Palestine and had been persuaded by the Americans to reconsider.[35] In any case the Russians now proceeded to do what they had not done before and have not done since—they volunteered to send Russian officers to a UN mission not authorized under Chapter VII. Offering five men to serve alongside nearly two dozen Americans, the Soviet ambassador to the UN, Andrei Gromyko, exclaimed, "No one will understand why the United States has the right to send its military observers to Palestine and the USSR has not. What justification is there for such a thesis?" Gromyko's Ukrainian colleagues at the Council table answered his rhetorical question: "Merely because these three countries happen to have Consuls in Jerusalem? This is a purely accidental factor—and a very weak one." "The point at issue," Gromyko said, "is that the United States in the

first instance—and also some other members of the Security Council—
oppose the very idea, the very principle, that USSR military observers
should be included among the observers."[36] Oppose it they did, by
easily outvoting a Soviet resolution introduced by Gromyko.

American influence in political councils was matched by American
technical dominance in the field. To some extent, the secretariat played
a support role in all early missions, but a relatively minor one compared
to the logistical services provided by participating countries. United
States help was indispensable, and U.S. officers filled key staff positions
at field headquarters. In absolute terms, U.S. contributions were
modest. The operations themselves were small but required specialized
communications and transport equipment, as well as maintenance
facilities that only the United States could spare and quickly send to
UN theaters. By mid-1949 disproportionate national logistical support
was the normal pattern.[37] Australia, China, France, the Netherlands,
and the United Kingdom provided an occasional ship or airplane with
crew, or light ground transport. Britain's presence in Palestine at the
time allowed it to contribute aircraft and assorted other logistical
services and hardware. But the United States was the prime supplier.
During most of the Greek mission's early days, nearly all transport,
communication systems, and other major support items were funneled
from U.S. sources. Throughout its life the mission in Indonesia was
underequipped and undersupported, dependent on hit-or-miss help
from the local consulates supplying observers, or relying on the Dutch
and Indonesians themselves.[38] The parties even gave defensive arms
and ammunition to the observers. The United States filled the major
gaps. Communications links—immensely complicated in this difficult,
vast territory—represented a case in point. Initially the field net's
central receiver was at the American consulate in Batavia, which also
lent portable equipment to the observers. Later a U.S. naval communications vessel in the Djakarta harbor serviced the entire mission.
In Palestine both the United States and the United Kingdom were
logistically active in routine support functions, with the United States
carrying the bigger load and also providing, along with France, the
ships needed for observation purposes.

All this still left room for field involvement by secretariat civilian administrators. It is often forgotten that from the very beginning the secretariat has dispatched personnel and services to support military peacekeepers. This began before the establishment of special-purpose units within the secretariat, such as the Field Service, and before UNEF. In 1956 the administrative demands were more massive than they had been, yet not qualitatively different. Comparison of an organization table for any early mission with that of UNEF demonstrates the essential similarities of secretariat-supplied personnel.[39] Every field headquarters contained an integral complement of civilians: political officers; legal, press, finance, and administrative specialists; technicians and maintenance workers; clerks, secretaries, précis-drafters, and editors; and occasionally photographers, interpreters, and translators. These services were not limited to military observer operations. During its first years the UN had also been asked periodically to send out diplomatic field commissions of various kinds, and these too were staffed and supported by New York. This represented a novel operational role that demonstrated rather vividly how differently UN practice in these respects was to evolve, as compared with the more restrictive approach of the League secretariat and its almost complete dependence on national administrative implementation.

As the UN secretariat took on more support responsibilities, improved its performance, and substituted itself for national sources, it progressively became the centralized coordinator and manager of field missions. This piecemeal, gradual evolution had a lasting effect on peacekeeping. One of the most far-reaching events was the secretariat's early claim, which eventually gained broad acceptance among member states, that its own capabilities for organizing and directing field missions had decisive advantages over any similar national capabilities. Greater assurance of political impartiality and command efficiency were said to result from international control. One of the secretariat's earliest defenses of this proposition in an official document was a memorandum on reorganization of UNSCOB to diminish national controls and reinforce its international character. The new modifications gave the United Nations explicit command preeminence throughout the entire field structure. Previously authority had been shared with national participants on various levels. "Experience has shown."

declared the secretariat, "that the dual control of the past months is unsatisfactory and should be replaced by an organization under one authority." Unified command was to be centralized by appointment of a "chief" of observation teams, and it was hoped that this would produce improvements in recruitment, support, and overall performance.[40] This episode was a preliminary but crucial step toward institutionalization of political impartiality, and toward applying its standards in practice to all political and command decisions.

With time and experience, the secretariat's support functions were regularized, though at first everyone did whatever was needed. Even secretariat civilians were on a few occasions detailed to observer duty until a military officer could replace them. But for the most part the secretariat's civilians—who were either detailed from UN headquarters in New York or recruited internationally—confined themselves to staff work at field headquarters, though top secretariat officials or special representatives were often engaged at the vortex of local negotiations, as Bernadotte and Ralph Bunche had been in Palestine.

Eventually the United Nations began purchasing some of its own equipment, especially communications systems, rather than using hardware on loan from national participants. And when loans were accepted, the secretariat started reimbursing suppliers. Before long its financial responsibility extended to paying maintenance costs for military and other equipment, as well as the extraordinary expenses, per diems, and transportation costs for observers.[41] The UN also took over certain backup functions from the military. In Palestine and Kashmir communications, the secretariat recruited its own commercial radio operators and assigned them virtually full responsibility for signals within the missions and to New York via a worldwide telecommunications network approved by the General Assembly in 1948. The secretariat also established standard procedures for some support services and for securing observers through national channels.

LIE'S PROPOSALS DEFEATED

As the secretariat began to acquire responsibility for operational performance and technical support, Secretary-General Lie hoped to systematize this de facto practice and to prepare for future peacekeeping. Tenaciously he campaigned for a standing international corps modeled largely on the early observer missions.[42] This was largely a failure, and he provoked a serious constitutional struggle with part of his constituency. It was the first attempt by the UN chief executive to enlarge preparedness officially, and it was done on very shaky constitutional grounds and with uncertain political support, even from Western and presumably sympathetic Council members. It was the first chance for the UN membership as a whole to take a stand on peacekeeping preparedness. And for the first time the Soviet Union went on record as opposing all preparedness, for whatever stated purposes, unless done explicitly within the Article 43 framework.

Lie admitted that his scheme, initially presented in the autumn of 1948, was "radical." He named the corps United Nations Guard. He tried to reassure critics that it was not a substitute for the enforcement army that the Military Staff Committee had failed to create, that it had nothing to do with Article 43 or Chapter VII, that it would not be physically capable of combat, and that it would be entirely non-military and consensual in character. Implementation of Lie's plan would have had the effect of reversing the decision of the great powers to reject internationalized forces for the UN. The UN Guard was to be recruited as a standing, organic unit of the secretariat, composed of personnel for technical support and for operational duties such as protecting UN property and personnel, patrolling cease-fire zones, or supervising elections. In time the Guard would number from 1,000 to 5,000 men. But as a start, Lie advocated a force of 800 international volunteers, 300 of them trained and permanently located at UN headquarters or somewhere in Europe, and the remaining 500 held in reserve in their own countries.

The secretary-general's mistiming was astonishing. It alone guaranteed communist denunciations. His trial balloon speech on the Guard was delivered at Harvard University as a commencement address in June 1948. Later that month he described the proposal in his annual report and soon submitted a more elaborate version, complete with a table of organization and job descriptions. In this same month the Security Council witnessed the Soviet-American exchange over exclusion of Russian officers from Palestine. Within the preceding twelve months, the United States had neutralized Soviet vetoes by transferring control of UNSCOB to the Assembly. Moreover, the Western majority persuaded the Assembly, over communist objections, to send a commission to expedite free elections in Korea, an issue the United States and the Russians had bilaterally been unable to resolve during nearly two years of negotiations. So the USSR must have taken very keen notice of Lie's stated intent to use the proposed Guard at the call of *either* the Council or the Assembly. It rejected the plan outright and unreservedly. Lie's reassurances were ignored. This Guard, the Russians charged, was to be all the things the secretary-general said it would not be. Many noncommunist states had doubts too, some serious: the Guard's costs would stretch thin the UN budget; 800 men were too few to do any real good; the Guard could grow into an enforcement arm of the UN; it was impractical; it would intrude on local police powers. Lie did not even enjoy the support of the United States, which expectedly balked at the proposed internationalization. "In the face of opposition by two great Powers, the doubts of three others, and the mixed response of lesser states, the Secretary-General retreated."[43]

Lie tried again in 1949, with countersuggestions more modestly designed and cautiously presented. There would be no standing, internationally controlled units with operational functions. Instead the secretariat would merely keep a list of names, a shadow observer force, composed of persons recommended by member governments. This innovation was approved by the Assembly but never implemented. Another part of the revised plan was new in name only. He proposed a Field Service section at headquarters that "would in fact amount to a systematization of the regular functions of the Secretariat" in providing administrative and technical support for field missions.[44] The communist states reacted no more favorably to this idea, but the membership voted it through.

The total result in the end was a minor bureaucratic consolidation with some new nomenclature. No other formal preparedness measures were attempted during Lie's tenure. It was, as he later recalled disappointedly, "something useful, but not at all what I had originally intended."[45] This remains the only Assembly resolution in UN history favorably affecting secretariat preparedness.

Debate on Lie's blueprints did provide still more hints of movement toward acceptance of international control and impartial performance. Lie had explicitly mentioned the advantage of the Guard's "ability to proceed with the necessary confidence and authority . . . without the suspicion of partiality," and he emphasized that "absence of an independent international body representative of the authority of the United Nations has seriously embarrassed the work of United Nations missions."[46] Paralleling changes already begun in the field, one member state further proposed that all nominees for the special panel of observers be required to take the standard loyalty oath of the UN international employee.* It is a revealing commentary on the time that objections to this reform were raised by a group of states that included the United States, which cited possible domestic constitutional impediments. Use of the oath was therefore not approved.

A STATUS REPORT ON EARLY PREPAREDNESS

Each of the three preparedness components fared quite differently during this first UN decade. Surely the most important trend was the steady growth of secretariat independence and of its responsibility for peacekeeping missions. The other two preparedness components—provision of logistics and availability of national suppliers of personnel—remained largely undeveloped. The reasons are obvious. Logistical demands were moderate and the extent of national participation similarly limited. If only the initial years of the first three missions, in which composition was restricted, are considered, the total number of contributing states was small and participants in more than one operation can be counted on one hand. Only UNMOGIP was theoretically open to participation by all UN members. There was little incentive, in logistical and manpower matters, to question the assumption that whatever became necessary could be done ad hoc. Naturally

---

* Each observer would have had to swear to act "with the interests of the United Nations only in view, and not to seek or accept instructions . . . from any Government or other authority external to the organization."

this complacency was reinforced by the absence of overall UN-approved international preparedness programs. Too, concern for peacekeeping was diverted by the Korean war and the renewed, if short-lived, concern for collective security preparedness.

Nevertheless, the early years left a rough impression of what was to come. Logistically the missions largely depended on American help. United Nations operations in Egypt and the Congo could not have survived without massive technical support from the United States. Subsequent supplier patterns in all UN missions became less like those in Greece and Indonesia and more like those in UNMOGIP, and in UNTSO after the 1954 inclusion of neutral and disinterested states. Standard practice later was for great powers to be ipso facto disqualified, along with any states having political or other interests in the outcome of the local dispute. These principles have remained intact despite exceptions in the Congo, where Hammarskjöld at first tried to "Africanize" the United Nations Congo Operation (ONUC), and in the United Nations Force in Cyprus (UNFICYP), where special circumstances allow an active British role.

During this decade there was no general stocktaking of preparedness problems after Lie's grandiose designs fizzled. Between the Korean war and UNEF there was little inclination to look beyond the current needs of ongoing missions. Preparedness would perhaps have been more fully developed by 1956 had the UN been called upon to engage in wider peacekeeping responsibilities before Suez. But it was not, despite occasional indications that new roles were being contemplated for the organization. For instance, at the Geneva negotiations in 1954, had the United States and the associated states of Cambodia, Laos, and Vietnam been given their preferences, the UN would very likely have been asked to supervise the Indochina settlements. Lie had suggested this possibility earlier to French Foreign Minister Georges Bidault,[47] but the French strongly resisted any UN role. The British, for a time favorably disposed to UN involvement, really had no choice but to play down the idea in the face of France's opposition; and China and the Viet Minh rejected any UN responsibilities in Indochina. At about the same time, in 1953 and 1955, private diplomatic discussions in and outside the UN also explored the possibility of replacing UNTSO with a larger peacekeeping force having firmer authority and a broader mandate. This too came to nothing.[48]

By the end of the decade the missions in Greece and Indonesia had terminated. Those in Palestine and Kashmir evidenced much plainer contours of true internationality. The secretary-general exercised genuine operational control through UN-appointed commanders, his civilian staff at mission sites handled all administrative and financial affairs, and a rough civilian–military division of labor emerged at local headquarters. Overall financial responsibility rested in New York. Peacekeeping support became "business as usual" for the secretariat, and its regular administrative departments integrated this function into their routine activities. Slowly, international command and control of peacekeepers were becoming constant companions of the secretariat's international administration. Slowly, practice was catching up with theory.

FIVE

Hammarskjöld, Middle Powers, and the Nordic Response

PARADOXES are found throughout the evolution of preparedness after the first generation. Against what might seem to be reasonable expectations, as United Nations peacekeeping increased around the globe, prospects for UN-sponsored preparedness became dimmer and dimmer. Between 1956 and 1968 the Security Council or the General Assembly authorized a new peacekeeping operation on the average of once every year and a half, and between 200,000 and 250,000 soldiers served under the UN flag. But not until 1967 did either political body formally initiate even such a minimal preparedness measure as a study of past experiences (see Chapter 7). Dag Hammarskjöld and U Thant were entrusted with ever larger peacekeeping responsibilities, and they took on increasingly heavy burdens as executive managers of field missions, though no formal action has ever been taken by the Assembly or the Council to strengthen the secretary-general's relevant staff capacities. Yet preparedness did make advances—and notable ones. What happened was that while peacekeeping services became more visible peacekeeping preparedness went underground.

Political and constitutional arguments about the conduct of peacekeeping are deeply rooted and have been set forth uncompromisingly. They have not, however, been strong enough to prevent peacekeeping operations from being launched when the need arose. But political discord has had real impact nonetheless. It erased reliable financing practices; it circumscribed the secretary-general's executive maneuverability; it divided UN opinion about the respective peacekeeping powers of the Council and the Assembly; it straitjacketed preparedness programs. Political disagreements have transformed preparedness into a do-it-yourself trade in countries willing to allocate national resources for peacekeeping. Both the financing of peacekeeping and the preparedness for it are today in phases of arrested development, both heavily dependent on member states' goodwill, voluntary assistance, and occasional cooperation for common purposes.

Nothing attests so convincingly to the controversy surrounding peacekeeping as the semiclandestine atmosphere that occasionally has enveloped preparedness efforts within the secretariat and, to a lesser extent, among national suppliers of peacekeeping personnel. They and others have repeatedly failed to get a UN stamp of approval for preparedness activities already being undertaken without official UN encouragement. In place of centralized pooling of resources, knowledge, and experience, there have been strictly unilateral activities, quiet exchanges of information, and several unofficial multilateral conferences, to which a secretariat representative might be invited. Peacekeeping's strongest supporters have been constantly preoccupied with how to alter this imbalance, how to get formal guidance from headquarters and involve it in preparedness.

Goals for preparedness programs and policies did not have to be defined in the abstract or on the drawing boards of military planners. For all who cared to look, a preparedness agenda was being drafted, based on the lessons learned from operations in Egypt (United Nations Emergency Force—UNEF), the Congo (United Nations Congo Operation—ONUC), Cyprus (United Nations Force in Cyprus—UNFICYP), and smaller but troublesome observer missions. All of these made the casual approach of the first preparedness generation obsolete.

The three components of preparedness now needed to be geared up to new and more demanding challenges. Even though seven of the initial ten UNEF participants had previously sent officers to early observer missions, they thereafter faced new kinds of commitments at new orders of magnitude. No longer could supplier states, as before

1956, perfunctorily survey their military establishments for a handful of officers willing to do short-term observer duty. No longer could planners make comfortable assumptions about the ease of setting up and supporting new missions. No longer could the secretariat expect to administer peacekeeping routinely. Unanticipated demands required vastly more manpower, more sophisticated military skills, more effective management, and more competent logisticians—the 20,000 men of ONUC, to cite what was perhaps the most extreme of the UN's operational nightmares, covered selectively an area one-fourth the size of the United States in which normal services and communications had almost totally broken down. Overshadowing expanding requirements was the need to devise politically acceptable preparedness methods in a diplomatic environment that radically narrowed areas of possible consensus.

Hammarskjöld and Preparedness

Dag Hammarskjöld indelibly stamped preparedness with his singular style of diplomacy and leadership. He and his concepts of the secretary-generalship pervaded the next generation of preparedness, even though he was killed before it ended in the mid-1960s. If Hammarskjöld was the prime mover, certain middle power members of the UN were his principal agents. To increase preparedness became one of their shared objectives, and together they moved it out of the doldrums into which it had slipped.

Hardly had UNEF been put in the field before Hammarskjöld turned his attention to the needs of the hypothetical next crisis. The tangible outcome of his concern was a pair of documents that became the guidelines for all subsequent preparedness activity. The first and more well known is his 1958 Summary Study of the UNEF experience.[1] It is a basic outline for the entirety of peacekeeping and the first elaboration of principles for comprehensive preparedness. The second is a letter from the secretary-general in 1959 to participants in Middle East peacekeeping missions. Its contents, known but never published, represent the only existing official communication between

the secretariat and individual member states urging specific preparedness steps. The history of these documents has been called by a Hammarskjöld biographer "an elegant example of the way he [could]
weave back and forth on the diplomatic gridiron and yet always move
steadily toward his objective."² Capacity for independent initiative
and a gift for conceptualization are two qualities recognized as
Hammarskjöld trademarks.³ Both were central to his preparedness
diplomacy. The secretariat, he once said, "has creative capacity. It can
introduce new ideas. It can in proper form take initiatives. It can put
before the Member governments new findings which will influence
their actions."⁴ He took precisely this generative approach to preparedness.

Soon after the dispatch of UNEF he suggested that this peacekeeping
venture be studied "should the Organization wish to build an agreed
standby plan" for a peacekeeping force that "could be activated on
short notice in future emergencies."⁵ He announced then that a study
would be made within the secretariat. Hammarskjöld did not explain
what such a "plan" might entail, but several months earlier Canadian
External Affairs Minister Lester B. Pearson, who won the Nobel
peace prize as Hammarskjöld's co-architect of UNEF, had described
what probably was the substance of the secretary-general's thinking:

> Member governments, excluding the permanent members of the Security
> Council, should be invited to signify a willingness in principle to contribute con-
> tingents to the United Nations for purposes that are essentially noncombatant, such
> as, for example, the supervision of agreed cease-fires and comparable peace super-
> visory functions.
>
> · · · · ·
>
> Even if governments are unable to give the United Nations a "fighting" force ready
> and organized to serve it . . . they should be willing to earmark smaller forces for
> [this] more limited duty. . . . We might in this way be able to construct a halfway
> house at the crossroads of war, and utilize an intermediate technique between
> merely passing resolutions and actually fighting.⁶

Hammarskjöld envisaged a sequence beginning with secretariat enun-
ciation of working principles for a preparedness system, proceeding to
an explicit, formal acceptance of these guidelines by the Assembly, and
ending with some fairly definite arrangements between the UN and
willing member states, as suggested by Pearson. Coupled with the
secretariat's own internal resources for supporting peacekeeping, these

were to be the foundation for his "agreed standby plan."[7] Hammarskjöld's strategy was to secure positive approval from the Assembly, and he seemed to imply that beyond formulating these principles his freedom to act was conditional on unambiguous Assembly consent.[8] However, once it became clear that no organizational backing would be forthcoming, the secretary-general pursued identical objectives semiofficially and strictly on the independent authority of his office. The 1959 letter originated in this context.

Hammarskjöld never had any illusions about the political problems still to be overcome if the Summary Study was ever formally accepted. Cautiously, he stressed that standby arrangements would not necessitate a permanent force or a sanctions army, and he was calculatedly vague at controversial junctures in the Study. He had to maneuver gingerly between a need to disengage his plan from any association with Article 43[9] and a need to find acceptable justifications for a preparedness system not explicitly provided for in the Charter. He left open a number of constitutional questions, while implying that Chapter VII procedures were not applicable—he never mentioned the Military Staff Committee or the Article 43 special agreements. He defined standby arrangements as loosely as he could. They were not so much a contractual scheme as "an approval of those general conclusions regarding principles which can be reached in the light of the UNEF experience." If these "were to meet with the approval of the General Assembly, they would provide a continuing basis on which useful contacts in a standby context might be established with interested governments, with the aim of being prepared for any requests" for peacekeeping forces in the future.[10]

He gave a significant role in the system to the secretariat. In place of the Military Staff Committee he substituted the secretariat as the executor of preparedness arrangements. Not only should it manage particular peacekeeping operations, said Hammarskjöld, it also should serve as the permanent center for all preparedness activities. But this goal would be approached slowly. The secretariat initially would take "soundings" from member states to determine whether "a number of governments in their planning would be willing to take into account the possibility of having to provide promptly—on an emergency basis, on specific appeal from the United Nations—men and matériel" to a peacekeeping operation. "Continuing contacts with the governments" that are possible suppliers would be maintained and the situation would be kept under "constant review." But beyond this the secretariat should not go without a signal from the Assembly. Hammarskjöld underlined the need "at some stage" for "a standing group of a few military experts" that "might be useful in order to keep under review such arrangements as may be made by Member Governments." But he considered this step still "premature," and added that such a "far-reaching understanding" would "obviously" have to be submitted "in appropriate form to the General Assembly."[11]

A combination of factors dissolved all hope that the Study would be approved. Automatic reaction by Africans and Asians against any international forces, suspicion on the part of the Soviet Union, Latin American apprehension about financial burdens, and wide skepticism about the intentions of the United States after President Dwight D. Eisenhower told the Assembly that, had a standby force been in existence, it rather than the U.S. Marines could have intervened in Lebanon during 1958—all these doubts cooled the Assembly to a point where it did not even wish to consider the Study.[12] Hammarskjöld, not relishing a confrontation, forwarded it to an Assembly committee, remarking only that members could comment on it, that public discussion of peacekeeping might be guided by it, and that "Member States needed to know as fully as possible" what might be involved if the UN ever needed their assistance as peacekeepers. Plainly reversing his earlier intention, he stated that "there was no need for the Assembly to take any action at the present time."[13]

This said and done, Hammarskjöld finessed the formal obstacles, and preparedness went into quiet and informal channels. Before long he made it known that he intended to pursue the matter regardless of the Assembly's attitude. Soon Pearson again urged the earmarking, training, and equipping of national units for peacekeeping. He suggested that medium-sized and small states implement on their own the preparedness principles of the Study, without waiting for the Assembly. Hammarskjöld, of course, responded favorably, calling it a "useful next step" and offering the opinion that if such voluntary commitments were made the secretariat could create a special staff to administer them.[14] In 1959 he took what under the circumstances was an extraordinary step. He lifted language from the Summary Study and inserted it in a written inquiry to the twenty-three states that had supplied peacekeepers in the Middle East, asking whether they were willing to take into account, in their national military planning, the possibility that they might be asked to provide personnel again in some future emergency.[15]

The Middle Power Constituency

By the time Hammarskjöld's letter reached the Scandinavian foreign ministers in June 1959, their governments as well as Finland had already begun accumulating peacekeeping experience, and the following summer found all except Finland sending units to the Congo.* During the years spanning the UN's second decade, these and the other countries that took part most frequently in peacekeeping operations succeeded in grafting a new meaning onto the notion of middlepowermanship. "Participation in peacekeeping," it has been said, "is by no means the only outlet for middle powers, but it has become a badge of middlepowermanship."[16] This same group, predictably, has shown the keenest interest in preparedness matters, and in it has been concentrated most of the spirited leadership and forward thinking about the subject. Hammarskjöld's initiatives, in part, were merely incremental stimulants that augmented and gave direction to an existing momentum.

Peacekeeping and preparedness were both a cause and a beneficiary of a burgeoning self-consciousness among middle powers. Awareness of this interrelation was crystallized for many observers at about the time of the Suez crisis of 1956, during which middle powers played so prominent a role diplomatically as well as militarily in UNEF. Reflecting the tenor of much contemporary reaction, one journalist, writing just a few months after UNEF had become operational, referred to

---

* The term "Scandinavian" properly refers only to Denmark, Norway, and Sweden. "Nordic" includes Finland as well.

the activity within the UN of a ginger group—a group of members of more than negligible weight, with enough detachment to win widespread confidence, enough concern for the general good to break out of the parochial pattern of geographical blocs, enough imagination to put forward new techniques, and enough generosity to set an example by contributing physically to the development of these techniques. . . . The ginger group is not confined to "uncommitted" countries. . . . Canada and the Scandinavian countries at present provide it with a hard core.[17]

While the immediate circumstances and needs of the Suez episode provided an unusually dramatic occasion for the exercise of a vigorous, highly visible middlepowermanship, the basic phenomenon is traceable to deeper causes. No single peacekeeping emergency, whether Suez or subsequent ones, can in itself explain why these middle countries were available, even eager, to take on peacekeeping and preparedness burdens, why they were able to forge such a close identification between these UN activities and middlepowermanship, and why they were at the forefront as innovators in preparedness diplomacy and institution building.

It is first necessary to understand that these particular manifestations of middlepowermanship are only a fragment of a larger process of evolution in modern international organization, in the course of which states other than great powers have progressively acquired more influential political voices and more active responsibilities. Indeed, international organizations have been viewed consistently by less powerful states as great equalizers in form if not in fact, and as principal vehicles for assertion and protection of their own identities and interests. The European great powers that helped bring into being the League of Nations barely concealed their nostalgia for the good old days of the nineteenth-century Concert, although they considered it unfashionable to be quite as frank as the British statesman who had complained sardonically at the Congress of Berlin in 1878 that his temporary residence had mosquitoes, that the Congress had minor powers, and that he didn't know which was worse![18] Great powers at Versailles left little doubt that they intended to dominate the new organization's structure and proceedings. One of the plainer indications of their expectations was their preference for a League Council on which they held a majority of seats and to which an Assembly representing all members equally but meeting no more often than once every four years or so would be subservient. Yet on these and other structural issues concessions had to be made by the great powers both during the drafting of the Covenant and subsequently in practice. Their wishes surely prevailed, but not without challenge. Moreover, the medium-sized states of the League soon demonstrated a capacity to make positive contributions to the organization's peace-maintenance activities: they frequently played important parts on the various commissions of inquiry or fact-finding bodies periodically created by the League, they were called upon to provide troops for Vilna and again for the Saar, and they were often actively involved in dispute-settlement diplomacy at Geneva. They also displayed a certain amount of cohesion even in the earliest years of the League, when some of them sought to form a political counterweight against the influence of great powers; the Scandinavians served as a kind of inner circle of this group, and Sweden's having a seat on the Council at that time allowed it to act as spokesman.[19]

In many respects the wartime planning that laid the groundwork for the United Nations and the San Francisco negotiations that produced the Charter were a rerun of the great power–lesser power encounters of a generation earlier.[20] Again, while accepting great power leadership as indispensable, the less powerful among the original fifty-one members had to press insistently to carve out their own place in the new organization. They made themselves heard, and on a number of important counts they were heeded: they managed to bolster the powers of the Assembly, to narrow somewhat the discretionary authority of the Council, and to turn the organization's purposes toward economic and social concerns that the great powers had shown signs of neglecting during their earlier planning.

Some second-ranking powers at the San Francisco conference added still another theme, urging that the proposed organization not be viewed simply as a composite of great powers plus an undifferentiated everyone else. The new United Nations, they emphasized, was going to include members with recognizable gradations of resources, ranges of interests, and political weight, and they ought therefore to be accorded commensurate status and responsibility. Canada was the leading proponent of this idea, even before the conference. The prime minister, W. Mackenzie King, had told Winston Churchill in 1944 that the Ottawa government wished to be treated "as one of the *middle powers*, medium powers that should be brought into the world organization in some way that would recognize that power and responsibility go together."[21] No such recognition was ever specifically awarded. The Charter, although it does say that nonpermanent members of the Security Council ought to be chosen primarily on the basis of the quality of their contribution to the preservation of peace and to other purposes of the UN, confers no special rights or responsibilities explicitly on middle powers per se. In practice a loosely defined middle-powermanship emerged nevertheless.

The term "middle power" acquired, in the UN context, a variety of connotations. At first it was used in an objective sense to identify those member states with comparatively medium-level resources, measured in terms of geography or wealth or military capabilities. It later took on a second meaning, according to which a middle power's endowments were seen as circumstantial and perhaps temporary. A state was so categorized not just because of what it possessed but also because of what it did. For example, this description was given to countries occupying a political "middle" on given issues, to those that appeared frequently as interlocutors in the UN's parliamentary diplomacy, or to those that often performed various mediatory and third-party functions in dispute-settlement efforts. A member state could be classified as a middle power for some purposes but not for others, at some times but not at others. Middlepowermanship thus has not taken identical forms in peacekeeping, in debates on colonial or racial or human rights questions, in disarmament negotiations, or in economic matters—although a Canada, a Sweden, an Austria, or an Ireland has repeatedly acted out the middle power role on a range of problems.

The willingness to wear the badge of middlepowermanship in peacekeeping was greatly facilitated by the refocusing of international organization concerns away from traditional collective enforcement. This objective has always created special difficulties for many middle powers when the great powers that were to be the bulwarks of any collective security system were not united behind it and when military measures were the system's ultimate weapon.

The League was barely a year old when Canada and the Scandinavian members took steps to reduce their collective security obligations that might entail involvement in military sanctions.[22] For these and other relatively powerful states with sufficient resources to be able to contribute to League operations, one of the central dilemmas of collective security—the need to make collective war in the name of peace—implied some very unpleasant possibilities. They did not wish to fight great-power wars, to become entangled in other quarrels in which they seemed to have no direct interest, or to commit themselves to a collective security system controlled basically by the big powers. How strongly such apprehensions were felt and expressed varied from country to country. In one case, that of permanently neutral Switzerland, League membership was accepted only with the proviso that the government be exempt from having to take part in any military sanctions. But not all lesser powers had reservations about League sanctions. For some that were certain to be drawn into any general European war, the League represented a potential added insurance or guarantee. It was for this reason that one of the most active and controversial small power statesmen of the period, Eduard Beneš of Czechoslovakia, campaigned vigorously at Geneva to put airtight and comprehensive sanctions powers into the League's hands, even proposing at one point that these powers be capable of activation by a mere majority vote of the League Council.[23]

In 1945 some middle powers, while not harboring any fundamental objections to the newly proposed collective security system, felt that the sanctions procedures devised at Dumbarton Oaks by the great powers paid insufficient attention to the interests of others whose mandatory participation in military sanctions was expected. Successfully, Canada, the Netherlands, and others pressed the big powers to modify their original outline, which would have permitted the Security Council to use the troops provided to it by any member nation for sanctions operations without those members having any voice whatever in the decision unless they happened to be nonpermanent members of the Council at the time. Canada warned that failure to assume some kind of consultation would endanger prospects for Charter ratification in many countries, and the Dutch insisted, "No military action without representation."[24] A number of middle powers also made it clear in later years that they had initially accepted collective security obligations on the implicit condition that wartime great power unity be sufficiently preserved. When this hope was shattered and especially after the United States had tried, with the Uniting for Peace Resolution, to construct a sanctions system that theoretically could operate over a great power veto, a reevaluation was felt to be justified. In 1952 a Swedish representative to the UN, referring to the originally projected great power agreement, said, "On that basis the smaller states undertook to conform to the decisions of the Security Council and to that extent surrendered sovereignty." "If the great Powers were not unanimous," he added, "other States would also retain freedom of action."[25] That same year, Stockholm's minister for foreign affairs put the matter straightforwardly: "Sweden cannot be expected to participate in sanctions in cases where a war between Great Powers has broken out or where she considers that she is in danger of being drawn into a general war."[26]

Middle power interest in peacekeeping and preparedness stemmed from positive as well as negative rationales. The counterpart to this disaffection with collective security thinking and its implications in the nuclearized cold war atmosphere was the more decisive conviction that identification with peacekeeping was both beneficial and suitable. Increasingly, a number of middle powers, for diverse reasons, came to regard peacekeeping involvement as supportive of their underlying foreign policy objectives in the postwar world, complementary to their general views about what the UN could offer in that setting, consistent with their attitude toward participation in international organizations, and representative of the kinds of peace-maintaining services which they in many ways have been uniquely qualified to render on behalf of the UN.

Some of the governments that became regular members of Hammarskjöld's "constituency"—notably the Nordic group, Ireland, and eventually Austria and the Netherlands—were among those European states surveyed in a brief but useful analysis written in the mid-1960s.[27] Several of its conclusions bear directly on why these and other non-European middle powers like Canada or India have been motivated and able to take leading parts in peacekeeping and preparedness activities.

A first conclusion reached was that as a rule these states have tended to prefer a UN whose main function is that of conciliator, as the term is broadly conceived. On a wide spectrum of political, economic, and legal questions, they have usually given their firmest support to steps that cast the UN as "a physician to its troubled Members, not a judge."[28] This translates into disapproval of using the organization as a crude propaganda forum, as a partisan in situations involving potential interbloc confrontation, or as a parliamentary device for rolling up majorities behind unenforceable decisions. Instead, emphasis is placed on UN policies these states regard as conducive to negotiation. This has meant, for instance, their support for the seating of mainland China in the UN on the ground that the principle of universality best conforms to their vision of the UN and their advocacy of tension-reducing measures in the disarmament sector. Politically impartial, noncoercive peacekeeping is seen as an especially apt extension of these preferences for the UN-as-conciliator. Active intermediary efforts to control local conflicts, particularly if these raise the specter of big power competitive intervention, are viewed as supremely appropriate tasks for the UN to undertake and for these states to support, with political backing, with money, and if possible with manpower or other facilities.

Significantly, the thinking of most middle powers on these issues fitted well with the conceptions of the UN's potential value that Hammarskjöld himself began developing after taking office in 1953, ideas that before long became embodied in catchphrases—"quiet diplomacy," "preventive diplomacy," "vacuum-filling" by the UN in theaters of local conflict—associated with the second secretary-general. While his "alliance" with the northern European peacekeepers may have been somewhat easier to establish because of cultural and personal links, undoubtedly even more important was that he and many middle powers drew from a common fund of convictions about the UN's international security responsibilities. It is striking that not once during his career did Hammarskjöld seriously try to revive his predecessor's campaign in favor of collective enforcement machinery. Hammarskjöld, rather, felt that "one of the most serious remaining obstacles in the way of public understanding of the true role of the United Nations today results from a . . . tendency to picture the United Nations of 1945 as establishing collective security for the world." He insisted that "true collective security, in the sense of an international police power engaged to defend the peace of the world, is to be found at the end, not at the beginning, of the effort to create and use world institutions that are effective in the service of the common interest."[29]

A second conclusion reached in the study of certain of these states' UN policies singled out what each, from its national point of view, gained from UN membership and from its mode of participation in the organization's work. While they have derived returns of varying type and scale, "perhaps the common element is that UN membership permits them to be independent in several different ways, an independence which these states tend to emphasize."[30] This does not refer, of course, to the basic national independence and self-determination to which "new states" of the postcolonial period have devoted their energies; for the middle powers that are identified with peacekeeping, these fundamental values have long been taken for granted. Most of them were members of the League, some even logging during those years their first experience as peacekeepers. In a contemporary context, national independence has implied a striving for wider opportunities to pursue distinctive, constructive policies in an environment shaped by the nuclear giants and their concerns. Particularly as the post-Stalinist thaw in the cold war moderated some of its harsher manifestations, North Atlantic Treaty Organization (NATO) members like Canada, Denmark, and Norway—each, once again, in individual ways —were able to use their positions in the UN and their devotion to peacekeeping goals as counterbalances to their association with the Western military alliance. European neutrals—Sweden, Finland, Austria, and Ireland—were able to rely on peacekeeping involvement not just to underline their apartness from either of the military blocs but also to reinforce it. Ideologically "nonaligned" peacekeepers like India or Indonesia (an early participant in UNEF) or Yugoslavia were likewise able to demonstrate cold-war detachment and to display peacekeeping credentials that improved their leadership standings in the eyes of the Third World.

That these reaffirmations of independence could be asserted through peacekeeping has been largely the result of the appropriateness of peacekeeping's image as an impartial profession and the middle powers' cultivation of reputations as intermediaries, as purveyors of political-military, third-party services not otherwise available. In this sense the self-conceptions of middlepowermanship and of peacekeeping have been mutually supportive, and the effect has been cumulative for those governments whose peacekeeping careers have been the busiest. Domestic support for this national avocation has usually been strong and steady. Foreign offices have come to regard it, despite occasional frustrations and sometimes substantial burdens, as an enlightened international role that brings greater respect and influence in international councils. Military establishments, though with far from equal enthusiasm, have gradually come to appreciate more fully that peacekeeping can be a respectable outlet for military expertise.[31]

A third conclusion concerning the UN policies of a number of these powers was that they have regularly contributed disproportionately large shares of men, money, and specialized skills to a broad variety of UN activities in political, economic, and humanitarian spheres. Perhaps this is testimony to the benefits that UN participation produces for their foreign policy ledgers; perhaps also it is evidence that their willingness is coupled with the ability to deliver the goods. Their names regularly are high on the list of those that furnish extensive backing for UN technical assistance programs, that give more than their share to various categories of UN budgets, that provide proportionately high numbers of international civil servants to the UN system, and that have occupied a relatively large number of the more important elective or appointive offices in the organization. Their equally conspicuous contributions to peacekeeping and to efforts to create and refine preparedness programs have been one more reflection of their consistent demeanor toward the obligations of membership in the UN. Along with this general disposition, more specific factors operated to strengthen the credentials of these countries in matters relating to peacekeeping. Most mundanely, they could bring to bear the necessary military resources for sustained participation in field operations. And for the most part they possessed few of the impediments that might disqualify them as peacekeepers in particular situations: no prejudicial political or economic interests in areas of potential conflict, no colonial histories, and no presumed imperial designs, to name a few. As a middle power statesman of the highest order, Lester Pearson, once put it: "We are big enough to discharge with effect the responsibilities that we undertake; we are not big enough for others to fear us."[32]

Nordic Activities to 1963–64:
The Second Preparedness Generation

Heavy material demands on the preparedness system after 1956 generated refinement of the secretariat's capabilities, just as they forced greater burdens on the few states, especially the United States, able to provide complex logistical assistance. But both of these preparedness components underwent only linear growth. Though the secretariat took on a much-extended diplomatic role, its administrative and support activities were essentially the same as those that predated UNEF. United States technical services were more of the same but on a larger scale. It was in the third component—national suppliers of manpower —that truly major changes occurred. Dominating preparedness questions was how to enlist politically impartial states with competent military establishments as potential peacekeepers on a more or less regular basis. National decisions to participate in peacekeeping or to establish national preparedness programs, for regular suppliers especially, required major financial, administrative, and resource allocations. Peacekeeping and preparedness had to be injected into domestic and foreign policy processes. Vague promises to "support UN peacekeeping" had to be converted into operative commitments and tangible outlays.

Developments relating to the supplier component delimit succeeding generations of preparedness. The second can be said to have begun with the germination of Hammarskjöld's standby concepts and to have ended with national announcements in 1963–64 that cooperative Nordic preparedness arrangements and unilateral programs by other states were being started. It was largely a generation of planning and study. The third, which began in 1964, has been largely one of implementation, bit by bit with mixed results.

Even before the Hammarskjöld letter of 1959, some thought had been given in Scandinavia to the possibility of creating special national units for UN peacekeeping—for the moment, call them standby forces. Per Haekkerup, former Danish foreign minister and strong advocate of the idea, wrote that the Suez experience originally prompted the project, that it was "discussed" at a meeting of the Nordic foreign ministers in September 1958, but that "the decisive contribution to the thinking on the subject" was Hammarskjöld's Study.[33] The Scandinavian plan seems to have been discussed confidentially with the secretariat in early 1959, before the Hammarskjöld appeal.

From this time on, the secretariat was occasionally active in designing and modifying the joint Scandinavian program, though this was never widely publicized. While the Scandinavians received important guidance from members of the secretariat, Hammarskjöld and later Thant made it very clear that they could have no official ties with national programs without political authorization from the Council or the Assembly.[34] But both executives, especially Hammarskjöld during the second generation, stretched discretion far enough so that member states interested in preparedness would not have to plan in a complete vacuum. Remarks were made by a ranking secretariat official in 1964 apropos of its modest role in preparedness. "It is quite extraordinary," he said, "how far, in fact, in a muddled kind of way, we have come, especially in the last ten years. The number of things which are purportedly not acceptable but which have been done and are constantly being done is remarkable."[35]

Hammarskjöld's 1959 communication was intended, in part, to encourage a receptive attitude among the Scandinavians, specifically a willingness to consider standby plans at a regular joint meeting of their defense ministers. In September 1960 such a session was held in Stockholm, and Scandinavian standby arrangements were officially discussed collectively for the first time, though only in a preliminary, tentative way. One month before the meeting, Hammarskjöld had surveyed the hectic improvisations of the new Congo force that summer and renewed his appeal that "governments maintain a state of preparedness so as to be able to meet possible demands from the United Nations." Accompanying this were broad indications of the secretary-general's changing attitude about preparedness. No mention was made of the need for prior approval from political organs. He urged a greater "state of preparedness" inside the secretariat itself, including, he said explicitly, a permanent staff of military officers. The "experiences" in the Congo "should be fully utilized by the United Nations, by appropriate informal planning within the administration."[36]

One of the things included in the "informal planning" was cooperation with Scandinavian military planners commissioned by their superiors to recommend a structure for the national standby forces. By March 1961, initial studies in the three countries had been completed and the results put before a ministerial meeting in Copenhagen. One of the important conclusions was that many types of specialists as well as full military units were likely to be most helpful to the UN. Experience had already shown that middle powers would have to be prepared to dispatch not only major components such as infantry battalions but also experts in engineering, communications, transport, movement control, medicine, hygiene, and other fields. The defense ministers authorized further national study and discussions at the UN.

Within a few weeks, Scandinavian ambassadors were asking the secretariat for estimates of the types of specialists most often needed by peacekeeping commanders. Early in May, they were given lists of personnel that the secretariat would probably hope to recruit from Scandinavia and told of strong secretariat interest in further discussions. At about this time plans were also being developed by the secretariat for an in-house training program for civilian and military peacekeeping personnel. (For a brief description, see Chapter 7.) Hammarskjöld approved it a few weeks before his death in September, but it was not implemented afterwards. In December 1961, the secretariat's suggestions to the Scandinavians were passed on to another ministerial meeting in Stockholm, and subsequently a three-power working group was appointed to draw up detailed plans for coordinated national commitments.

Rough outlines of possible national contributions were presented to the next defense ministers' meeting in March 1962, along with recommendations concerning political conditions for offers to the UN. The working group was instructed to prepare complete specifications, constructed on the basis of alternate cost assumptions. In October the ministers received these reports and decided to expose them to full examination by their home departments. Further consultations were conducted between their UN missions and the secretariat.[37]

The decisive steps were taken in Stavanger, Norway, on April 24, 1963. Each minister agreed to propose to his government the creation of standby forces to be made available to the UN under specified conditions. Further planning assignments were given to the working group, which today remains an active and important middle-level instrument for Nordic peacekeeping cooperation. It was decided, too, that limited, joint training for observers and staff officers could be undertaken. A working syllabus for a coordinated staff officers' course had already been prepared at the secretariat, and the curriculum for observer training was later drafted by the UN division of the Swedish army staff. The Stavanger decisions were immediately reported to the press, and U Thant was unofficially briefed.

Soon afterward the secretary-general made his first public remarks on preparedness, breaking a three-year official secretariat silence. He repeated the gist of Hammarskjöld's 1959 letter and expressed "appreciation" to the Scandinavians for their recently announced efforts, adding, "It would be a very welcome development if other countries would consider following the lead of the Scandinavian countries in this matter."[38] In October 1963, Scandinavian cooperation acquired a Nordic flavor when Finland sent a representative to observe sessions of the working group. In December, after consultations with its regional partners, the Finnish government confirmed earlier indications that it would contribute a standby force.

Nordic Programs: The Standby Concept

In 1964 special legislation was enacted in each Nordic country to pave the way for establishment of standby units for the UN. Although for shorthand purposes this collective effort is often called a "Nordic standby force," it is properly understood as a design for coordinating four strictly national components. This is the first multinational, systematic attempt to provide a global organization with military forces for peacekeeping. By 1964 each country had developed plans for its own contribution to a 4,500-man force, and by 1969 the overall design included the elements identified in Table 1. One infantry battalion apiece from Denmark, Norway, and Finland plus two from Sweden are to make up the bulk of the manpower. Specialized units, staff, and observer detachments are included in the plans. Some army, navy, or air force elements are to be provided by each country, with Norway and Finland contributing all three. The units, composed almost entirely of volunteers, could be deployed either in separate national formations or together as coordinate components in any given UN theater of operations.*

Conditions were attached.[39] The standby units are not to be literally on call to the UN but can be dispatched only after the supplier government decides to take part in the particular operation. The national forces are not substitutes for Article 43 contingents, and they can be used only for peacekeeping actions with the consent of the host state. Collective enforcement is explicitly excluded from possible force missions. Until actually turned over to UN command, the units remain under national control and responsibility.

The word "standby" became jargon before it became accurate. In the closing years of the 1960s major portions of the Nordic countries'

* Available published surveys of detailed information on national standby programs are mainly two: publications of the International Information Center on Peace-Keeping Operations (IPKO) and memoranda submitted in recent years to the United Nations Special Committee on Peacekeeping Operations. Relevant materials from both sources are cited where necessary in the present chapter. Data in the chapter's country reviews are also based on interviews conducted in April and May 1967 with civilian and military officials in each Nordic government and with officers of their peacekeeping units in UNFICYP, UNEF, and UNTSO (United Nations Truce Supervision Organization).

TABLE I

National Standby Forces Organized or Planned
by the Four Nordic Countries, 1969

Components	Country			
	Denmark	Finland	Norway	Sweden
Army				
Infantry battalion	1	1	1	2
Signal company	1			
Workshop company			1	
Maintenance platoon	1			
Medical company	1	1		
Antiaircraft platoon		1		
Movement control	1	1	1	1
Transport platoon		1		
Military police	1	1	1	1
Surgical emergency unit			1	
Hygienic unit			1	
Navy element				
Frigate		1	1	
Harbor command			1	
Air force element				
Helicopter platoon				1
Air transport unit		1	1	
Other units				
Technical contingent				1
Special personnel				
Staff officers	15	15	25	15
Observers	15	25	25	26

Source: Adapted from unpublished sources.

standby force did not exist, not as designed by the Nordic states themselves earlier in the decade and not by any reasonable definition of
"standby"—even the nonmilitary, commonsense one in Webster:
"held near at hand and ready for emergency use." This is not to say
that the Nordic states do not deserve the kudos bestowed on them
from so many quarters. They do. With the Canadians, they have been
the backbone of most UN missions. They have funneled officers and
men in an unbroken flow to UN service. Overall Nordic capabilities
for participation in peacekeeping have surely grown as a result of their

detailed national planning, their extended regional cooperation, their long experience, and their accumulated exposure to peacekeeping's unique properties. Yet their standby concepts have not been fully translated into practice despite heavy, actual UN commitments—and to some degree because of them.

What are the standby forces supposed to look like? How are they supposed to be raised? What relation are they supposed to have to contingents that these countries are supplying to existing UN operations at any particular time?

The large majority of standby soldiers are to be volunteers, mostly men who have completed their national conscript service and have returned to civilian life. A smaller proportion, mainly officers and specialists, may be volunteers from the regular standing military establishment. Each volunteer signs a contract by which he agrees to hold himself in readiness for a specified length of time after brief training. During the contract period—and this is an important point—he must be prepared to respond rapidly to an emergency call-up, at any time, for duty anywhere. As a Nordic source describes this obligation, "those who sign up for such forces do not know beforehand where they will be sent, nor when their services will be required."[40] These are large unknowns. A mobilization call would mean leaving one's family, job, or school. To offset these risks, the governments generally have offered volunteers a financial bonus for placing themselves on standby, laws protecting their jobs until they return from the usual six-month UN tour, and attractive pay while on UN assignment.

As planned, the standby contingents, therefore, were not to be the same units as those already in UN service or those periodically rotated to relieve them. In fact, in their original designs, all four countries had expected to set up their standby forces only after existing UN commitments were discontinued—a decision reached early by the working group, accepted by the defense ministers at Stavanger in the spring of 1963, and presented to the respective legislatures in early 1964.[41] At the time, some five hundred Scandinavians were in the skeleton force remaining in the Congo. One Swedish battalion plus a larger mixed Danish-Norwegian unit was in Egypt, and all four countries were posting observers to the Middle East or Kashmir. The Danish Folketing (parliament) was told that the relation between these various commitments and the proposed standby units "is subject to further negotiation among the [four] countries concerned since it is deemed correct that a common Nordic position be adopted on this point."[42]

But then the Cyprus crisis erupted and upset nearly all initial calculations about when the standby plans could be implemented. Existing commitments, it now appeared, were going to continue for some time. In March 1964 the Swedes and the Finns sent major infantry units, and were soon joined by the Danes. By midsummer, together they were contributing about 40 percent of UNFICYP troops.

What then happened to the standby force concept? There are really four separate answers, because after UNFICYP all pretense of a "common Nordic position" splintered into different interpretations and practices among Sweden, Denmark, and Finland. Norway, not involved in UNFICYP and only minimally committed elsewhere, was able to go still another route.

Of the three UNFICYP suppliers, only the Finns have remained constant to the original Nordic intent: they make no claims whatever to have established any standby units, and they do not hope to do so until the Finnish battalion in Cyprus is substantially reduced or brought home for good. Sweden departed substantially in practice from the original assumption that creation of standby forces would await cutback of existing commitments. Instead it simply decided to regard as the two standby battalions those units already serving in UNFICYP and UNEF. In effect this meant that ordinary rotation battalions which had to be sent frequently to these two missions—as had been done routinely for many years in the case of UNEF—were now to be rechristened "standby contingents-in-service." Thus, so long as Sweden's UN commitments included both of these missions, her two standby battalions were considered as being "on assignment." This near-equivalence of rotation units and standby units blurs the initial Nordic concept of standby. The capability for raising rotation units is of course important, and all Nordic states have demonstrated that they can do so over a sustained period. However, routine replacement contingents generally are recruited, organized, trained, and equipped differently than genuine standby battalions. To be able to mobilize one is not necessarily to be able to mobilize the other, and the two are not functionally exchangeable. The most obvious difference—though not the only important one—has proved to be that it is relatively easy to recruit qualified men for rotation units where there are few unknowns about the time, place, and circumstance of a tour of duty; it is vastly more difficult to recruit genuine standby units where the uncertainties and personal risks are numerous. The Nordic states all appreciate these differences, and their awareness is unmistakably evident in the original standby designs, which had nothing to do with mobilization of rotation battalions. The Danes chose a third and even more complicated practice. Their Cyprus units contain mostly rotation personnel recruited by ordinary methods plus a smaller number of men that the Danes prefer to call standby soldiers, who are sprinkled throughout the periodic rotation units. The Norwegians were the only ones in a position to go ahead with the original standby plans. They tried, failed, redesigned some of the program, and have had initial successes with a second try.

These variations are not trivial. The widely accepted view that there is in the Nordic countries a fully developed standby force ready to respond to an emergency call from the United Nations for duty in an unanticipated crisis is not entirely consistent with the facts. To call the Nordic force "now a reality"—as one knowledgeable Scandinavian officer did in a prominent European military journal in 1966—is to invite serious misunderstanding of what has happened in these countries since 1963–64.[43] More important, it diverts attention from the magnitude of the job still ahead for most of the Nordic governments if they are ever to create a standby program that meets the goals initially agreed on, for it is not certain that the original design is adequate, and there are signs that Nordic planners now acknowledge this. Furthermore, it hides the important lessons Nordic experience ought to convey to other countries contemplating standby efforts and likely to encounter many of the same difficulties.

The structure and procedures chosen for the Nordic standby force are heavily influenced by the similar patterns of organization in the military establishments of the four countries, two of them NATO alliance partners and two of them neutrals. These common features have shaped their approaches to UN obligations. None of the four maintains large permanent armed forces in peacetime, as do, say, the United States, the United Kingdom, Canada, or India. In varying degrees, their armed services are based on several important principles: relatively small professional cadres for peacetime staff and training functions, rapid mobilization in emergencies, heavy tactical emphasis on home defense rather than on overseas commitments, general conscription, long-term reserve obligations, and active service with periodic refresher training. The Norwegian army's peacetime nucleus consists of 19,000 men, which would be rapidly swollen to 130,000 in time of emergency. Sweden's 12,000 regular officers and noncommissioned officers provide leadership for armed forces numbering almost 700,000 in wartime. Denmark's 28,000 can be expanded by 72-hour mobilization into 150,000.[44] In these armies there exists in peacetime a combination of training personnel, support and logistical units, and operational components. Length of training and of obligation differ somewhat in each country. Sweden's conscripts undergo initial training of anywhere from eight and one-half to twenty-three months, depending on rank, and are liable for reserve duty until they are forty-seven years old. Norway's army conscripts serve twelve months initially, as do Denmark's, and retain reserve obligation until the age of forty-four. Finland's military organization is shaped by the terms of the Finno-Russian Treaty of Paris of 1947, which restricted the size of each branch of the armed services and prohibited their use abroad, the latter making it necessary for Finnish UN units to be organized outside regular army channels. The army's quota is 34,400, though it, the navy, and the air force have always remained understrength. Finland too has national compulsory service, requiring training of eight to eleven months and reserve obligations to the age of sixty.

United Nations military commitments must be met within these organizational frameworks and with sufficient regard for the military traditions common to rapid-mobilization, militia-type armies everywhere. Above all, there is a strong disinclination to send conscripts abroad, except for what is considered national defense, unless they volunteer to go. This is an age-old limitation for countries with such military establishments. The moral basis of this system is the citizen's civic obligation, and privilege, of defending his country. Armies organized on mobilization principles face the prospect that long wars or expeditionary ventures will severely, perhaps fatally, disrupt the social and economic structure left vacant by the mobilized manpower.

By the time decisions had to be made about supplying the UN with peacekeeping forces, this tradition was deeply ingrained in Nordic countries and embodied in constitutions, military service acts, or other legislation governing the raising and use of armed forces. Indeed, during the League years Sweden used a volunteer system in the Saar and would have used it earlier in Vilna. For Nordic states today, this method is natural as well as consistent with historical experience and contemporary security needs. Furthermore, it alleviates most internal competition for military resources between the recognized national defense missions and UN requirements, a choice that could arise if both were met fully by the regular army. And of course, in domestic political terms, it is far more palatable to call for volunteers than to compel reluctant citizens to don UN helmets and go abroad for six months or more. In spite of these advantages, the volunteer solution has not been applied with equal vigor in the four states. Nor has it escaped internal criticism. It is not immutable in law or absolute in practice.

Each government has faced different problems, experimented with different approaches, and set different short-term goals for standby programs. Each has had successes or failures since 1964 that are illuminating for different reasons. Most available analyses of Nordic preparedness have stopped far short of the mark in merely pointing out (correctly) how broad has been the popular, legislative, and executive consensus behind the standby concept—and leaving it more or less at that.[45] One is left with the sanguine but grossly misleading impression that, once the enabling laws were passed, all there was left to do was to allocate the money, draw up the organization charts, and move ahead unobstructed. True enough, the initial legal and policy decisions provided the essential impulse, but the later obstacles to implementation were numerous, in Nordic and other standby states as well. Human and material factors, plus plain bad luck, slowed down the rate of execution. Unexpected legal or financial snags, lack of volunteers in high employment economies, the stubbornness of a critically placed minister, resistance from unconvinced ranking members of the military establishment, overly optimistic planning—all of these have had negative consequences in one or another Nordic country. Some have shown up in other standby states; others will most certainly be found in countries joining the standby club in the future.

Norway

Norway's case is unique. It is the closest thing to a controlled experiment for examining how the standby system was to have worked in every Nordic state if the Cyprus crisis had not intervened and forced major changes. Norway does not participate in UNFICYP, and only occasionally since 1964 have Norwegians in UN Middle East service at any one time been very numerous. When UNEF disbanded in 1967, it had only 60 Norwegian personnel. Thus current commitments have not distracted the Norwegians too far from their standby planning of a tri-service unit totaling 1,300 men.

Several important developments had already occurred by June 1964, when the Norwegian Storting (parliament) approved standby legislation submitted six months earlier. The Norwegian military had successfully insisted that all Nordic partners contribute basic infantry units to the combined force, demonstrating equal willingness to share the burden. Original Nordic working group plans included only Norwegian technical units (for instance, transport, hygiene, and maintenance) of 300–400 men from all three services but no infantry battalion. After the Norwegian army showed its displeasure at being the only Nordic country not scheduled to provide an infantry component, a full battalion was included in Norway's contribution.

The issue of payment to volunteers had a prominent place in Norwegian background planning, and in 1964 Oslo alone among the Nordic standbys expected to get contractees without paying them anything at all unless they were sent abroad. The working group had previously agreed that *some* remuneration to volunteers would be necessary to compensate for the possible inconveniences. Nevertheless, the Norwegian minister of defense—a firm, optimistic advocate of peacekeeping—rejected the advice of his chief of the army and chief of defense, both of whom advocated a bonus equivalent to that being offered in Denmark and Sweden. Other contract terms were also debated thoroughly in government councils. The army, interested in having UN units turn over as infrequently as possible, opted for a three-year contract under the terms of which the volunteer would obligate himself to serve no more than six months abroad but still be available for service at any time during the long contract period. The minister of defense agreed to a compromise, and the legislation pro-vided for alternative contracts of one, two, or three years, without pay during the contract period. Norway, like Sweden and Denmark, agreed to propose job-protection laws, and Finland was to do the same, but with coverage limited to government employees.[46]

Probably no Nordic military establishment has gone on record as strongly as Norway's in favor of peacekeeping preparedness. This was their position before the Storting in 1964: "The Chief of the Army, with the support of the Chief of Defense, has stated that participation in this cooperative undertaking is of such importance that it should be carried out even if it involves certain adverse effects on the defense activity."[47] The two chiefs wanted no doubts left that Norway would be able to deliver the necessary resources when the time came. But their detailed proposals to this end were far too ambitious, at least for the Storting. The Defense Ministry's draft bill included two important items rep-resenting the views of the military authorities. One said simply that the chiefs believed "the Norwegian contribution might be made in addition to the present Norwegian UN contingents" in peacekeeping service. Second, they suggested, and the defense minister accepted with seeming reluctance, a far-reaching clause reading: "The King is granted the authority, to the extent required, to order officers and enlisted men to serve the UN outside the borders of the country."[48] The military, then, were willing to go further than had been tentatively agreed to in the working group, by setting up standby forces irrespective of ongoing obligations. And they were willing to leave open the possibility of modifying for UN peacekeeping purposes the practice of not sending conscripts abroad involuntarily, in much the same way that conscripts in regular mobilization units can be used for certain NATO duty.[49]

The Storting said no to both suggestions. The 1,300-man standby forces were to be reduced by the number of Norwegians serving abroad at the time, and the authority recommended for the king was flatly denied. A report of the Storting's military committee was the basis for the final decision, and on both counts, Danish and Swedish practices to the contrary were cited.[50] All government and opposition parties agreed with the committee,[51] so the prospect of nonvoluntary UN service was solidly quashed by legislators accountable to the voters whose lives might be affected by mobilization for the UN.

By the end of 1966, nearly 13,000 Norwegians had seen UN service. Like the other Nordic states, Norway has never had any real difficulty rounding up the volunteers needed for rotation battalions. Some men remain in the field for additional tours, others come from home every six months. They go through a predictable and relatively risk-free process: they sign up for a known place, for departure on a known date, for a known financial allowance during service. Plans can be made. Students can take off a semester in advance, a construction laborer can schedule a UN tour during an off season, a farmer can adjust to the harvest cycle, and so on. But Norwegian standby contracts under the 1964 system were an altogether different matter. A year or more on standby could be a period of some anxiety except perhaps for the adventuresome or the unemployed. A volunteer's personal life was subject to disruption at any time—and for these uncertainties the contractee was to receive no bonus, though he would of course be paid, and quite well, during an actual tour if he were called up.[52] (Even the amounts paid to standbys in Sweden and Denmark were to be small, amounting to about $150 each year of standby.)

An American commentator on the Nordic contract system observed in 1965: "One may well question whether a young man, just starting his civilian life, with his required military service behind him for the most part, can be expected to sign a contract which is seemingly so one-sided. The answer is that they do not sign."[53] This describes almost perfectly the state of affairs in Norway during the first two years of the standby program. By late 1966, the essentials of the system—especially the no-pay feature—spelled failure. For the infantry battalion, 750 slots were to be filled by volunteers. In May 1965, 55 men had signed up,[54] and by October 1966, 202.[55] Fewer than 10 percent of the naval contract personnel were available.

Unlike the lower ranks, which were to be filled mostly by civilian volunteers, the officer rosters were adequately manned by volunteers from the regular military establishment. For many of them, this was an opportunity to get useful career experience abroad, with their usual pay plus special overseas allowances. Staff and observer openings were and still are easily filled.[56] Organization of the infantry battalion staff was far enough along to permit initial officer training in December 1965, which the battalion commander emphasized was not in any way related to current commitments in the Middle East, but to "a separate battalion which may be used anywhere."[57] Some twenty regular officers and twenty reserve officers took part. By then, however, everyone realized the bulk of this battalion was simply not available, and was not going to be without some basic policy changes.

A start had already been made as a result of a change of government in early 1965.[58] The newly elected coalition was neither more nor less positive about UN peacekeeping or the standby concept. Top-level personnel changes accompanying the shift simply made reevaluation of the existing policy more convenient. Growing concern in 1964–65 about the lagging recruitment provided a catalyst. Not long after the new government's installation, for example, a press campaign by an influential journalist focused attention on the situation by criticizing the 1964 plans and their execution and by suggesting the possibility that Norway would be unable to fulfill its UN commitments in an emergency.

The new defense minister permitted wholesale stocktaking. It took over a year, and it was thorough. Motivations of potential volunteers were studied in greater depth than ever before. Some 4,000 men in the Norwegian army during 1966 were professionally surveyed to determine why they did not sign UN contracts and what might make them do so. Alternative recruitment methods were reconsidered and the reasons for recent failures were isolated as accurately as possible.

In October 1966 the Storting received and quickly passed new proposals for a reconstructed standby system. Now, compensation about equal to that in Denmark and Sweden would be given to signatories. There were to be more sophisticated and aggressive recruitment techniques, new contracts, and emphasis on the recruitment of volunteers during conscripts' regular twelve-month stretches. The new legislation established several types of standby contracts.[59] The two in widest use may be signed either during conscript service or anytime after it has been completed. Either way, the contract period is two years, with up to six months of UN obligation. If a volunteer is called up, his contract is nullified after the standard half-year tour.

Earlier recruiting methods were of a passive, slap-a-notice-on-the-bulletin-board variety. Under the new program, recruiters with a support staff that included a screening psychologist visited every army command in Norway, equipped with specially prepared lectures, films showing Norwegian soldiers in UN service, and slick new pamphlets. Strong sales talks were aimed at senior army commanders, urging them to encourage their men to sign the new contracts.

The results were very favorable. Since then Norway has been the only Nordic country to form a standby infantry battalion according to original plans and for genuine standby-emergency use. The army units—the battalion and related elements—consist of about 950 men, some 750 of which are other ranks; that is, privates and corporals who are contractees. In the spring of 1967, nearly 475 of these lower slots had been filled. By midsummer a second recruiting drive had brought the units up to full strength. At the beginning of 1969, all officer and senior NCO ranks were filled, largely by volunteers from the regular Norwegian army, and there was a surplus of other ranks recently recruited to anticipate expiration of older contracts.[60] In the long run, of course, the test of the refined system will be whether it continues to attract the needed replenishments of volunteers, especially among the other ranks.[61] Estimates are that replacement contracts will eventually have to average between 100 and 200 every three months.

Thus in the summer of 1967, two years later than originally hoped, a full Norwegian standby unit went into training, one week for officers and NCOs and two for the entire unit. There were just over a hundred hours of operational exercises, about half devoted to strictly UN tactics and problems, the remainder to ordinary infantry brush-up drills. Subsequent sessions were scheduled to train half the army contingents annually, each half being composed of revolunteers and new recruits in their first contract year.

It was largely the success of this army program that allowed the Norwegian ambassador to the UN, Edvard Hambro, to report in 1968 "the recent completion of the arrangements to make this force operational and ready for participation in peace-keeping operations."[62] But this was not meant to imply that all contract slots were filled in the three services of the Norwegian UN commitment. There are no contracts signed for the air force's 87-man units and only a fraction signed for the navy's standby unit of about 210 men—in 1967 there were only eighteen navy contracts in force; in 1969, forty-five; and none of these were other ranks. Both services seem to recruit less vigorously than the army. In the navy's case, especially, the new contract bonus probably makes little difference to conscripts whose navy experience generally qualifies them for high-paying jobs, after their conscript tour, in Norway's merchant marine. Yet these two services maintain that, despite poor contracting, the necessary units could be raised in an emergency without too much difficulty.

Contingency plans assume that the infantry battalion plus supporting units could be ready to go in a minimum of three days, a maximum of seven. The call-up process would resemble that of the regular national mobilization forces, but with one critical difference. The regular units, which can be readied in a matter of hours, are regionally recruited. This is characteristic of militia-type forces, and it cuts their response time to the minimum, whereas members of the standby unit might have to be assembled from all parts of the country.[63]

Two highly developed, dedicated, and widely respected army standby units are the small medical components. Organized and trained separately, they consist of a field hygiene section (human and veterinary) and a sophisticated surgical unit. The Norwegian government has told the UN that both of these are available for peacekeeping operations or for natural disasters requiring international assistance.[64]

A long tradition in Norwegian international medical service has given these military men a special place in peacekeeping affairs. Some of the officers responsible for designing UN units have had individual experience as far back as the 1930s, and Norwegian medical units served in Korea, UNEF, and the Congo. In both units, recruitment procedures, contingency planning, and overall readiness are far advanced—and were even before 1964.

The recruitment system for the medical units represents a creative solution to a persistent Nordic standby problem: how to make it easier for skilled, even professional, civilians to leave their lucrative, secure jobs to serve in peacekeeping missions. The Joint Medical Service of the Norwegian Armed Forces has successfully done this by creating a two-track standby program. The first goes into high gear at the outset of an emergency. For every position in the surgical unit one person, who expects to be mobilized first, is on standby and three or four others are on reserve. Most have jobs in civilian hospitals. Administrative personnel are usually from the regular military establishment. The doctors, if not professional soldiers, have completed their conscript service, almost always in a medical capacity. Nurses are available, including males for hazardous duty. All personnel are volunteers. The secret has been to assure them that their service will be limited to the early, critical stages of a new mission, probably not longer than a few months. Under most conditions the unit can depart from Norway in eight to ten hours, equipped with facilities and drugs usable in the climate for which they are bound, and capable of performing as many as fifteen major operations a day and providing postoperative care and numerous lesser services. With departure complications the readiness time might stretch to twenty-four or forty-eight hours.[65] In anticipation of doctors' need to communicate accurately with foreign patients, Norwegian universities are being tapped for language students willing to serve as interpreters for short periods of time.

The second track would be activated when the new mission stabilizes and medical services become more routine. From the reserve rosters, replacements for the standbys would be sent according to well-tested procedures. Because of their compulsory military obligation, most doctors or medical students put on a soldier's uniform early in their careers. At the end of their first several months of conscript service they are given a choice: complete the eight-month conscript tour or leave the service now in return for agreeing to six months' duty in the future as a UN doctor at an ongoing mission. Although there have been periodic shortages of volunteers, virtually all Norwegian doctors for UNEF were recruited this way and future operations are expected to follow a similar pattern.

Denmark

Since 1964 the number of Danish troops in UN service has often exceeded, by 500 or 600 men, the planned number of about 900 standby personnel. Danish officials reported to an international meeting of peacekeeping experts in 1965 that, because 1,500 men were currently in Cyprus, the Middle East, and elsewhere, the government would use all units being prepared in Denmark as rotation battalions and would not set up the specialized standby contingents that were scheduled, such as communications and field hospital units.[66] Some efforts had already been made to enlist general standby personnel on the original model, but according to one account only about 75 young Danes had signed on as of May 1965. This skimpy response resulted not only from the standard inconveniences of standby contracts but also in part because Denmark provides no job-protection laws like those in Sweden and Norway.[67] Little has changed since then. A reduced battalion staff cadre had been created in Denmark "to handle current tasks" of "forces in the field, as well as the formation, training, etc., of new forces."[68] Most of its output is concerned with current needs of UNFICYP, where the Danish battalion carries the burdens of order-keeping in the heart of Nicosia.

About 600 strong in 1968—400 fewer than at the beginning of the operation—the Danish unit has been replenished by an unusually complex rotation system, one purpose of which is preservation of certain standby procedures so they will be available whenever standby units are set up. Four categories of personnel make up an ordinary rotation battalion, and the one that went to Cyprus in the spring of 1967 is typical. Approximately 100 of its members were repeaters, men already in Cyprus and wishing another six-month stint. This is common; it is not unusual for Danes to do three or four tours. Another 75–100 transferred from a Danish unit in Gaza. A third segment was recruited by news media advertisements in Denmark asking men who had completed the final two months of their conscript service, or were about to, to volunteer *specifically* for Cyprus tours. These totaled approximately 200, although nearly 700 applied after the advertising began in February for the May rotation. The fourth component, about 150–200 volunteers, is drawn from what Danish officials call "normal standby."

This last category complicates the system, for it is a more or less fictional standby component. The Danes do establish every year a unit the size of a company or slightly larger which is put on standby and eventually integrated into a Cyprus rotation battalion. Volunteers for this unit sign a contract containing standby terms like those anticipated in 1964. They obligate themselves to one year on standby in addition to four weeks of training, and are subject to six months of UN duty beginning anytime during the contract period. The contract does not mention Cyprus or any other existing mission, and to all outward appearances it constitutes an obligation to go anywhere, anytime. But in fact the signatories are given oral assurance—described by one Danish official as "90 percent guarantees"—that they will receive on a specified future date an assignment to one or the other operation currently using Danish personnel. This is how these men get into the Cyprus rotation battalion. In effect these volunteers, assembled and readied before other rotation personnel, suffer little risk of surprise disruption but are nevertheless awarded a contract bonus. The explanation given for this circuitous process is that it preserves a precedent for reconverting the contract system back to its genuine standby purposes.

The practice of using only volunteers for UN service has not been strictly adhered to in Denmark, and the relation between Danish conscripts and peacekeeping duty abroad has been the subject of significant legal scrutiny. The 1964 standby laws said that "it is presumed" that UN personnel "will be recruited on a voluntary basis."[69] This same presumption had been voiced in the Folketing (parliament) years before, during the 1956 debates on Danish participation in UNEF.[70] In purely numerical terms, the presumption has in fact guided the selection of most of the 18,000 Danish soldiers who have seen UN duty. Nevertheless, a higher proportion of them have been nonvolunteers than in any other Nordic country. Only a small number of Danish officers with Cyprus service ribbons have volunteered and the same is true of many UNEF personnel. Technically, perhaps, these are not truly volunteers, since any professional officer finds it difficult to refuse a request from his superiors that he offer himself for UN assignment.[71] Danish regular army officers all have a status equivalent to civil servants and they are expected to serve wherever required, even though this strains somewhat the presumption of voluntarism. For many years now, UN service has been a well-nigh inescapable interruption of many officers' home regimental duty, but for the up-and-coming young captain or major, it can be a career asset.

But there is a second type of Danish officer, the conscript who usually performs only his minimal national service with a local regiment. Except that it is of longer duration, his obligation is essentially the same as that of the drafted private or corporal. Over the years some conscript officers have also been ordered into UN units, but none resisted or complained until 1966. The one who finally balked set off a chain of events with implications that go considerably beyond the personal status of an obscure Danish officer.

The complainant was a physician, a conscript student-officer at the military medical school who was inducted for Gaza duty in May 1966 after the medical corps could not find an acceptable volunteer. He was very qualified, very available, and absolutely determined to get his orders rescinded. He first tried military channels, and eventually his case reached the Defense Ministry, which maintained, as it had for years, that nothing in Danish law prevents ordering conscripts to UN duty if volunteers are not at hand. The doctor had already reluctantly gone to the UNEF hospital, and after the ministry's unfavorable ruling he took his case to the Ombudsman, the successful and much-touted

Nordic institution that defends the rights of citizens against arbitrary or unlawful government action.*

The doctor won his appeal. After considering the Ombudsman's judgment, the Defense Ministry said it would rely in the future exclusively on conscript volunteers for UN assignments, recalled the doctor from Gaza, and informed the Ombudsman that it might ask the Folketing for a revision of the military service regulations to explicitly permit the use of conscripts for the UN, whether volunteers or not.[72] The ministry made this request in late 1968, and in June 1969 the legislature took the significant step of granting to the government the authority to order any conscript into UN peacekeeping service.[73]

The rationale of the Ombudsman's ruling could have important consequences for Danish practice and, by example, perhaps for the rest of Scandinavia as well. Behind the issue of personal rights in this case was a more fundamental public policy question: Is the Danish government willing to affirm politically and legally that UN peacekeeping is an essential defense priority directly in the national interest? If not, if a conscript's UN service cannot be broadly construed as defending his country's interests, then UN duty must be entirely voluntary. If so, there are solid grounds for fulfilling UN commitments with the regular military establishment, including its conscripts, whenever necessary. This was one implication of the Folketing's decision to amend the military service rules as requested by the Defense Ministry.

To focus attention on this choice, the Ombudsman singled out Article 81 of the constitution, which states: "Each man fit for military service is committed to contribute in person to the country's defense according to the detailed rules the law prescribes." The Defense Ministry's customary position, explained the Ombudsman, assumed in effect that a Danish unit under UN international command preserves Denmark's security. The Ombudsman neither rejected nor approved

* This institution is analyzed in "The Ombudsman or Citizen's Defender: A Modern Institution," *Annals of the American Academy of Political and Social Science*, Vol. 377 (May 1968), entire issue. The Ombudsman's findings are not legally binding but are always weighty and never ignored. His jurisdiction extends to all government agents but judicial ones, and he may take up the case of anyone with personal interest in a matter. This doctor's complaint was one among 1,106 in 1966 and one of the several dozen in which the Ombudsman chose to issue detailed findings. Ibid., pp. 56–59.

this idea, but merely said new law would have to be enacted if this interpretation were to be maintained. In a key sentence he added: "I wanted to give the Folketing an opportunity to consider if participation in the UN forces can be classified as 'the country's defense.'" An affirmative answer would put the government's UN involvement on the same footing as military responsibilities within the NATO alliance, for which the regular establishment and conscripts would of course be used.

This issue of ordering conscripts abroad is not new in Denmark, although it had never been raised in a peacekeeping context. One precedent mentioned by the Ombudsman was the special Danish regular army brigade that went to Germany in 1947, during the Allied occupation, for which special legislation was passed.[74] A few years later, after the General Assembly adopted the Uniting for Peace Resolution, Denmark promised a unit for its standby system. Because the Resolution's preparedness structure never took shape, this promise never had to be fulfilled and the necessary legislation was never presented to the Folketing. But at the time the conscript question became a partisan issue, it appeared that the government might decide to use regular army contingents for this commitment, and it was criticized for this intent by one of the left-of-center parties.[75]

Irrespective of the recent decision about conscripts for the UN, Denmark is likely to continue sending professional officers to UN battalions even if they do not volunteer. Now that the authority exists to order conscripts into UN service—and essentially this is the same option that the Norwegian parliament declined to make available in 1964—Danish UN planners will be able legally to deploy for peacekeeping any person or unit from the standing or mobilizable armed forces. This would be a radical departure from the practice of other Nordic states. Even though available, the new authority presumably will be used sparingly, probably only in emergencies where time is at a premium and no volunteer forces can be readied, or when specialists from the regular military establishment are needed. Some Danish experts are convinced that when the time comes to recruit for genuine standby, it will be necessary to raise the contract bonus perhaps as high as two or three months' potential wages, to design new and more appealing recruiting methods, and to experiment, as Norway has, with ways of enlisting conscripts near the end of their compulsory service.[76]

Sweden

Like Denmark, Sweden's standby plans were interrupted by heavy demands on the Swedish military establishment for UNEF and UNFICYP. Sweden is eventually to have the largest Nordic standby force—two full infantry battalions and fairly large technical units, plus the usual observers and staff officers. Even while the original legislation was being drafted, it was apparent that some targets would have to be adjusted. Sweden at that time had men in Egypt and was also providing the Congo force with the largest Scandinavian unit, which from January 1963 to January 1964 decreased gradually from 1,056 to 396 men. Legislative proposals for the 1,600-man standby contribution recalled that the working group had "agreed to request the establishment of standby forces" only after "the dissolution of the existing Nordic UN forces," and concluded that "should Sweden have military contingents participating in UN peacekeeping operations, the size of the standby force should be proportionately reduced."[77]

The proportional reduction formula was never applied literally, and it is difficult to trace exactly what the Swedes intended to do. The Riksdag (parliament) approved the government's proposal in May 1964. A month earlier Swedish spokesmen had left no doubt that the standby force, whatever its actual total, would not be used as replacements for current commitments but rather as a rapid-response force, usable anywhere on emergency notice.[78] Had proportional reduction been used in the spring and summer of 1964, even as a rough measure, Sweden would have had to defer nearly all standby preparations, for at that time more than 1,400 Swedes were already on active UN duty. For reasons not altogether clear, the government accordingly decided in June to alter the original design, and the Swedish mission at the UN announced in July that a standby force "consisting of about 1,000 men" was going to be "provisionally organized." In October this same unit was rotated to Cyprus.[79] Six months later this battalion and another in Egypt had to be relieved, and after this time the replacements were simply identified as "standby units" or as "the organized part of the Swedish UN standby force."[80] No longer did the government mention proportional reduction of any kind, and nothing more was heard of the 1,000-man ceiling.[81]

These relabelings tend to create the impression that the units in question are essentially the same as the originally planned standby battalions, except that they end up being used as relief contingents. In reality they are unlike them in most essential respects. Volunteers for these units came forward not on the understanding that they might have to go anywhere anytime, but on the assumption that they would go to Cyprus or Egypt on a specified date. The standard volunteer applications even contained spaces where the recruit indicated which of the two units he wished to join. Between 1964 and 1967 all battalion-level training was oriented specifically to these operations, and most units spent two weeks getting ready and departed at the beginning of the third week for one or the other theater. For those on this tight schedule there was not even a pretense of being on general standby after training.[82] They were actually very much like the units Sweden had periodically been rotating into UN missions since 1956. While continuing to rotate a unit to Cyprus since the demise of UNEF, Sweden has recently been able to make some progress in setting up a standby battalion at home on the original model—although a Swedish report to the UN in 1968 left the status of the standby program unclear.[83]

The Swedes probably would be less inclined than the Danes or the Norwegians to consider revisions in the volunteer system. None of the tendencies toward change inside these neighboring states has had a counterpart in Sweden. The Military Service Act of 1941 is controlling in law and practice: "Conscripts belonging to the army may be used outside the frontiers of the country only for the defense of the country." The 1964 legislation commands, therefore, that "the forces should be recruited on a purely voluntary basis."[84] And they are, officers and privates alike.

An adequate supply of Swedish volunteers has usually been available for rotation battalions, often three or even four times the number needed. Many are recruited near the end of their conscript service, and final selection of unit members, most of whom apply through their regiments, is left to a small commission of officers at the UN Army Department in Stockholm.[85] By mid-1969, just over 30,000 Swedes had done at least one UN tour. No other Nordic state has supplied this many, though the Danes point out that they have provided a larger proportion in terms of national population. Since 1964 occasional recruiting shortfalls have been reported,[86] and in 1967 the chief of the UN Army Department acknowledged that Sweden's uninterrupted heavy UN commitments have caused "certain problems which have not been easy to overcome. With the shortage of labour which has been prevailing during the past few years and still prevails in our country, it has accordingly been difficult to spare personnel for service abroad."[87] If, here and elsewhere in Nordic states, high employment affects recruitment patterns, so do seasonal factors to some extent. The Scandinavians have been most willing to volunteer for service abroad when the climate at home is most rigorous, and they have tended to volunteer for one mission rather than another because of preferences for its working and living conditions.[88]

Swedish experience shows how easily a small military establishment can be somewhat strained by UN commitments even when only volunteers are used. The UN Army Department chief admitted that "it has been particularly difficult to free officers in active service" as UN volunteers, and that the number of regular officers "who have in the last few years been continuously working in UN units abroad, corresponds to the training officers of two regiments" in Sweden. Moreover, "the burden on the regiments which—in addition to their ordinary tasks—have had the responsibility for the organization, equipment and training of the UN units, has also been heavy at times."[89]

These twin requirements, personnel and time, can cause particularly serious strains when the regular military establishment assigns peacekeeping-related activities a comparatively low priority. At one time this made it difficult for Swedish regular officers to volunteer for UN duty. Some years after Sweden had become a frequent peacekeeping supplier, the UN Army Department noticed unexplained imbalances in the statistical histories of professional officers volunteering for UN duty. An exceptionally large number were coming from a small number of the army's regiments. It turned out that other senior regimental commanders were actively discouraging their young officers from volunteering. Loss of subordinate staff and command officers for six months or longer was naturally resisted by those responsible for overall regimental performance. Although this situation improved gradually, not enough active officers can be regularly made available to UN battalions. Consequently, most contain greater proportions of volunteer reserve and conscript officers than of active professionals.[90] In UNFICYP it is not always possible for the Swedes—or the Finns, who must also use many officers not in active service—to match the man with his job. A schoolteacher becomes an intelligence officer, a farmer a logistician, or a graduate student a public information officer. By contrast the Danes can more easily order a regular officer to do in Cyprus the same job he does with his regiment in Denmark.

Swedish standby units that have been almost completely recruited and prepared included, as of 1969, a complement of staff officers and observers, a movement-control team, a helicopter platoon, and a military police unit. All except the military police unit form the 202-man technical contingent, which has its own command and staff element and a 56-man technical team capable of maintaining or reconstructing essential civilian services such as ground transportation, telecommunications, sanitation and drainage installations, and electrical and refrigeration systems. Heavy equipment and supplementary local labor would have to be acquired in the area of an operation. This is the only specialized standby unit to have existed continuously since 1964, the others having been organized gradually in recent years. Like the Norwegian medical elements, it has been offered for UN disaster-relief work.[91]

If Sweden were ever to consider, for UN purposes, revision of the 1941 conscription regulations, legislative historians would have to search back a quarter of a century for apposite discussion in the government and legislature. Sweden has been a UN member since 1946 and, like others, expected this to entail responsibilities in the collective security system, most concretely the provision of Article 43 enforcement forces. Most member states were to remain in the dark about the size and nature of their contributions and the procedures for negotiating special agreements with the Security Council until the Military Staff Committee had completed its work. It was assumed, however, that offers from middle and small powers would pale in significance next to the larger forces anticipated from the Big Five. In view of these uncertainties Sweden decided to participate in the new organization but to await results of the preliminary Military Staff Committee recommendations before deciding how the Swedish contributions would be recruited and organized. Implications at the time were that regular Swedish armed forces might be used for Article 43 and the 1941 regulation revised to this effect.

A few years afterward, during UN debates on the Uniting for Peace Resolution, the issue had to be faced again, and this time Sweden was obliged to adopt a definite position. The initial step came in October 1950, when the Swedish ambassador to the UN reacted to the preparedness paragraphs of the Acheson Plan. He advised an Assembly committee about the military service law and said that, if the Resolution were adopted, "the matter of revising those provisions of Swedish legislation would arise as an important question."[92] For this reason, though Sweden favored the Resolution as a whole, it abstained in the vote on the paragraphs in question. Within a month the commander in chief of the Swedish army was instructed to examine the question of setting up a 1,000-man standby force. He recommended that the law not be revised, that the force be available only under specific conditions, and that all personnel be volunteers enlisted for a three-year contract period. Apparently these conclusions were not expected by the government, which had intended "to put forward a proposal in Parliament in 1951 concerning 'the United Nations Battalion,' and at the same time to present a proposal for the necessary alteration of the conscription law" so that active servicemen could be used.[93] The matter became quite controversial, with some of the press and some officials strongly favoring a revision of the conscript law. But before it reached the parliament, the dismal fate of the Resolution became clearer and the Korean armistice undercut enthusiasm for all collective enforcement proposals. Standby preparations were not considered again in the Riksdag until 1961, when Sweden, earlier than any other Nordic state, took formal legislative action to anticipate training needs for continuing UN operations.[94] Before long attention shifted away from unilateral programs and toward the blossoming Nordic regional cooperation in standby planning.

Finland

Finland makes no pretense of having set up any of its Nordic force quota, or even of having made final decisions about how this will be done after the Finnish contingent in UNFICYP is no longer needed.[95] The Finns are intensely interested in the standby activities of their neighbors, from whose failures and successes Finland can learn, borrow, and adapt. They are especially concerned about personnel problems, for Finland has not yet tried to recruit general standby troops. Since 1964 all recruiting has been for Cyprus volunteers, but experiences of other Nordic states have alerted the Finns to the possibility that volunteers might be more reluctant to commit themselves to a general standby obligation.

Blueprints for the Finnish standby force are still rudimentary. Initially, it is to be an infantry battalion, and under current law the total force, including reserves and observers, must not exceed 2,000 men.[96] The Finnish constitution implies that volunteers may not be sent abroad, and the peace treaty of 1947 restricts military missions to internal and local defense, to be performed by armed services numbering no more than 41,900 men.[97] The more than 5,000 Finns who have served as UN soldiers have all been volunteers, as any standby recruits will be. They will sign renewable one-year contracts and before their six-month standby period will be given up to forty-five days of training. The 1964 legislation did not provide for bonus payments to volunteers, but government employees who enlist are assured of job security if they are called up.[98]

Cyprus commitments have absorbed most of the energies that Finnish planners had decided in 1963 to expend on standby preparations. This is Finland's first large and sustained involvement since becoming a UN member in the 1955 East-West package deal—an arrangement that also brought in two other potentially important peacekeeping suppliers, Ireland and Austria. Only a year passed before Finland was asked to provide a small UNEF contingent, which served during the initial thirteen months of the operation. In New York, former Finnish chief of staff, Major General I. A. E. Martola, who a decade later was to command UNFICYP, was the informal chairman of the informal UNEF military advisory committee and acted simultaneously as the personal military adviser to Hammarskjöld. Between then and 1964, Finland's participation was small, limited to the sending of observers to Lebanon and Kashmir.

More than anything else, scarcity of resources has shaped the administration of Finnish participation in UNFICYP, and these economies will constrain standby efforts later. It is first a matter of money. Finland alone among the Nordic states takes part in UNFICYP on the condition, laid down by the Eduskunta (parliament), that reimbursable costs be paid promptly by the UN. This insistence is vital to the Finns. To mid-1967, Helsinki's total reimbursable outlay for UNFICYP was about $13.7 million, slightly exceeding 10 percent of the entire defense budget for 1968. As a comparative measure, consider that Sweden's total reimbursable costs for UNEF, ONUC, *and* UNFICYP, over the entire decade between 1956 and 1966, amounted to a little less than $50 million, or about 5 percent of the total Swedish defense budget for 1968.[99]

Except for the lower grades, manpower has not been plentiful. The Finns also consider it detrimental to deplete their regular officer and NCO ranks and, like the Swedes, employ exceptionally high ratios of reserves and civilians in their UN battalions. The first four Finnish battalions in UNFICYP numbered nearly 3,000 officers and men, yet among them were only 50 regular officers and 53 NCOs. In 1968, only 5 percent of Finnish battalion higher ranks were members of the regular armed forces.[100] Such professionals as can be spared for Cyprus duty may stay no longer than six months, although others in the battalion may remain a full year. These others, all from civilian life, have been readily available since UNFICYP was formed, when 5,000 applications were received for positions in the first Finnish battalion. Subsequent volunteer surpluses have fluctuated with unemployment levels and seasons, but a 20 percent excess of applicants has not been uncommon. Many revolunteer while in Cyprus for three or six months, a practice that leads to irregular quarterly rotations of fractions of units, occasionally as few as one or two hundred men at a time.

Whenever conditions permit formation of their standby units, the Finns will be austere. Sophisticated, expensive military hardware is not likely to be siphoned from the regular defense establishment; the navy and air force are already underequipped for lack of capital. Procurement for the standby unit probably will be pared to indispensable items. Procedures for supplying the contingent with officers and specialists will in all likelihood resemble the Cyprus pattern of heavy dependence on nonprofessionals.

Swedish and Danish Civilian Police

If the Nordic standby plans had been developed after rather than before the initiation of UNFICYP, they would probably have included some civilian police components. By summer 1964, a 175-man police element (United Nations Civilian Police—UNCIVPOL) was integral to the force. It has included contingents from Sweden, Denmark, Austria, Australia, and, until 1967, New Zealand. In the police hierarchies of most of these suppliers, this novel role has grown steadily in popularity, particularly in the Scandinavian states.

U Thant did not get all the policemen he wanted in 1964, nor was he able to enlist all the states he approached for offers of police. In addition to the five that did take part he requested police units from Canada, Finland, Ireland, and the United Kingdom, hoping the nine together could muster 200 men.[101] When they declined to participate for various reasons, several of the five suppliers overcame the nearly universal scarcity of policemen and managed to provide 40 men apiece, resupplying them at this level consistently after 1964. The Danes and the Swedes have been in this category.[102] By 1969, together they had provided UNCIVPOL with something like 600 to 700 policemen, and central headquarters in Stockholm and Copenhagen have established routine recruitment and training programs for rotation volunteers.

The inclusion of policemen in UNFICYP was a last-minute move. Senior police officials in Sweden and Denmark had little advance notice that anything was to be asked of them.[103] The secretariat began circulating its plans for the organization of UNFICYP soon after passage of the March 4 resolution authorizing the force. A report issued on March 12 makes no reference at all to civilian police but rather conveys the distinct impression that only military peacekeepers were envisaged at that time, which was about two weeks before UNFICYP was to become operational.[104] Abruptly and with minimal explanation, secretariat progress reports on UNFICYP in late April and early May began mentioning UN civilian police.[105] During the final weeks of March, one fact about power on the island had become clear to secretariat planners: the police of both communities, heavily armed, partisan, and well trained, were among the critical potential sources of disorder and intercommunal violence. The rationale for UNCIVPOL, one Danish policeman wrote much later, was that "the local police personnel would be more receptive to cooperation with their fellow policemen, even though they are from foreign lands, than they would be to military personnel."[106]

Similar policies have governed the preparation of Danish and Swedish police. Surpluses of applicants—far in excess of the number of men who could actually be spared at any one time—permit high selection standards. Even the lowest ranking UN policemen generally have at least several years of national experience in good standing and a working knowledge of English. In the beginning both Swedes and Danes rotated their policemen every three months, but the Swedes later extended this to six months because the shorter period left too little time for familiarization with Cyprus, an especially pressing requirement in view of UNCIVPOL's unique closeness to complicated local police affairs. Both countries have set up brief training periods at home, structured on the presumption that the trainee's activities in Cyprus are going to be functionally much the same as his domestic police work, with allowance of course for the differences in political contexts and degree of police authority. Even though traditional police powers—arrest, interrogation, and so on—are not available to members of UNCIVPOL, most of their time is spent exercising skills to which they have been habituated since police academy days. Investigation, reporting, collecting and filing evidence, and mediatory services are the standard fare, and wrongdoers, an UNCIVPOL member has remarked, "fear our pens more than our swords."

Nordic Cooperation

Joint activity is an accepted and time-tested feature of the Nordic way. In many economic, social, and technical sectors a complex web of interconnections, including both public and private interchange, has been spun since the beginning of the twentieth century. Among the highly visible institutional successes of this cooperation, the intensity and effectiveness of which were enlarged dramatically after World War II, is the Nordic Council, a quasi-parliamentary consultative and coordinating device with recommendatory powers over the five national members (Iceland is included here). Proposals for cooperation have aborted too—notably the failure to create a Scandinavian defense alliance in the late 1940s and the dead-end attempt to form a Nordic common economic market. Yet whether or not institutions are built or policies executed jointly, it has been true that in practically all substantive fields, even defense and foreign policy, "joint consultation almost assumes the sanctity of an ethical principle in the inter-Nordic relations."[107] That in peacekeeping affairs this consultative bent has generated joint military preparedness programs is at once explainable and remarkable. Explainable because convergent Nordic national interests are strong regarding UN peacekeeping; remarkable because, as a result of Nordic cleavage between NATO and neutral states, military togetherness has been rare. The first time Nordic military students engaged in joint training of any kind was when all four sent officers to Sweden in 1965 for the premiere session of a new combined UN observer course.

During the second half of the sixties, regional cooperation in peacekeeping was increased cautiously but steadily, and now three forms of official intra-Nordic activity are talked about or exist in practice. The one likely to have the least long-term impact is the system of fielding peacekeeping units that mix national soldiers in Nordic battalions. Convention and military convenience have so far dictated, and reasonably, that at the battalion level most UN units ought to be nationally homogeneous. An exception for eleven years was the so-called DANOR battalion in UNEF, which mixed Danish and Norwegian companies under alternating command. The battalion gave the two partners a good deal of political mileage because of the cooperative spirit it displayed. But militarily the battalion was inefficiently organized, top-heavy with separate support and administrative personnel for each nationality, and a technical headache because of the petty and not-so-petty frictions that plagued even the compatible Danes and Norwegians. In 1966, as part of a secretariat effort to streamline the force and make it more economical, the Scandinavian states considered proposals for a three-nation battalion incorporating a Swedish contingent as well. This was the litmus test for the idea of wider regional mixing. It showed that the pleasant patina of cooperation is marred by the stubborn fact that two Nordic states are NATO members and two are not. After multilateral discussions, the Danes and Norwegians were affirmative but Sweden rejected the plan, reportedly to avoid possible compromising of Swedish neutrality. The Danish military command said later that its planners "appreciate the Swedish objections. Perhaps there is nothing to say to the fact that a non-NATO power refuses to place soldiers under the command of NATO countries."[108]

A more significant form of Nordic interaction is the now-regularized, high-level Defense Ministry collaboration. Twice yearly, the four ministers, supported by six- to ten-man delegations, meet for a few days to plan and coordinate peacekeeping matters (but nothing more). Lower level preparations are the task of the Nordic working group composed of majors and lieutenant colonels who get together three or four times a year. Finland's participation in all this has been piecemeal. Only an observer was sent to the working group sessions in 1963, after which Finland took full part. In 1967 the Finnish defense minister attended the biannual meeting, held for the first time in

Helsinki; before this, Finland had been represented at the ministerial meetings by its local ambassador at whichever Scandinavian capital the sessions were held. Now these consultations range over all standby and current peacekeeping problems of common interest; and every agenda devotes time to the Nordic UN training programs—the third category of regional cooperation.

In the spring of 1965 a Swedish army training center at Strangnas, a small town near Stockholm, received a modest parade of visitors that included distinguished Nordic military and civilian officials, the Swedish army staff, media representatives from the four countries, and even an American news team from the National Broadcasting Company. The occasion was the first session of the joint Nordic training course for UN observers.[109] A total of thirty-six students and six permanent instructors explored, mostly in English and with the advantage of teaching personnel with UN experience, the major problems of being a UN military observer. Students and teachers alike came from all four countries. Since most students had already been handed orders for UNTSO or UNMOGIP (United Nations Military Observer Group in India and Pakistan), the subject matter emphasized requirements in these two missions, whose standing operating procedures and other documents were adapted as background and study materials. In addition, general training exercises based on fictional conflict situations were prepared. To complement operational instruction in communications, incident-investigation, reporting techniques, and the like, the students completed special oral and written exercises in English.

Plans for this course had taken shape over a period of several years, beginning during the joint consultations of the early sixties. After the trial session in 1965, the curriculum branched out to include separate training for staff officers, movement- and transport-control technicians, and military police. Other fields of possible future joint UN training have been considered. The project has expanded geographically, so that each Nordic state hosts at least one of the courses; and in 1967 its membership was broadened to admit a few students from the non-Nordic countries Canada, Austria, and Switzerland.[110] The center of activity is still Strangnas, where every year some seventy students (with a high proportion of Swedes) and fifteen instructors converge for two 120-hour sessions, one for observers, the other for staff officers. Most students are captains, majors, or lieutenant colonels. Sweden pays all administrative costs, each country assumes the financial burden for its own participants, and they divide the labor in preparing the courses. Only the observer curriculum is offered twice a year, once at Strangnas and once in Finland.

The distance between Hammarskjöld's first concerted attention to preparedness problems and the fruition of Nordic training programs spans the greater part of a decade, the creation of three major peacekeeping operations and assorted lesser ones, the accumulation by more than four dozen states of at least some brief peacekeeping experience, and political crises and calms over peacekeeping in UN diplomatic councils. Throughout these years, under a UN flag somewhere, tens of thousands of Nordic officers and men have served. While strictly national preparedness efforts have matured as fully elsewhere, perhaps most outstandingly in Canada, the collective Nordic record of preparedness planning and training is unique, their history of patient collaboration in peacekeeping affairs unequaled, and their development of a deeply imbedded UN habit unsurpassed.

SIX

The Wider Fellowship

T HE admissions committee of a hypothetical future peacekeepers' club would have a difficult time going about its business. Charter memberships could hardly be denied Sweden, or Finland, or Norway, or Denmark, and Canada would also deserve founder status; but beyond these five, selection would be tricky.

To admit only states that have promised or established standby programs would seem a fair criterion, opening the doors to the Netherlands, Austria, Iran, New Zealand, Italy, the United Kingdom, and even tiny Malta.[1] So constituted, however, the club roster would ignore how little its members' preparedness activities have in common except the "standby" adjective customarily lumping them together and how unevenly perfected their preparedness plans are. Worse, the roster would exclude a country like Ireland, a frequent and valuable supplier whose internal procedures for preparing United Nations units are far more advanced than those in some standby states. Or it would exclude India, Brazil, and Yugoslavia, all participants in both the United Nations Emergency Force (UNEF) and the United Nations Congo Operation (ONUC) and all, as late as the end of UNEF in 1967, displaying comparatively well-developed preparedness capabilities because of the need to fill rotation requirements.* As a group these nonstandby coun-

---

* Logically the list could be extended to countries with substantial experience, such as Pakistan, a principal supplier in the Congo and the only contributor of operational units to the United Nations Security Force (UNSF) in West Irian; to Ethiopia, Malaya,

tries are disparate both in the importance they attach to peacekeeping and the resources they can bring to bear. In recent times, for example, a large portion of Ireland's small army, which numbers fewer than 10,000, has seen service in the Congo or Cyprus. For this otherwise uncommitted establishment, UN peacekeeping is a central mission. On the other hand, India regularly keeps a million men under arms, and although ONUC literally could not have done without large Indian contributions, the output from New Delhi's perspective was small— no more than 1 percent of total army personnel ever went to the Congo at any one time. But whatever their proportional sacrifice, countries that supply forces without setting up standby systems—and others of this type surely will contribute to future operations—deserve consideration along with the standbys. While a "standby" label may be a badge of extraordinary effort or achievement, it is not yet necessarily so; and these nonstandbys have augmented overall UN preparedness in important ways without claiming to have established standby contingents.

Of additional importance for preparedness are the providers, those states whose visible contributions to operational, front-line units may be negligible, even nonexistent, but whose logistical and technical support are crucial. Of course the United States historically has been *the* provider. Canada has been both supplier and provider, and other medium-sized but militarily sophisticated nations may someday do the same. Because of special circumstances, the British wear both hats in Cyprus, supplying infantry units as well as nearly all logistical services and making the United Nations Force in Cyprus (UNFICYP) the only large mission not critically dependent on U.S. technical support. The United States did, however, provide a large part of the initial strategic airlift and has been financially generous ever since.

Nigeria, Tunisia, Ghana, Morocco, and others in ONUC; to Indonesia, which took part in the early UNEF and in ONUC. During the early 1960s, however, these involvements were mostly one time only. Internal mechanisms for servicing UN commitments have since disappeared, or detailed information about them is not available. All of the states dealt with in this chapter had units in active UN service as recently as 1967. Much of the country data used here are based on interviews conducted mostly between April and June 1967 with civilian and military officials from each government; sometimes at both national capitals and field units (Canada, the United Kingdom, Ireland, and Austria are in this group); just at the capitals (the Netherlands); or just at UN missions (India, Yugoslavia, and Brazil in UNEF).

Canada

Canadian leadership in preparedness is incontestable. By its national example, its persistent preparedness diplomacy, and its historic association with peacekeeping, Canada is universally recognized as a prime mover in efforts to put UN peacekeeping capacities on a more solid footing. Canadian military and foreign policy outlooks have been saturated with peacekeeping and preparedness concerns, more so than any other UN member's. It is perhaps a measure of this importance that Canada's peacekeeper identification, long thought sacrosanct, has been recently touched by national controversy, as conveyed a few years ago (March 4, 1967) by a skeptical caption in the Toronto *Globe and Mail* reading, "Canada's Dilemma: How Blessed Is a Peacekeeper?" Since this query, Lester Pearson has stepped down as prime minister; UNEF has disintegrated, and Canada's frustrated embarrassment over its collapse has scarcely been concealed. The new prime minister, Pierre Trudeau, began to challenge the conventional, uncritical versions of Canada's future as a peacekeeper. Nevertheless indications are strong that the government's answer still is, "Blessed enough."

The peacekeeper, the disinterested yet outward-looking intermediary, is a fairly new role for Canada. During the Suez crisis of 1956, the Canadians unearthed a seventy-year-old retort from their prime minister Sir John A. Macdonald, who had been asked for a Canadian military contribution to Britain's Sudan expedition in the 1880s. "The Suez Canal," Macdonald said, "is nothing to us," and Canada has no wish to sacrifice its blood and treasure "to get Gladstone and Co. out of the hole they have plunged themselves into by their own imbecility."[2] Just as Macdonald wanted no part of far-flung imperial wars in the nineteenth century, later governments sandwiched between the world wars were complacently inward-looking and convinced, in the inapt metaphor of one Canadian legislator, that a man living in a fireproof house only wastes his money on insurance premiums.

Canada's career in peacekeeping began in 1949 with the United Nations Military Observer Group in India and Pakistan (UNMOGIP) in Kashmir, and Canadians have taken part in every UN mission since then, as well as in the International Control Commissions (ICC)—all absorbing some 25,000 men. Few Canadians, though, remember how different the style of their involvement was in the beginning, how sharply it contrasted with recent practices. Now it is common to send off Canadian UN soldiers with some measure of patriotic publicity and even a dash of fanfare. But twenty years ago the first Canadian officers left virtually unnoticed, only once were they discussed in the House of Commons, and not until 1955 did the Defense Ministry mention the Kashmir observers in its annual reports. The UN's initial request for officers to serve in Kashmir was evidently received without much enthusiasm in Ottawa. According to one Canadian historian's account,[3] several factors explain this cool reaction. Despite some stimulation of Canadian interest in the UN as a result of a first, active term as a nonpermanent member of the Security Council in 1948-49, there was growing disillusionment with the world organization during this period, perhaps aggravated by the recent collapse of the Charter-based collective security system. Canada was now paying greater attention to the negotiations for a new North Atlantic treaty. The military establishment was not eager to deplete understrength officer ranks, so when the government did decide to participate in UNMOGIP, reserve officers rather than regulars were used for the first year or so. No one relished getting into a dispute between India and Pakistan, two fellow Commonwealth members. Canada's affirmative response to the UN request was partly credited, even in those days, to Lester Pearson, who only three months earlier had taken the External Affairs portfolio.

Two Defense White Papers were to tell the story of the coming decades. One, in 1952, cautiously admitted that for Canada peacekeeping had some respectability. Twelve years later a second one gave peacekeeping a priority place in Canadian defense policy in a systematic way that no other government has matched.

Canada rates numerous distinctions as a peacekeeper. It was the first to set up a standby battalion. It is the only state ever to use one—in Cyprus. Among standbys it alone earmarks for the UN fully formed units of professional soldiers. It alone over the years has kept a standby battalion always on call for emergencies and unrelated to rotation contingents. It alone has sponsored a general intergovernmental conference for suppliers. If the word "standby" overstates most Nordic programs, it vastly understates Canada's, because in addition to its single standby battalion, Canada ensures that a substantial part of its 100,000-man armed forces is able to take on peacekeeping assignments if necessary.

The standby battalion is a quick-response unit likely to be the first to go in any crisis. Although its chronological history is somewhat blurred, its origin ought to be reckoned in the late 1950s. Canadian sources occasionally give 1950 as the date because in that year Prime Minister Louis St. Laurent earmarked a brigade called the Special Service Force, available either for the North Atlantic Treaty Organization (NATO) or for the UN. This unit later went to Korea. But preparedness planning for peacekeeping rather than for collective enforcement did not begin until after UNEF, probably in 1957 when Pearson published his standby proposals.[4] Either then or in the following year the standby contingent was actually designated from the regular army.[5]

A light infantry battalion plus supporting elements, the standby unit has a combined strength of approximately 750 men. Its priority mission is standby duty, to which it might be assigned for as long as three years at a time. Already highly competent and well trained, it receives two to six months of additional orientation in peacekeeping skills. There are of course no special recruiting problems when the regular military establishment is used, and the earmarked unit is of the same quality as any infantry outfit in the armed forces. All men and equipment are transportable by air on short notice. Readiness is tested annually, if possible in a full-scale peacekeeping exercise involving emergency airlift to a distant Canadian location and mock operations designed to sharpen peacekeeping tactics.

The first Canadian unit in Cyprus was a standby battalion, supplemented by an armored reconnaissance squadron.[6] As soon as it left Canada, another was appointed to replace it, and when the time came for twice-yearly rotation, this new standby force remained untouched. Other infantry units have been successively assigned as rotation battalions and given training related to UNFICYP that has even taken them to the Canadian Rockies, where a site has been chosen for its resemblance to the rugged Kyrenia range of northern Cyprus, bailiwick of the Canadians on the island.

This standby system, which Ottawa once considered expanding to two infantry battalions, represents only a fraction of Canada's preparedness capabilities. Although the standby battalion is exposed to the most intense UN training and kept at a higher state of readiness for UN use than any other Canadian unit, Canada's peacekeeping experience plainly shows that its infantrymen are often less in demand than its versatile military specialists in communications, logistics, transport, and the like. Therefore the watchwords for Canadian planners are "diversity" and "flexibility." They anticipate UN needs for technical resources from virtually any support sector in the armed forces, and this enlarged preparedness assumes the gradual evolution of a military establishment suited to a wide variety of peacekeeping requirements.

By the early 1970s Canada will have completed its "military revolution," for which the closest thing to a bible is the White Paper dated March 1964.[7] It is a document that "tells us how the Department of National Defence sees its world,"[8] and like the other Bible it invites interpretation and counterinterpretation by friends and critics alike. At the center of the controversy was the government's decision, announced in the White Paper, to make Canada the first advanced nation to abolish triservice military organization, replacing the separate army, navy, and air force with a unified, one-uniformed Canadian Armed Forces. The case for unification was a complex blend of desires to economize within a defense budget remaining constant; to rationalize a top-heavy, triplicate military administration; and to tailor military resources to Canada's foreign policy and defense position. When the newly elected Liberal government of Lester Pearson surveyed its world, it saw that Canada's military priorities were very likely to need readjustment away from the contingency of central conventional war in Europe and toward growing requirements at the "lower end" of the conflict scale, including peacekeeping. Whether this readjustment was going too far too fast became the primary issue in the ensuing defense policy debate. Moreover, the unification controversy, which led to stormy resignations in high places and opposition by threatened service interests, "raised the question of whether 'peace-keeping' is a role to which the Canadian military organization can or should be tailored."[9]

In 1967, on the defensive against a recurring theme of his critics, Defense Minister Paul Hellyer assured the House of Commons that "the purpose of our defence policy is not and never was to create simply a giant peacekeeping force."[10] Any suggestion to the contrary, he told a magazine editor, "is tommyrot."[11] There is no denying, however, that the White Paper elevated peacekeeping to a position of remarkable prominence in Canadian defense thinking. It was listed among the top priorities of defense policy, though the government was intentionally ambiguous about the precise relation among them.[12] The impression given was one of considerable multitasking in allotment of missions and responsibilities. Thus the White Paper admitted that while preparations for UN peacekeeping "may be of a special nature, the best results can be accomplished through the establishment of regular military formations, which need not be earmarked exclusively for United Nations service and which can be used for other roles as required." Multiple readiness was a logical corollary: "The combined land, sea, and air forces normally stationed in Canada and at Canadian ports will be sufficiently flexible to satisfy almost any conceivable requirement for UN or other operations."[13]

The creation of these flexible military assets was a major purpose of reorganization.[14] The operational workhorse of the system is the 29,000-man Mobile Command, the largest of the new, composite "functional commands" and the one that Hellyer regarded as essential in the design of Canada's new defense policy. Mobile Command "has the responsibility for providing operationally trained and combat-ready land and tactical air forces, capable of rapid deployment in circumstances ranging from service in the European theatre as part of Canada's contribution to NATO, to U.N. and other peacekeeping and peace-restoring operations."[15] In part, this statement is oversell intended to pacify a range of critics concerned about whether Mobile Command can do everything they want it to do, and in one form or another it has been frequently heard in Canada since the White Paper. It is easily misinterpreted. Mobile Command is not mainly a UN peacekeeping standby reservoir, as many non-Canadians seem to think. Nor is it composed of units equally uncommitted, equally flexible, or equally mobile.

Mobile Command incorporates four brigade groups, each roughly 5,000 to 6,000 men, and certain smaller units. Until Canada completes a "planned and phased reduction" of its NATO forces, which is expected to happen by 1972,[16] one of these brigades is in Germany and another serves as its backup in Canada. They are both crack mechanized infantry formations with tanks, armor, artillery, and other heavy hardware unsuitable for peacekeeping. The other two brigades, both stationed in Canada, are light, air-transportable, flexibly equipped for quick modification, and rapidly deployable outside the country; from them two battalions are also earmarked for special NATO duty. Additional, smaller units in Mobile Command are a 1,200-man parachute regiment and a tactical fighter and transport group. The deployment capabilities of the NATO brigades and the general-purpose ones are not alike. One Canadian analyst has warned against literal acceptance of frequent government allusions to the "global mobility" or the "global parish" of Mobile Command:

> Insofar as these comments may suggest that Mobile Command is a flexible force, adaptable to a wide variety of tasks, they are misleading. The [brigades] committed to NATO have *combat* mobility—in the sense that they are able to move on the battlefield under fire—but very little tactical mobility, and very little capability for re-deployment, or multi-tasking.[17]

He also demonstrates that while Canada's strategic mobility will grow in the near future it will remain relatively small, and major technological improvements, such as acquiring the jumbo long-distance C-5A military transport, are likely to be prohibitively costly for Canada.[18]

What this means is that even though the government has had to avoid detailed commitments Canada retains a large UN capability, far outdistancing the single standby battalion but not equivalent to the entirety of Mobile Command. Canada confirmed this unspecific but finite potential in a report to the UN on preparedness in 1968. As a statement of intent, it emphasized (1) that the standby unit and "other elements of the Canadian forces are assigned a number of responsibilities" that preclude large-scale earmarking for single tasks, although peacekeeping is the standby battalion's main job; (2) that all naval and air elements are "liable for possible assignment to peacekeeping tasks, subject to other peacetime commitments"; and (3) that the provision of land forces is limited by the absence of "inherent strategic mobility," by the limited rotation ability in this small standing military establishment, and by the need to take "into account" current UN commitments. The Canadians expose "all headquarters, formations, and units of Canadian regular land forces, at every level of command, to some degree of training in peacekeeping or security operations," although the amounts of specialized training vary. In all, resources are matched flexibly with responsibilities against a "background of uncertain requirements."[19]

Lester Pearson: An Exercise in Preparedness Diplomacy

Canada's preparedness has also shown a multilateral side, through the encouragement of cooperation among principal supplier states. At about the time Nordic decisions were being made in 1963, the Pearson government took office, and in a matter of months ideas for multinational activities began to jell. The result was the first and the only instance of preparedness conference diplomacy at an intergovernmental level, the Ottawa conference of 1964. More than a hundred delegates from twenty-three countries assembled there in November, though this was not the kind of meeting it was supposed to have been.

Earlier, in 1963, not long after U Thant delivered at Harvard his speech welcoming standby programs, Pearson told the General Assembly something of Canada's plans, proposed "an examination by interested governments of the problems and techniques of peacekeeping operations," urged "a pooling of available resources and the development, in a coordinated way, of trained and equipped collective forces" for UN service, and said that Canada "would be proud to initiate steps for this purpose."[20] What he had in mind originally, apparently at the suggestion of Canadian General E. L. M. Burns, was a small and select group of six: the Canadian hosts, the Nordic four, and the Dutch, all of whom were quietly invited early in 1964 to meet in Ottawa that July. Even before plans were leaked, the Finns and to a lesser extent the Swedes expressed reservations about the predominance of NATO members. Word soon got out, the Soviet Union objected, and U Thant reportedly was uneasy over the absence of non-Caucasians.[21]

Pearson would not be put off—yet. In an article in a Canadian popular magazine (a serious piece billed a little irreverently alongside

"What's So Hot About Being a Rich Playboy?"), Pearson urged, as compensation for the UN's inability to centralize preparedness programs, "a number of middle powers, whose credentials and motives are above reproach, to work out a standby arrangement among themselves." They might also "set up their own consultative machinery to watch over developments, as well as a small military staff to coordinate the roles of separate contingents."[22] And in a major foreign policy address, he announced that "we have been considering plans for confidential discussions with certain other governments, primarily of military problems" in peacekeeping. He acknowledged the criticisms but hoped he would not be "misunderstood." "There has been some disposition," he explained, "to interpret my proposal as an intention to turn away from the United Nations. The whole point of it was to strengthen the capability of the members concerned to serve and support the United Nations." He then backtracked, but not very far, by suggesting meetings among the six standbys as merely a "first stage," a preliminary to subsequent "extended" discussions in which eventually "all the continents would be represented."[23]

Pearson's tenacity drove Soviet critics into high gear. Not much is known about their private diplomatic objections—except that they had their effect—or about the reactions of the invitees, but *Izvestia* delivered a rambling, gruff censure of the plans, zeroing in on the NATO "tinge" of the group of six and castigating peacekeeping, present and past, as Western connivance and circumvention of the United Nations Charter.* Shortly before the scheduled summer meetings, Canada redesigned the conference and postponed it until later in the year. To qualify for an invitation, a country needed only to have set up a standby force, planned to do so, or supplied the UN with one hundred peacekeeping personnel—criteria permissive enough to embrace such "politi-

---

* The commentary appeared June 7 and was reprinted in *Survival* (Great Britain), Vol. 6 (September–October 1964), pp. 240–41. For the most part it was a direct reply to Pearson's speech, from which it quoted. It is possible that the Russians also had in mind the *Maclean's* article, and if they suspected the Canadians of engineering a takeover of UN preparedness by NATO members, an exuberant editor of the magazine fueled their worst fears. His captions promised that "on the following pages one of the architects of NATO sets out an equally original initiative—but one to be taken within rather than outside the UN—by which Canada could lead the world."

cally acceptable" conferees as the United Arab Republic, India, and Ghana.24 The agenda was sanitized by removing troublesome items such as the creation of permanent military staffs and coordinative machinery. A Canadian statement of conference objectives was only a faint echo of the original ambitions: the Canadian government "has no preconceived ideas" about conclusions that might emerge; no "prior commitments as regards future developments" would be expected of the participants; the topics discussed would be "practical and technical" and anything with "political implications" would be avoided. Although the proceedings were informal and confidential, a press communiqué listed the countries in attendance and outlined the final agenda—a step everybody hoped would ease any suspicions.25 The Russians were still not satisfied.26 But their objections to the larger conference were not vigorous enough to discourage states from attending.

Anyone looking back over this episode can hardly avoid noticing how inauspicious the year 1964 was for Pearson's proposals. There is strong reason to believe that the Soviet Union was not merely using the occasion of an inoffensive conference to vent its characteristic mistrust of peacekeeping institutions. The main event, it seems, was not in Ottawa, but in New York, where the Article 19 crisis was about to come from a simmer to a full boil. Its immediate cause was Moscow's nonpayment of peacekeeping dues, for which it became legally delinquent on January 1, 1964. Similarly in arrears were ten other states, and France was to join them at the beginning of the next calendar year. All were sufficiently behind in their dues to be threatened by the application of Article 19's penalty—loss of vote in the General Assembly. Whether, how, and when to impose this sanction were the immediate issues at stake in the crisis. Moscow and Paris, arguing different paths to similar conclusions, insisted that Article 19 was completely irrelevant to these peacekeeping costs. To Washington, each of these issues had an answer that was, at least initially, clear and straightforward: Article 19 must be imposed, it must be imposed automatically, and this must happen on the very first day of the Assembly session opening in autumn 1964. On each point in this triad, Washington eventually found itself with no responsible option except to back away from its original hard line. The Russians had skillfully brandished a threat to withdraw from the UN and thereby wreck it in response to any disenfranchisement. A majority of the Assembly were unwilling to risk a showdown—as was the United States before too long—that would prove whether Moscow was bluffing or not. Washington's case gradually lost its credibility, momentum, and political support as opinion in the organization placed ever-higher premiums on compromise over confrontation. In August 1965, the United States recognized the inevitable by reserving its legal position on the issue but indicating that it was prepared to drop the entire question of enforcing Article 19 against nonpayers.

It was understood throughout that money was not the crux of the dispute. More fundamentally, it was a test of Soviet versus American concepts of UN peacekeeping. Contrary to the logical implication of Washington's case, the whole affair demonstrated that no state, surely no great power, could be compelled to support financially any peacekeeping operation of which it disapproved politically. Washington, in any event, was hardly willing to sanctify such an implication, in case it might find itself one day on the receiving end of a politically unpalatable assessment by the Assembly. (Indeed, when the United States announced that it would no longer press for application of Article 19, it reserved its right to refuse payment for future UN activities which it did not support.) But neither was the United States prepared to endorse the proposition, which the USSR was then putting forward even more vigorously than usual, that all aspects of peacekeeping, including financing, be brought under the exclusive authority of the Security Council.

Because these and other bedrock issues were involved, the Article 19 crisis touched everything to do with peacekeeping, including Canada's attempt to multilateralize preparedness in a way that insulated it from direct Soviet control through the Security Council. This may have been the strongest yet least traceable influence on the Russians—all the more so because Pearson's initiatives were assumed to have had the backing, even the encouragement, of Washington and London.[27] Canada's timing unwittingly stimulated Soviet skepticism, as did Pearson's practice of vaguely linking his plan with the financial impasse in New York, hinting that if Soviet stubbornness was going to grind things to a halt inside the UN all the peacekeepers ought to band together outside it. Or so it appeared to Moscow. Reinforcing this attitude was the energetic attempt in early 1964 by the United States and Britain to install a NATO peacekeeping force on Cyprus. A meeting under Canadian sponsorship convened a few months later, with four out of the six in attendance holding NATO membership, could only seem to the Russians like anticipation of a next NATO peacekeeping venture.

After this event Canada's approach to multinational programs shifted. The Ottawa conference was not considered a failure; exchanges of information and opinions took place, personal contacts were established, and many of the delegates came away better informed. But there were too many of them, too little time, too wide a variation in expertise and educability, too little possibility for follow-up efforts, too many political complications, and too much reciting of a litany of familiar problems. Although three years afterward Canada remained officially "ready to carry further this process of informal consultation outside the strict framework of the UN whenever circumstances appear to warrant it,"[28] the government was lukewarm and convinced that "circumstances" were inappropriate. Canada has since concentrated on another technical role—articulator and dispenser of doctrine. This is not new. At the Ottawa conference, discussion of main problems was aided by Canadian-authored papers analyzing Canadian experience and offering suggested improvements. In recent years, when the UN has been unable because of diplomatic sensitivities to draft or circulate technical documents, such as provisional standing operating procedures and national training data, Canada has informally done so in New York.[29] Ottawa has shown a similar willingness to supply technical information on a bilateral basis if requested. In the early sixties Canada gave some thought to unit-level peacekeeping training with other interested nations, but little is heard of this idea now. Even modest cooperative training of officers is viewed warily, though Canadian students have attended the Nordic courses recently. The Canadians provide their UN officers with a general orientation course, and proposals to invite other supplier countries have been rejected by the government.

In its preparedness and peacekeeping careers Canada's middlepowermanship has been singularly durable. If one were to draw up a theoretical balance sheet showing Canada's pluses and minuses for these roles, both columns would be filled, unlike a similar tally, say, for Ireland or Sweden, whose credentials seem somehow more natural, more obvious. Of course, Canada shares important minuses with other principal peacekeepers—white skin and a Western liberal democratic outlook being perhaps the most manifest badges of exclusivity. (But it is noteworthy that Canada and other principal peacekeepers have demonstrated that white skin and a Western liberal democratic outlook do not constitute—as many commentators expected they would—inherent impediments to peacekeeping eligibility or effectiveness.) More to the point is that Canada's association with NATO is more intimate in some ways than Denmark's or Norway's, even though all three have a special reputation for flexibility and eagerness to stress the alliance's diplomatic leverage for détente more than its military potential for deterrence. And Canada alone among major peacekeeping suppliers has nuclear responsibilities, both in NATO and NORAD (North American Air Defense Command), Norway and Denmark having refused to accept nuclear weapons in their territories. On the plus side, Canada's world image is unencumbered by the colonial traditions of some of its alliance partners, whose presence in the Third World in a UN peacekeeping capacity is unwelcome. Moreover, Canada has no worldwide economic or political interests of a kind that might disqualify it as an impartial third party. These complicated detachments and loyalties were embodied fully in the personal history of Lester Pearson, a prime mover in NATO and at the same time a proponent of UN peacekeeping capabilities and of the Commonwealth. He often said he envisaged Canada as a middle power—in all three.

Canada's associations have given its peacekeeping face a Janus-like quality. When the ICC was set up, Ottawa was chosen as one-third of the troika to "represent" the West, to balance politically the Indians and the Poles. Under UN auspices Canada neither expects nor is expected to act in this implicitly partisan guise, but Western members, particularly the United States, have occasionally shown a tendency to view Canada's involvement as safe, protective, and reliable; as a very indirect form of quasi representation.

Canada, finally, is an enormous medium-sized country—a Nordic military officer once said that to his country Canada seems a great power—and this bigness produces the necessary goods and expertise for peacekeeping. But even here, resources have been strained and allocations stretched.[30] Thus far, material constraints have had more to do with shaping Canada's peacekeeping policy than serious doubts about its wisdom, though these have cropped up in official and private circles.[31] It appears that, barring erosion of Canada's relative security, the reorganized military establishment should continue to be a potential source for peacekeeping talent on a major scale.

The Netherlands

The Dutch were one of the first half-dozen UN members to make standby offers in 1963–64, but they, unlike the others, had chalked up almost no peacekeeping experience. Instead of counting their UN veterans in thousands or tens of thousands, they could list fewer than 200, most of them former observers, the rest specialists or medics with brief Congo tours. Nevertheless The Hague gradually upped its original standby totals—even after having been passed over as a possible UNFICYP candidate because of Archbishop Makarios's automatic resistance to the participation of former colonial powers. The Dutch program has become a hybrid of the Nordic and Canadian programs. Three separate offers have been forwarded to the United Nations over a period of five years, eventually resulting in a flexibly organized interservice commitment that can include as many as 1,500 to 2,000 men.

Recruits for Dutch UN contingents come from a fairly large military establishment—over 100,000—which is sophisticated and highly skilled. Since the early 1920s the armed forces have been an amalgam of a small proportion of professionals and a large block of eighteen-month conscripts whose obligation after basic service extends to between the ages of thirty-five and forty-five, depending on rank. The ratio of conscripts to volunteers is highest in the army, where draftees may make up as much as 80 percent of all manpower. Technical arms of the services attract the most career soldiers.[32] Holland's military organization differs from Canada's all-volunteer service and from the Scandinavian pattern of small standing cadre armies. The Dutch standby unit resembles Canada's, however, in that only active service personnel are used. There is no volunteering from civilian life, and as far as possible the Dutch will try to supply the UN with units that already exist for other purposes.[33]

When the Dutch foreign minister announced to the Assembly in 1963 the earmarking of marines from the Royal Navy, a long history preceded the announcement.[34] From this same marine corps, League peacekeepers were chosen for the abortive Vilna operation, and later the then-neutral Dutch served in the Saar force. After the Second World War the marines assumed some of the responsibilities of the former colonial garrison army that was dismantled when Indonesia became independent. They brought a strong, old tradition of overseas duty, reminiscent of the Dutch imperial navy's global spread. Even the modern Netherlands constitution, in Article 191, singles out the navy as the service whose "conscripts shall be intended for service in and out of Europe." The decline of imperialism that whittled away the navy's colonial outposts was almost complete in the early sixties when the Dutch evacuated West New Guinea in the Pacific. Marine contingents returned home and in 1963 found themselves without a mission, faced with the possibility of deactivation unless another role, perhaps for the UN, could be found. There was irony in all this: departure from West New Guinea was accomplished with the assistance of a UN peacekeeping force, the United Nations Security Force (UNSF), and this same process made the withdrawing marines available for UN standby. The Dutch did not earmark a unit merely because there was an uncommitted unit available, without a job or a future. Rather, the Foreign Ministry was definitely interested at the time in asserting a new and constructive external identity beyond either its colonial or its NATO role. This was a convenient congruence of foreign policy leanings and ready availability of military personnel, though the Dutch might not have gone ahead just then with this UN initiative had not the marine command shown considerable enthusiasm for the idea.[35]

The initial offer of marines was not very specific about upper limits. A first contingent of about 300 was to be kept ready for action on twenty-four-hour notice, while unspecified additional units could be available within a few days. The foreign minister did not say so in the Assembly, but the Dutch privately indicated later that the marine unit used in the first instance might be dispatched either from Holland or, if geography and logistics necessitated, from a Caribbean-based marine post in the Netherlands Antilles.

There was less ambiguity at the second stage of the Dutch commitment, in the autumn of 1965, when the government again used the Assembly as the forum for an announcement. Standby programs had undergone a greater measure of internal scrutiny, detailed planning, and discussion of political, constitutional, and military ramifications. To Dutch planners, this second stage was far more significant than the almost perfunctory one two years before. Now all three services earmarked support and technical units, the army joined the navy in providing up to 900 troops, and the marine contingent was increased to a firm 600.

The officially stated rationale for this second initiative was sensible but unrevealing. After recalling the earlier offer, the foreign minister explained: "Experience since then has demonstrated that the United Nations will in the future need more elaborate and more diversified military contributions from its Members if it is effectively to exercise its peacekeeping task."[36] The important developments that had in fact joined to bring about this new situation were three. First, the UN secretariat conveyed serious doubts that Royal Marines so closely associated with Dutch colonial pursuits would be politically acceptable as peacekeepers in most conflicts. The secretary-general's military adviser, besides personally communicating this skepticism to government leaders at The Hague, opened up a range of alternatives for the Dutch by emphasizing that their most useful contribution would probably be support facilities from their technologically advanced resources, instead of marines, however well-trained and ready. Second, the Cyprus crisis drove this point home. By all standards of logic and operational imperative, during those critical weeks of March 1964 when mounting the operation was hampered by lack of national readiness, the available, able, and eager Dutch marines would have been given the nod if they had had the proper political credentials. The third factor was internal to the Dutch military establishment. The army and air force, as well as nonmarine elements of the navy, wanted a share in the action. This—call it constructive interservice rivalry—had become apparent by the time the Foreign Ministry in early 1965 formally requested the Defense

Ministry to consider an all-service supplement to the 1963 offer. Some senior military officers and some politicians were afraid that UN commitments might downgrade Dutch NATO readiness, but the decisive inclinations were overwhelmingly positive, especially at middle levels of the military, from the defense minister (later prime minister), and in the Foreign Ministry.

During the months leading up to the offer of a triservice package, legal and constitutional arguments were raised by a prominent academician, among others, who assailed the proposed extension as unconstitutional in employing conscripts for prohibited purposes. According to the constitution, Article 188, the armed forces, "composed of volunteers and conscripts," shall be raised "for the protection of the interests of the State." But there was no general support for the proposition that UN peacekeeping operations were not in Holland's interest—this being of course the same issue that has had to be addressed in Scandinavia. In the States-General (parliament) it was not seriously questioned, though the government was braced with counterarguments drafted by the Foreign Ministry and resting on amendments to military service legislation enacted by the States-General shortly after World War II. This legislation had provided, partly anticipating requirements for Article 43 forces, that Dutch conscripts could be used for international peace and security operations. This is now the prevailing constitutional opinion, and apparently it was firmly accepted by the time the government arrived at the third standby stage in May 1968 when thirty members of the Royal Marechaussee, the military police corps, were earmarked for duty on the condition that Dutch military units also be attached to a UN mission.[37]

Concern for its NATO obligations and about the political implications of the conscript issue have been evident, even if not controlling, in the management of the standby force. Like the Canadians, the Dutch expect it to be understood that the press of other obligations, alliance and national, may in some circumstances shrink resources available for the UN. Yet neither Canada nor any other standby who is also a NATO member has quite so emphatically covered itself as the Dutch Joint Chiefs of Staff did in a press conference at the time of the 1965 offer. Standby units in Holland are dually earmarked for United Nations peacekeeping and for NATO—except for the marines, who have never had NATO responsibilities—and the Joint Chiefs assured any doubters that these units would not be sent into UN service without first considering NATO obligations. Assignment to the UN of dually earmarked forces would, the Chiefs added, be a matter for consultation with the NATO supreme commander. How or when this would take place was not elaborated, and probably would depend on circumstances. The method of organizing the army standby units recognizes the touchiness of ordering conscripts abroad against their will. The government does not say it will not do this, but only that it will try not to: "As far as the Army contingents are concerned it is the aim to enlist as conscripts mainly those who prefer to serve in units earmarked for UN peace-keeping tasks."[38] This applies only to army units. Marines, it has been noted, all expect to have to serve abroad. Too, their standby units have fewer conscripts than the army's.[39]

Lack of substantial peacekeeping experience has had its effect. In designing standby arrangements, the Dutch have had at their disposal little of the information that is at the fingertips of a more experienced supplier. Files on national participation or the personal experience of veterans can often tell a Canadian or a Swedish planner what he wants to know. Not so for the Dutch, and in the future countries starting to earmark will surely encounter the same liability—all aggravated by the absence of a centralized information flow from UN headquarters. The Dutch information gap, especially at first, related to mundane items like pay practices and methods for sharing costs with the UN. In training and staff matters the Dutch have felt a little more comfortable with what they could do on their own. The assumptions, which remain to be tested in a UN mission, are that their officers are already practiced in working with a multinational system, that their technical units are normally at an adequate readiness level, and that their usual training curriculum is sufficiently relevant to peacekeeping tasks. This last is said to be true for the army infantry contingent. Its national and NATO training is thought to include sufficient riot control and paramilitary exercises to make any special UN work unnecessary. The marines, however, even though skilled in internal security jobs, conduct much more extensive, specifically UN programs for units and individual officers.[40]

Some officer orientations cross service lines, such as the periodic briefings given to all standby officers by the Foreign and the Defense ministries' representatives.

The Dutch have had selective and minimal external contacts on preparedness matters, relying mostly on Canada as a direct bilateral source of information. They went to the Ottawa conference, and Dutch nationals have attended private international meetings in Scandinavia. Tentative consideration (never more than that) was given to the possibility of arranging participation for Dutch officers in the Nordic training courses, as much for the exposure and interchange as for the benefit to individual students.

Austria

In mid-December 1960, fifty Austrian men and one woman, all volunteer members of a hastily assembled medical team for ONUC, arrived in the Congolese town of Bukavu, the capital of Kivu province, and set about establishing a UN hospital. Before they had been there twenty-four hours they were besieged by the local gendarmerie, promptly incarcerated, and rescued only after Nigerian peacekeeping troops fought a pitched battle in order to reach them. Though none of the Austrians were seriously hurt, many of their personal effects and nearly all of their equipment were lost. (Thinking a water-filtering apparatus an exotic weapon, the thorough Congolese efficiently "disarmed" it by dumping it into Kivu Lake.)

This incident, surely a lesser one in ONUC annals, might very well have reversed what in 1960 was only the initial, cautious show of active Austrian support for UN peacekeeping. The furor in Vienna over the indignities suffered by the volunteers was not strong enough to force withdrawal of the unit from ONUC, but it must have been a difficult time for those Austrian officials who, months before, had urged this participation in spite of some misgivings about the whole idea—misgivings that had less to do with the well-being of Austrian nationals than with the integrity of a corporate Austrian identity: permanent neutrality. It had been thought possible that the government, by becoming involved in unpredictable and controversial situations like the Congo disorders, might be jeopardizing its international legal status and its consistently neutral foreign policy. After all, only five years had elapsed since Allied occupation troops had withdrawn from Austria, enabling it to regain full but precarious sovereignty. Popular and governmental sentiment was sufficiently solid behind peacekeeping to keep the medical team in the Congo, and the first half of the sixties saw Austria's step-by-step movement toward fuller readiness to take part in future operations.

Immediately after independence in 1955, Austria, on the basis of an understanding reached earlier with the Russians, declared itself perpetually neutral and anchored this status in a formal constitutional law.[41] Within these confines Austria has become the fourth European neutral to prepare for military responsibilities in UN peacekeeping. Even though in origin, form, and substance Austria's neutrality differs from Sweden's, Finland's, or Ireland's, each country in its own way has demonstrated the compatibility between neutrality and peacekeeping. Particularly in Austria, as in Finland, special attention has had to be paid to the possible effect of peacekeeping on relations with the Soviet Union. The preparedness programs in these states also have been closely watched by another permanent neutral, Switzerland, which, though not a UN member, has been scrutinizing its own possible future as a peacekeeper.

Austrian peacekeeping preparedness is but one extension of the foreign policy image of "active neutrality" that the country has energetically cultivated ever since becoming a UN member in late 1955.[42] Acceptance of its application had been promised by the Big Four in the Security Council, and Austria interpreted the circumstances of its membership to mean that the Council, having acknowledged this permanent neutrality, would not subsequently prescribe violation of it by ordering Austria to take part in any Chapter VII enforcement action. However, the presumption has been that peacekeeping is not a threat to neutrality but rather a vehicle for expressing it. Activism motivates Austria to seek out intermediary roles, in traditional diplomatic mediation, in conciliation, and of late, in peacekeeping. A former foreign minister put it very plainly: "Austria joined the UN and thus affirmed her intention to take part in the solution of the political problems of our time—whether they be her immediate concern or not."[43]

Austria's interest in peacekeeping grew rapidly. Although its General Assembly delegation abstained on the UNEF enabling resolution and took no part in the operation, Austria by 1958 expressed a willingness to participate in peacekeeping forces, while qualifying this inclination by saying Austrian law did not permit such a step.[44] The movement toward Austrian standby preparedness over the next decade involved first bypassing the legal obstacles to Austrian nationals' participation in peacekeeping, then eliminating them entirely, and finally devising, under the new legal situation, a politically acceptable formula for raising UN manpower in Austria.

Legal and treaty arrangements of the 1955 settlement were not directly at issue, except to the extent that peacekeeping policy had to be consistent with permanent neutrality. What mattered was the constitution in force at the time, which was a slightly modified version of one drafted and amended in the decade following the end of the First World War. The legal theory inherent in this constitution, together with the specific provisions covering military activities, restricted the use of the armed forces to maintenance of internal order and frontier defense. This was the legal situation when Austria received a request to participate in ONUC. Instead of flatly refusing, the government issued a complicated legal interpretation permitting participation by Austrian nationals as contracting private individuals rather than as police, or gendarmerie, or as representatives of Austrian sovereignty. Several purposes were served. The government, as the contract partner, could and did restrict involvement to noncombatants, the acceptability of Austrian participation could be tested without yet taking the drastic step of constitutional amendment, and Austria could begin constructing another limited outlet for active neutrality.

Because the dispatch of the medical team was experimental, the Bukavu incident acquired exaggerated importance. As the months passed, the effects wore off, Austrian peacekeeping participation came to be taken for granted, and even before the Cyprus crisis, plans for constitutional revision had been formulated within the government.

The Austrian inability, legally, to contribute military units to UNFICYP even evoked some mildly invidious internal comparisons between the limited Austrian UNFICYP commitment of medics and police and the full military formations provided by the Swedes, the Finns, and the Irish.

Cyprus merely injected a sense of purpose into the already favorable outlook for constitutional reform. It was completed a little over a year later in the summer of 1965. By revising the constitution and adopting a special military service law for the army (the only branch of service, though with an air arm), the parliament made it possible to respond to a request from "an international organization" for "a unit" or "a number of units" composed of volunteers from the regular army or the police, or of citizens who have finished normal military service. Any such response must be "in strict conformity" with permanent neutrality and preceded by consultation with the appropriate parliamentary committee.[45] To facilitate readiness the government followed the lead of countries that had recently established UN forces. Austria's standby system, however, is quite different.

In the final months of 1965, now on firm legal ground, the Ministry of Defense took the first step, issuing a call for UN recruits. At this stage the ministry was not putting together a standby group; it was drawing up a list of men who were only volunteering to volunteer should need arise. To get on the list, applicants filled out a form indicating how long they would like to remain on it (six months, one, two, or three years) and to what parts of the world they were willing to go (anywhere, or one or more of five continents)—all this conforming to regulations governing "exceptional" foreign military service. Droves of these "advance enlistees" came forward, almost 1,800 during the first several months, leveling off at about 2,000 by mid-1966 and 2,300 a year later.[46] To make such an application does not entail personal commitment and uncertainty comparable to, say, Nordic standby status. Thus Austrian enlistees do not get paid any bonus at this stage, and they undertake no significant obligation until a second call, for actual volunteers, is made, which technically and "in the legal sense" can happen only after the government has "responded positively to a request for assistance."[47] The popularity of this program, at least initially, can be gauged not only by the absolute numbers but also by the source of enlistees: about 80 percent were either professional, serving soldiers or active-service conscripts from the 50,000-man army.

In 1965, this two-phase system was, it seems, the least common denominator acceptable to political parties and others wanting to give Austrian citizens ironclad assurances that UN service would be totally voluntary. Even a direct contract system modeled on Nordic practice was rejected, and assignment of regular active service units was out of the question. However, to speed up UN mobilization as much as possible, Austrian planners have tentatively begun setting up a 628-man standby battalion, which can be called up and dispatched in two to four weeks. Manpower is drawn from the pool of enlistees, presumably those who have volunteered to volunteer for service anywhere. Active soldiers make up two-thirds of this battalion, and reserves the other third. All of them must legally revolunteer for the specific mission in question, even though they are in the standby battalion. But on the assumption that most will do so, which is pretty certain since Austrian UN allowances are extraordinarily attractive as compared with military pay and because the prospect of out-of-country travel and experience is similarly appealing, the Defense Ministry has conducted about twice a year brief administrative orientation sessions of less than five days for the entire battalion. For officers and specialized personnel longer substantive training has been arranged, and by 1968 several Austrian students had attended the Nordic courses.

Like the Dutch, the Austrians have been faced with an information shortage resulting from lack of army peacekeeping experience beyond the medical personnel and a handful of officers on observer duty at the Suez Canal after 1967.[48] Austrian military officials have had to go to some lengths to learn what they could about standby programs elsewhere and about the financial practices of the UN. Once in recent years Austrian officials explored the prospects for giving their battalion a taste of service in Cyprus by substituting it for another UNFICYP contingent, but a suitable opportunity did not present itself. When the United Nations India-Pakistan Observation Mission (UNIPOM) was being hastily put together in late 1965, Austria was requested to provide ten officers; however, by the time political and procedural clearances were completed, the mission had been adequately staffed and the Austrians were told, much to their annoyance, that they no longer would be needed.

When asked to supply men for UNFICYP, Vienna police headquarters reacted almost as if nothing out of the ordinary had been requested. There were none of the initial reservations that marked, say, the Danish police reaction, none of the worries that perhaps this was the wrong kind of work for Austrian policemen, from whose ranks the UN secretariat's field service had long recruited men for protective and custodial duty around the world. Enthusiastically the Austrians had sent, by 1968, nearly 120 individual policemen to the United Nations Civilian Police (UNCIVPOL), each serving on the average about fifteen months. Future provision of policemen, national needs permitting, is said to be possible in numbers no larger than the 45-man contingent in UNCIVPOL.[49]

Standby Promises: Iran, New Zealand, and Italy

All three of these countries announced standby plans during 1964. Iran and New Zealand said they would set aside military units, but neither has implemented its programs. Italy's offer of individual officers has produced a small roster of men for staff or observer duty.

Iran acted first, during an official visit by the Shah to the United States in June. He endorsed the standby offers already forwarded to the UN, promised U Thant his country's "full cooperation," and said that Iran was prepared to assign a contingent for peacekeeping and to provide money and instructors to train peacekeepers from other countries.[50] There was a brief series of follow-up steps. An aide-mémoire detailing units and personnel that might be most valuable to the UN was delivered later that month to the secretary-general, and contact was quietly established with Canadian military officials, who in July prepared a special briefing on their own efforts for the Iranian mission at the UN. In November Iranian representatives, now eligible by virtue of their recent offer, attended the Ottawa conference. Little seems to have been accomplished since then. Before 1964 Iran's peacekeeping experience was confined to a short tour by some forty-five soldiers in ONUC during mid-1963. As a Moslem state, Iran was automatically disqualified for UNFICYP service and is similarly unsuitable for other Middle East peacekeeping chores. Iran's marginal cultural and political ties to peacekeeping states of northern Europe and to Canada give it a sense of being "odd man out" among the standbys, an isolation that may account in part for the rapidly dissipated interest.

If Iranian officials could assume that the relative sophistication and size of their military establishment—a triservice organization of a quarter of a million men—would permit them to take part in future UN operations without extensive advance arrangements, the same could not be said by New Zealand, whose entire armed forces number about 13,000, fewer than half being army personnel.

New Zealand's prime minister, Keith J. Holyoake, announced in October 1964 that U Thant had been informed of the government's intention "in principle to designate a unit for participation" in future peacekeeping missions. It "might be drawn either from the armed services or the civilian police." "No firm decisions as to the exact nature or size of the unit" had yet been made, he explained, "but these questions are under active consideration, and a range of possibilities is being examined." Hinting at one of the explanations for the timing of this move, the prime minister said that it entitled the government to participate in the Ottawa meetings that were to begin in a few days, an opportunity that "will be extremely valuable at the present stage in our planning for the establishment of a standby unit."[51] Results of this planning were never disclosed, and New Zealand's earmarking offer has not been fulfilled.

In 1964 the apparent momentum building up behind preparedness seems to have pushed New Zealand into a quick decision. Only six months earlier the government had disqualified itself as a possible contributor of military units to UNFICYP because other national security considerations, principally those connected with the Malaysia-Indonesia confrontation, were priorities that might tax its small military resources. Yet in the offer in October, by which time the regional situation had not improved, the prime minister could say that the standby commitment "could be implemented in a meaningful way without detracting from

New Zealand's capacity to meet its other defense needs." In the interim UN preparedness diplomacy had appeared to be taking hold. Lester Pearson's proposals came in May, and the Scandinavian legislatures were moving ahead. Sir Leslie Munro, former president of the General Assembly and one of the first supporters of Pearson's 1957 initiatives, used his June debut in the New Zealand parliament to urge establishment of a national standby force. The following month the Commonwealth prime ministers pronounced their collective determination to strengthen UN preparedness. Too, the Cyprus mission had been successful on the whole, and New Zealand civilian policemen, the only New Zealanders to see UN service except for small detachments of observers in UNMOGIP and UNTSO, were participants.[52] These pressures lost their force partly as a result of the malaise surrounding the Article 19 crisis and partly because other military obligations eventually demanded attention, mainly Vietnam and regional defense cooperation to compensate for British retrenchment east of Suez.

The third country in this category, Italy, has told the secretary-general that twenty-two officers will be maintained on standby at home. Eight will be ready to take up staff or observer duties on forty-eight-hour notice, and fourteen or more on twelve-day notice. In addition to writing off all charges for UN use of a storage depot at Pisa since the late 1950s, the Italian government provided ONUC with large components of air staff and ground support technicians and supplied five observer missions with officers.

Nonstandbys: Ireland, India, Brazil, and Yugoslavia

Somewhat arbitrarily, these four are singled out for illustrative convenience. They have in common a history of unit-level military participation in at least two of the UN's three big peacekeeping operations. None has earmarked national forces, all give somewhat different reasons for not doing so, all have set up regular training and orientation procedures anticipating periodic rotations, all were engaged in active UN service as recently as 1967, and all have had to deal with many of the internal organizational problems that in the future will face other nonstandby suppliers. In short, all demonstrate the inadequacy of a conception of national preparedness that takes account only of standby states. Actual participation in itself breeds some degree of preparedness, and though this usually disappears when participation ends and therefore is decidedly inferior to active standby programs, it nevertheless can be valuable in a crisis. If, for instance, Brazil had gone ahead with an original intent to go to Cyprus in 1964, the army could fairly rapidly have put together a unit by using methods then available for supplying UNEF with rotation battalions. Similarly, the Irish military, when word came that they would be represented in UNFICYP, converted internal procedures previously used for ONUC contributions. Even after all active participation ends, as it did for Brazil, India, and Yugoslavia after the collapse of UNEF, a residue of experience and a feel or sensitivity for peacekeeping remain, which probably can be of use if not too many years elapse. Obviously, an especially busy UN peacekeeping period, as in the early sixties, creates a larger group of possible suppliers in this nonstandby category.

IRELAND

There are two especially pertinent commentaries on Irish preparedness: one underscores its limits, the other its intensity. The first is a conversation some years ago between an Irish diplomat and a foreign guest, which touched on Ireland's exemplary peacekeeping career since the first Irishmen went to Lebanon in 1958. After a quick volley of queries on Irish policy was fired at him, the diplomat is said to have interrupted his visitor, cautioned him against equating Irish resources with those of most other peacekeeping states, and counseled that perhaps the best approach when dealing with Irish preparedness was to "think small." A second, less anecdotal incident took place in 1964 during a Dail Eireann (lower house of parliament) debate on a government motion to send a unit to Cyprus. The leader of the opposition Labour party, in the course of a lengthy speech supporting the motion, called to Foreign Minister Frank Aiken's attention the fact that "many Deputies have been plagued, unofficially, of course, by various members of the Army who want to be allowed to go to Cyprus." The speaker proceeded to praise this unprofessional behavior as "a very good spirit."[53]

Presumably without backhanded assistance from legislators, Irish soldiers have seen a great deal of UN duty. In addition to providing over 100 observers to five missions, the Irish by 1967 had supplied ONUC manning tables with 5,300 men and UNFICYP ones with nearly 5,000.[54] These are weighty figures for an army establishment generally several thousand men below its authorized strength of 12,000. Ireland has made enormous contributions even in absolute terms, ranking seventh, for example, in ONUC manpower. In 1964, counting a large early unit in Cyprus topped only by those of Britain and Canada, fully one-sixth of Ireland's standing, all-volunteer army was on peace-keeping duty.

Until the recent changes in Danish law, Ireland was the only supplier to alter its internal law in such a way that all armed service personnel are liable for UN peacekeeping tours whether they want to go abroad or not. This is not the practice but the law, available if needed but never yet used. For largely political reasons much like those in other supplier countries, Ireland asks its regular soldiers to volunteer specifically for each UN unit. Under the terms of this special legislation, passed in December 1960, any Irish citizen joining the armed services is automatically, as Prime Minister Sean F. Lemass then said, "volunteering for service outside Ireland with a United Nations force, if the occasion should arise." He and the army predicted—and hindsight has proved them correct—that this knowledge would have no "other effect than to popularize Army Service and to help their present recruiting campaign."[55] The new legislation effectively overturned a fifteen-year-old law obligating Irish soldiers only to serve inside Ireland. But in not actually using the 1960 legislative authority the government has accepted the advice heard often in the legislature that it "ought as far as possible to adhere to the volunteer idea, even if it has the power" to do otherwise. Thus, a few years later, the government carefully explained that the emergency units being mobilized for Cyprus would "of course" be recruited from volunteers.[56]

There is no practical need, the government explains, to force soldiers abroad. Surpluses of volunteers are always high. The lead-off battalion for UNFICYP was selected from among three to four times the required personnel. United Nations duty customarily gives long-term

Irish regulars experience not otherwise available, younger ones get some excitement and travel, and all get relatively generous extra pay, though their emoluments fall far below those of other European UN soldiers. Also, military officials say that the volunteer system gives all willing soldiers a chance at UN service, whereas for various internal reasons many existing national units might not get the opportunity. To spread the recruitment base, the army fills rotation battalions with roughly proportionate numbers of volunteers from Ireland's three territorial commands and one training command. About four months before departure, subunits at each command begin getting ready, and these component parts combine two months later for battalion-level training and orientation. The entire routine is informal and by now quite second nature to the military administrators, who have also developed a three-week training course for officers going on observer duty.

In view of the reluctance to order units abroad unless absolutely necessary, some suggestions have been advanced for a standby arrangement to assure Ireland a rapid-response capability.[57] Though seemingly natural and suitable, this step has been avoided by Dublin, largely in line with the preferences of strong-willed former Foreign Minister Aiken, whose opinions on the matter had been closely tied to the stalled peacekeeping diplomacy at the UN. The nub of Ireland's argument seems to be that a formal standby offer would be tantamount to de facto approval, a blessing of sorts, for what the government considers a totally unsatisfactory diplomatic impasse over the constitutional and financial aspects of peacekeeping. Furthermore, Ireland insists that national support programs ought to be consequent, perhaps even conditional, on progress toward more efficient military planning and staffing at UN headquarters. Concern remains about whether placing units on standby would somehow lessen the government's freedom to evaluate each UN troop request on its merits. This notion, that it would be harder to say no once standby forces are set up, is part of the thinking of other nonstandby suppliers as well. A final recurring theme among Irish officials is that there simply is no real need to earmark. The armed services are small and not otherwise committed, men have shown themselves ready to volunteer for the UN, and as Aiken once said, "Standby profirams can be expensive propositions."[58] With somewhat less conviction, the Irish say that by not earmarking, the Defense Ministry can organize UN units more flexibly, that it would be diplomatically unwise to rub shoulders regularly with NATO members who are standbys, that earmarking proposals would unnecessarily invite partisan parliamentary opposition—though none appears as instrumental as discontent with preparedness diplomacy. The looseness of understandings, such as they are, for authorizing and financing peacekeeping operations and the failure of so many states to "do their part" have cooled the Irish toward taking any national initiatives, even though Ireland was in 1956, just after becoming a UN member, one of the first countries to endorse enthusiastically the concept of peacekeeping standby arrangements.

Peacekeeping financing is Ireland's favorite target. Actively, some say stubbornly, the government has prodded UN members to accept financing formulas that it has sponsored, but to no avail. During the first year of the Cyprus operation, Ireland's criticism of unequitable and unenforceable cost-sharing found an outlet in taking a stand that was concrete, demonstrative, principled, and self-sacrificing, though with the passage of time it turned out to be self-deception. The government's tactic was to refuse UN reimbursements owed to Ireland for the costs of overseas troop allowances and per diems—expenses ordinarily paid back by the organization. What was unacceptable was the source of these reimbursements, the UNFICYP budget, which consisted at that time of voluntary payments principally from the United States, the United Kingdom, West Germany, and a small complement of other, mostly Western supporters. Foreign Minister Aiken informed the legislature that Ireland regarded this voluntarism as "a grave and unwise departure from the principle of collective responsibility" and that the government would take none of the money it deserved unless the force's budget was "levied on all members of the United Nations in the normal way."[59] He meant normal assessment, the method that precipitated the looming Article 19 crisis and that was eventually set aside by the UN to avoid facing down the Russians and the French. The Irish also thought their stance would avoid the possibility of political pressures from the major contributors and would avoid stigmatizing Irish soldiers as just so many mercenaries at their hire. This was Aiken's own decision, made with minimum consultation inside the government, and it ran into fairly strong objections in the legislature from deputies who thought the taxpayers would suffer unnecessarily and who felt that Ireland was already doing enough. The policy, however, stuck until June 1965, by which time the Finance Ministry and some legislators had complained more and more vigorously that Ireland just could not afford the luxury of this principle. When the government finally abandoned its position, it had cost nearly $2,000,000.

INDIA

India leads all suppliers in gross manpower provided for peacekeeping—in the neighborhood of 45,000 soldiers, roughly two-thirds of them in ONUC and one-third in UNEF.[60] All have been professionals on active duty with India's all-volunteer army of nearly one million men, and most UN units have been regular national formations detailed in toto to peacekeeping theaters. In major respects, then, the system is like Canada's in execution. India has for many years, however, consistently opposed attempts, such as the Uniting for Peace Resolution, to institutionalize UN military forces other than under Chapter VII of the Charter. Apparently the government views establishment of standby forces by other countries as in "broad conformity" with its own preference for ad hoc international forces, though India can display this tolerance "without accepting any obligation to contribute forces towards this experiment."[61]

The most recent Indian unit to do a UN tour was the last one in UNEF. That this particular Sikh infantry battalion should have drawn a Middle East peacekeeping assignment was, incidentally, a nice historical twist: generations before, during the First World War, a parent battalion to this very unit had been stationed in Gaza and billeted not far from the UNEF camp site; and not two years before, in 1965, this same battalion had received a special citation for excellence during the India-Pakistan war, which was terminated partly by the intervention of UN peacekeepers.

The preparation of this Indian contingent was similar to that of its ten predecessors in UNEF, each of which usually contained around 1,000 men. Anticipating October rotation, the replacement unit arrived in July at Poona, the location in west-central India of the UN training camp, and for the remaining two and one-half months until departure by ship for Egypt the unit was put through operational drills and administrative checks appropriate to UNEF. While in UNEF service—and this factor sharply distinguished the Indians from all other UNEF infantry, which were one-time-only outfits—the Indian demeanor and routine were as far as possible unit oriented down to the last man. Testing for promotions, standard infantry performance exercises, marksmanship practice, the usual spit-and-polish requirements—all these continued during UN tours, and unit symbols and loyalties remained central to men and officers alike.[62]

BRAZIL

Just as India has stressed the need to organize UN military forces strictly in conformity with the Charter, Brazil exhorts the UN to raise its armies not according to the Charter as it stands now but according to an amended version favored by Brazil. In the absence of explicit Charter authority for peacekeeping, the government argues, a new section ought to be inserted. The repeated failure of this proposal (dubbed a campaign for Chapter VI-and-a-half) has apparently influenced Brazil's decision not to earmark UN units from its 200,000-man army, the largest in Latin America. Like some of its hemispheric neighbors, notably Argentina and Jamaica, Brazil has shown mild interest in earmarking, saying at one point that it would prepare a standby unit once its UNEF commitment ended, but it has been put off not only by Charter-revision preoccupations but also because its views on authorization and financing have not been generally accepted. With Ireland, Brazil wants peacekeeping financing to be assessed and, in diametric contradiction to India, advocates revitalizing Uniting for Peace procedures.

Brazil was one of the countries asked by U Thant early in March 1964 to contribute a unit to UNFICYP. Even from the simplest chronological evidence, it seems clear that Brazil initially responded affirmatively and then quickly reneged. This initial willingness must have been conveyed during negotiations at UN headquarters on the setting up of UNFICYP, for at least one supplier government, Finland, informed its legislature that Brazil was going to contribute a specific unit.[63] Inside Brazil during these March weeks a political crisis was mushrooming; it peaked April 1–2 in the bloodless military coup that toppled the government of President João Goulart. Events preceding the takeover apparently forced Brazil to opt out of UNFICYP sometime in early March. Though some press accounts had it that the decision was made for financial reasons, it was also reported that Brazil refused even after being promised full reimbursement. (Two other Latin American states, Mexico and Chile, had been sounded out by Thant, and both declined to take part.) Thant reported on March 12 only that "the Government of Brazil has found it virtually impossible at this time to respond favorably to my request for the provision of a contingent" for UNFICYP.[64]

Brazil was invited to UNFICYP for the obvious reason that it had more UN experience than any other Latin American UN member and by then had evolved routine supplier procedures. Like India's, the last Brazilian peacekeeping units were those in UNEF. To resupply them, the Brazilians used a system resembling that of Ireland in some respects: all were volunteers and the organization of UN units was based on shared responsibilities among army regional commands. Brazil, however, is one of the most expensive suppliers while Ireland is one of the least expensive. In UNEF battalions, all Brazilian officers and senior NCOs were regular army personnel, and all other ranks were reservists who had completed conscript service or men who volunteered to complete their draft obligations by spending time in Gaza. Surpluses of volunteers were high for all ranks, and everyone was restricted to a single tour, which in UNEF was one year, although some staff officers stayed longer. In putting the battalion together, the army called for officers and NCOs to volunteer from anywhere in Brazil. Other ranks were recruited by the regional command responsible that year for preparing the UN contingent—an assignment that was rotated annually. Several months before rotation, after the senior officers had been designated and oriented, unit-level preparations began. About 5,000 soldiers went through this process between 1956 and 1967, and a half-dozen or so standardized training manuals, tactical and administrative, were compiled over the years.

YUGOSLAVIA

With an army slightly smaller than Brazil's, Yugoslavia also formed one-time-only units for Sinai duty. The members of the contingent were all regulars and volunteers, at least in the technical sense used by, say, the Danes for their UN officers—the men find it difficult to refuse to volunteer if asked. The central army command in Yugoslavia selected senior personnel, and subcommands were designated to fill out the unit with a proportional number of volunteers, again much like the Irish practice. Some of the volunteers for the other ranks were ordinary national conscripts finishing the last portion of their eighteen-month service, and a desire to avoid obligating them beyond their required time was one reason for Yugoslav rotation every six months.

The readiness cycle was very nearly continuous. Commanding officers were named two or three months before departure, and all members underwent one and a half months of preparation. For one month of this time, as a formed unit at a Yugoslav UN training base, the contingent ran through exercises common to suppliers with long service in a particular mission, using movies and still photographs taken in Sinai and other visual aids. Training and briefing staffs always included officers who had been in the battalion that had returned home six months before the unit in training was scheduled to leave.

This system has never been translated into a regular standby system, partly because Yugoslavia tends to believe, like the Irish, that more flexibility in deciding whether to participate in an operation is retained if the government gives no formal indication of advance readiness, no semipromise that might make it harder to refuse. Beyond wanting to avoid extra expense, the Yugoslavs prefer to wait until the political underpinnings for preparedness are more solid, perhaps even until other Eastern Europeans can become suppliers. One manifestation of this go-slow attitude was the government's reaction to the Ottawa conference, which they declined to attend because it was poorly timed politically, because its original design aroused such suspicions, and because they preferred at the time to confine preparedness diplomacy to UN auspices. They adopted this position despite admitted curiosity about the activities of other supplier states with which they had served in the Congo, Egypt, and Yemen.

Providers: Great Britain and the United States

Hammarskjöldian precepts placed as much distance as possible between the Security Council great powers and the actual functioning of peacekeeping missions. Nonparticipation of their military contingents and noninvolvement of their nationals in top political or military positions at field headquarters are intended to ensure impartiality. Big power aloofness is thought, in principle, a precondition for effective peacekeeping. But in practice compromises have been inevitable.

Great powers influence, even dominate, peacekeeping diplomacy in the UN and they determine the fate of preparedness proposals in the Assembly and the Council. They affect the thinking of the secretariat decision makers, who are so sensitive to political crosscurrents. The Americans and British contribute heavily to peacekeeping coffers, and they give the logistical support, the technical advice, and the emergency planning skills without which the major peacekeeping operations could never have been started or sustained. Since these services have been indispensable and are likely to be so in the future, the international civil servants in the secretariat are both blessed and burdened. Blessed, because they are probably not going to have independent logistical wherewithal under foreseeable conditions; burdened, because they must apply high political skills if they are to rely on great power help without inviting charges of overresponsiveness to the political interests of these national providers.

GREAT BRITAIN

This was, in autumn 1964, the election campaign promise: "Labour will reassert British influence in the United Nations. We will seek to strengthen the UN by . . . making an effective contribution to the creation of an international police force."[65]

This was, in February 1965, the policy position taken by the new Labour government of Prime Minister Harold Wilson: "If so requested, and subject to our national commitments, we will help to provide logistic backing for a United Nations force of up to six infantry battalions. This could include, for example, short-range aircraft, engineering and signal troops, and ambulance, ordnance and motor transport units. If it were desirable, suitable units of these categories would be earmarked for use as available. Her Majesty's Government also hope to take share in providing long-range aircraft for the transport of peacekeeping forces."[66]

What did this statement mean? At the very most it was a general description of the kind and magnitude of assistance that might be forthcoming from the United Kingdom. As explained, it was not an offer to earmark such units, either by setting them aside or by designating them for double duty. The government was saying that if all stated conditions were met—and these were neither more nor less stringent than those of other standbys—it would canvass its logistical resources for facilities of the sort listed. It also hinted at the possibility, sometime later, of a more concrete and firm offer. This prospect was linked ambiguously with the United Nations Special Committee on Peacekeeping Operations, which in early 1965 was just beginning painstaking deliberations that were to last for years. The government forecast: "When the peace-keeping committee gets to its work and we, together with the other nations, are able to see what general structure for peace-keeping is emerging, we shall be able to make our own offer in a more precise form."[67]

In communications to the Special Committee three years later, most standbys reported as much national program detail as they could, but Britain devoted only a single sentence to its 1965 offer, recalling merely that it had been made and not referring again to the possibility of definite earmarking or to the original hope that Britain could provide strategic transport.[68]

Had Labour not come to power in October 1964, Britain probably would not have shown even symbolic interest in a national preparedness initiative. As the opposition party, Labour had flirted with the idea and occasionally twitted the Conservative government for its failure to lend any concrete support to the preparedness campaign in evidence during

1963–64. Labourite internationalists had ritually backed a standing UN army, and in its absence calls were heard for a permanent, unified Commonwealth force, a variant urged by former Labour Prime Minister Clement Attlee in 1963. The UN was "always a winner with the Labour Party,"[69] and with the development and publicizing of the Nordic, Canadian, and Dutch standby plans, these sentiments acquired a precise target of opportunity. In the House of Commons, Labourites asked, "Why not Britain too?" Harold Wilson, M.P., suggested to Prime Minister Sir Alec Douglas-Home that Britain earmark specifically for UN peacekeeping "perhaps two thousand or more" operational and support troops "at present in Germany."[70] At about the same time private proposals were circulating in Britain, urging that the sizable British navy be given responsibility for supporting UN peacekeeping operations.

These proddings had had little effect on the Conservative government. A number of suitable occasions for a gesture presented themselves; all were passed over. In early 1964 Britain, now aware of the efforts of standbys, told Geneva disarmament negotiators that it was encouraging greater secretariat preparedness, yet no mention was made of any British measures. More controversially, the foreign secretary omitted from the distributed text of an important speech in Washington a suggestion that all UN member governments earmark peacekeeping units. Wilson took the government to task for this omission by asking whether the oral or the printed version of the speech represented British policy, to which the prime minister replied, "Both."[71] Like others, Britain could have earmarked and made itself eligible for the Ottawa conference, but chose not to do so—even after the Commonwealth ministers met in July and collectively declared themselves ready "to consider practical measures" for strengthening UN preparedness and said they "agreed that consultation and cooperation among interested Governments in this matter could be of great value."[72] This endorsement smacks of Pearson's influence, all the more so since this was his first opportunity as a new prime minister to attend a Commonwealth caucus. The Conservatives, though, did not follow up, and in their campaign manifesto several months later took a far more uninterested and passive position on peacekeeping than their Labour adversaries.

After making its logistics offer, which probably had been discussed beforehand with secretariat officials, the Labour government took two supplementary steps. For possible mobilization of British UN personnel, it decided to use reserves rather than regulars. They are to be drawn from a category of reserve personnel numbering 1,600 men, which would have national tasks and "which might be needed to cover the logistic support of a United Nations peacekeeping force."[73] The second step was to set down on paper a possible combination of logistics units adequate to service six peacekeeping battalions. These estimates, which have been forwarded to the secretariat, comprise not quite 1,400 personnel organized in headquarters elements, workshops, communications, medical, engineer, supply, and other administrative and support units. Beyond this paperwork, no action has been taken to implement further the 1965 blueprint. The scheduled units have not been drilled or briefed, and no effort has been made to consult with planners from supplier states that might be involved in manning future UN missions logistically supported by Britain. Staff work in London has focused mainly on what resources will be needed after multinational contingents arrive at a UN mission and have to be serviced. For planning purposes the initial idea about strategic transport has been dropped, and it is not now assumed that British overseas bases would be made available for UN support.

Base conversion for the UN has often been advocated in Britain, and its supporters usually single out the sovereign base areas in Cyprus now supporting UNFICYP, the sprawling Singapore complexes, or even the "baselet" staging posts in the Indian Ocean. But now, half a decade later, British capabilities for any such agency on behalf of the UN have been greatly curtailed. Pressures on the pound in late 1967 compelled devaluation and general economic belt tightening. And during the following year radical changes modified the British defense position. Withdrawal east of Suez had been in the cards, but for the mid- to late 1970s. It is scheduled to be sooner. Except for a garrison at Hong Kong, British presences in the Far East will disappear, as they will in the Indian Ocean and the Persian Gulf. Only the Cyprus bases will remain, though greatly scaled down. Orders for the F-111 fighter bomber, symbol of British reach outside Europe, will be canceled; the 425,000-man armed services will be cut by 75,000; civil defense and reserve units at home will be either dismantled or streamlined. Even before the cutbacks, the reserve units from which UN logistics personnel would come were expected to be no more than 1,350 by 1970, instead of the 1,600 originally planned. The 1968 Defense White Paper announced a review of this outfit's training and organization, but it is not anticipated that the mode of fulfilling British UN support commitments will change essentially. However, this reserve category will have to be kept at fuller strength to avoid the 1968 situation, when fewer than 700 men were actually available.

All things considered, the 1965 offer probably deserves the summary judgment rendered at the time by *The Economist*: "At least, a timely gesture of encouragement."[74] The offer was directed less at military planners than at the diplomatic audience in the UN and the political one at home. Labour found additional avenues to demonstrate genuine concern for the UN, steps of no small importance for a member whose post-Suez attitudes toward the organization had been indifferent, lukewarm, or politely hostile. The elevation of Britain's Lord Caradon to full Minister of State for Foreign Affairs while ambassador to the UN symbolized the new government's seriousness of purpose, and in mid-1965 Great Britain helped to alleviate the UN financial squeeze by making a sizable voluntary contribution.

Whatever the motives were in 1965, it is a mistake to measure British preparedness now by referring only to this conditional promise of logistics. The United Kingdom has sent thousands of soldiers—regulars, not reserves, mostly on six-month tours—to UNFICYP in operational and support capacities.[75] From a top of about 7,500 British troops, which were on the island at the beginning of 1964 before the UN's arrival, their number leveled off by August to between 1,000 and 1,200 and has remained more or less constant since then. The bulk of British manpower has been in infantry battalions and reconnaissance units, the rest in UN administrative and logistical components backed up by the British bases in southern Cyprus, mainly the one at Dhekelia. Britain sent no civilian police to UNFICYP, though certain remarks in the House of Commons imply that they were asked to do so.[76] The support bases have carried the responsibility for UNFICYP's basic logistics since the beginning. Together, this peacekeeping experience in a UN context and the exposure to the difficulties of supporting a multinational force not entirely accustomed to British army procedures will probably prove to have increased U.K. preparedness more markedly than anything done since the 1965 offer.

THE UNITED STATES

Like the British, the United States has also been both provider and supplier, but much earlier and under markedly different historical circumstances. Ever since the 1940s the United States has been taking new preparedness roles. Sometimes a giver of men, sometimes of hardware, sometimes of money, sometimes of all three, the United States has had to adjust to the fundamental changes in peacekeeping institutions. The year 1956 was the divide. Previously the United States could fairly certainly expect to be an active and visible peacekeeper, if it wished, as it was in early observer missions. At one time both UNTSO and UNMOGIP had American chiefs of staff. But UNEF and Hammarskjöld's guidelines joined with the requirement for political impartiality to produce restrictions on the conduct of peacekeeping operations. The UN could neither organize peacekeeping in ways that might prejudice international command and control nor *seem* to be doing so. No longer could the United States be a supplier of operational personnel, and its massive provider services began to produce in the secretariat a transparent but necessary sleight-of-hand about who does what. Thus in his landmark report on UNEF, which never would have materialized without U.S. help, the secretary-general could write paragraphs about logistics, airlift, and supply, without once even mentioning the United States.[77]

In 1949 Congress amended the United Nations Participation Act, the basic legislation governing U.S. activity at the UN. A good picture of preparedness policies and assumptions existing then is provided by the text of the proposed changes and by executive branch testimony.[78] The State Department, for one, anticipated that American military men and equipment would be regular features of the UN peacekeeping landscape. Accordingly, several purposes were served by the amendments. To assuage scattered congressional fears that the United States would bear a disproportionate share of manpower burdens—while also paying.

as it then was, almost 40 percent of the entire UN budget—a ceiling was inserted restricting U.S. contributions to 1,000 men at any one time. This was considered adequate for future contingencies because up to that time American UN personnel had never exceeded 450. Men and equipment committed according to the amendments cannot be used for Chapter VII enforcement or for any other UN combat operations. A major purpose of the revisions was to authorize the government to ask routinely for UN reimbursement of extraordinary expenses incurred during U.S. support or participation. This right of reimbursement can be waived, but only by the President if he thinks it in the "national interest." Congressional intent was to stress the presumption of repayment, not the possibility of waiver; the language emphasizes that "the President shall require reimbursement from the United Nations."[79]

This intent has been honored. Only modest fractions of the reimbursable amounts to which the United States has been entitled have been waived.[80] Shifting and arbitrary criteria seem to have been applied in deciding whether to invoke the "national interest" clause. The record of practice reveals little, other than the understandable reluctance of the U.S. armed services to cover even relatively minor expenses not programmed in their operating budgets. When the United States airlifted contingents to Cyprus in 1964, the President instructed the Defense Department not to ask for reimbursement. Congress was informed that this was justified because "we thought it was in our national interest to prevent a war between Greece and Turkey."[81] Yet, unexplainably, when the United States transported UN military observers to the India-Pakistan border in late 1965, a crisis surely touching the core of U.S. national interests in South Asia, the Air Force billed the UN for the hourly costs of a single C-130 aircraft.

The amended manpower authority and ceiling in the Participation Act had lost much of their relevance by the mid-1950s, though they are still in effect. No intention of earmarking or otherwise preparing in advance the 1,000 men permitted by law had ever existed. The figure was strictly a quantitative limit, and one not even closely approximated in the years to come. By 1955 UNTSO was the only mission containing U.S. officers, and never since have permanent members of the Security Council been invited to participate in observer forces; however, the

United States continues to supply UNTSO with small numbers of observers and a colonel who has filled the second-in-command slot at Jerusalem headquarters.[82]

Hammarskjöld's revised, enlarged edition of peacekeeping obliged the United States to rethink its relation to preparedness. Fitfully, a broad design for a modernized U.S. preparedness policy emerged. Its main elements were three, each related to one of the preparedness components. The first (and the most concrete) was the government's decision to accept larger responsibility for the one preparedness component with which Washington could still be directly involved: provision of logistical services. Of course, this was not a new role; early missions had depended heavily on the United States. Yet now the scale was bigger. Before 1956 requests from the UN were neither very substantial nor very complicated to administer. Afterward they were both.[83]

Second, the United States quickly asserted itself as a leading advocate of secretariat reforms aimed at improving executive, administrative, and planning resources within a bureaucracy not specially geared for major peacekeeping assignments. It was thought that some but not enough relevant talent and experience had carried over from the UN's first generation of preparedness. A chief target for reform was the lack of a permanent military staff in the secretary-general's executive office. Temporarily, in connection with UNEF, Hammarskjöld brought in a senior officer and three assistants to act, he said, as military "consultants," and military representatives from troop-contributing countries constituted an "informal military advisory committee."[84] The United States and others were hopeful that some of this machinery would be a preliminary to more lasting staff arrangements. When UNEF was a mere seven months old, Ambassador Henry Cabot Lodge tentatively recommended a "permanent higher headquarters."[85]

Closely linked with secretariat reforms was the third U.S. theme—strong political support for the standby concept. In later proposals secretariat reform and standby themes were often paired, but American officials in the years just after UNEF treated them quite separately and mentioned secretariat reform more frequently and more approvingly. At that time proposals for standby forces tended to be automatically associated with a frequently proposed permanent peacekeeping force, which the U.S. government most emphatically did not favor. Furthermore, U.S. officials were none too sanguine about the willingness of potential suppliers to place units on standby. The tepid response to the Uniting for Peace Resolution was an uncomfortably fresh memory (even though one contributing cause of the generally unfavorable response was Washington's own reneging on those standby provisions of the 1950 Resolution which the United States had originally sponsored), and not much more enthusiasm was expected from UN members in the second half of the decade. In addition, the idea of standby programs was then only vaguely comprehended, even in Scandinavia and Canada. The strengthening of the secretariat seemed to be the more promising tack. Events soon rebalanced these priorities when, early in the 1960s, standby and earmarking planning had progressed far enough to elicit increased U.S. interest.

Translation of this design into viable policies has been full of problems. It has given rise to a pair of particularly troublesome issues: whether the United States should place any of its own logistical resources on UN standby, and whether the United States should, or could, somehow give more than verbal backing to standby programs in other member states. Both have left Washington vacillating and inconsistent.

The issue of U.S. standby arrangements must have aroused a fleeting sense of déjà vu for decision makers in the 1960s. It had been thrashed out a decade earlier, in quite another context to be sure, and had resulted in an embarrassing U.S. about-face. After championing earmarking by all UN members under the Uniting for Peace Resolution and after persuading the General Assembly to give its approval, the United States refused, in effect, to make any contribution of its own. This much-chronicled reversal has been attributed to a bureaucratic tug-of-war between State Department advocates of U.S. earmarking and Defense Department detractors, as well as to the general argument crossing departmental lines that, for any UN action viewed favorably by the United States, its defense establishment would be available anyway, and a specific earmarking would only be a pointless, perhaps inhibiting gloss.[86]

After 1956, the issue was entirely changed. Exclusion of military and operational units of the great powers was taken for granted. Thus for a time in the late 1950s U.S. support of earmarking was in the form of encouragement to nonpermanent members. This was the import of President Dwight D. Eisenhower's recommendation to the Assembly in 1958, at the height of the Lebanon crisis, for a "standby United Nations Peace Force." This recommendation received no elaboration until 1960, when enormous logistical demands were made on the United States for ONUC, when Hammarskjöld came down firmly on the need for national preparedness, and when, apparently, it seemed politically and technically sensible for the United States to think seriously about earmarking its own logistical units—but only these—for the UN. Again before the General Assembly in his farewell address in September 1960, Eisenhower made this pledge: "To assist the Secretary General's efforts, the United States is prepared *to earmark* also substantial air and sea transport facilities *on a stand-by basis*, to help move contingents requested by the United Nations in any future emergency."[87] (Emphasis added.) This is, admittedly, not a definite commitment, because of the phrase "is prepared to." But it resembles, in form, the British logistical offer five years later and, like it, suggests that the United States will take *some* internal steps as a consequence. It says more than merely, "We will see what we can do when the time comes."

The origin of the Eisenhower proposal is not known. Nothing like it had even been hinted at in executive branch congressional testimony on peacekeeping preparedness two years earlier. From State and Defense Department presentations then it could be inferred only that the United States would consider, ad hoc, any requests from the UN for logistical assistance. If the antecedents of the idea are unclear, its subsequent course is equally mysterious. Though confirmed officially in a letter from the secretary of state in December 1960, the standby offer was omitted from a relevant section of President John F. Kennedy's 1961 address to the Assembly recommending earmarking by all member states.[88] In autumn 1963, addressing the same forum, he welcomed the recently announced preliminary standby plans in Scandinavia, adding only that "this nation remains ready to provide logistic and other material support."[89] This is where the matter still stands. Not once in countless later expressions of support for UN preparedness programs has the Eisenhower offer been explicitly renewed, referred to, or rescinded by the government—it is as if it had never been made. A standard phraseology, basically no different from Kennedy's in 1963, has replaced it, omitting the words "earmarking" or "standby." As delivered by the secretary of defense in 1968, it says: "The United States will continue to provide logistical services, notably airlift [and] communications support, for UN peacekeeping operations, when appropriate."[90]

Without saying so, the United States seems to have scrapped the Eisenhower approach and decided to make no commitment beyond the above-quoted statement. Implicitly, this decision was an answer to a much-publicized proposal originally sponsored by six liberal Republican congressmen in 1965. Released on the eve of the San Francisco Conference commemorating the UN's anniversary, it urged the United States to earmark military transport as well as a "brigade" called FIRST—an acronym for the awkward "Forces for International Relief on Stand-by." In justifying the proposal, the sponsors pointed to stand-by efforts in progress elsewhere and to the logistics offer of the British Labour government and charged that "the U.S. Administration has applauded these steps by others but as yet has not taken similar action of its own." They tried to anticipate a response that had often been voiced. "We know that the U.S. Armed Forces may be able to provide most of these services relatively quickly without a special unit," they acknowledged, but insisted that the FIRST brigade would, nevertheless, "maximize" efficiency and stand as "a symbol" of U.S. faith and commitment.[91] A two-legged offer was suggested in a few brief paragraphs. The U.S. Military Air Transport System (MATS) was to be "placed on permanent call" for UN strategic transport needs. A declaration to this effect would "give assurance to UN personnel and would alert MATS personnel to the vital nature of their UN functions." Next, the FIRST brigade should be formed as "a small volunteer unit of approximately 1,000" personnel (technically not a brigade at all). Apparently the existing legislative ceiling determined this total. The unit would contain diverse logistical and support capabilities representing "technical skills at which the U.S. Armed Forces excel." Listed were communications, army and navy engineers, medical teams, quartermaster and MATS advisers, and multilingual interpreters. The brigade would have a "permanent headquarters" and be composed exclusively of volunteers from the active services. This "politically feasible" contribution would also be available, as are some of the Scandinavian standby units, for natural disaster relief services. Though terse and general, the proposals were on the whole well thought out, except for a lapse here and there, such as having the entire membership of the unit be given "basic language skills in order to facilitate communications with all nationalities"![92]

In 1965 there was little reason to expect this idea to be taken up by a Democratic administration, or for that matter any administration, given the diplomatic standstill in New York. In 1966 the prospects were even worse, because the plan had been incorporated into a GOP broadside against the administration's UN policies several months before off-year elections. A Republican task force accused the "Johnson-Humphrey Administration" of "inept and totally inadequate" UN diplomacy, charging "retreat" during the Article 19 confrontation. It swiped at the handling of Vietnam in New York and warned against any "similar retreat" from the U.S. position opposing membership for Communist China. Appended to this indictment was a recommendation for "study and consideration" of a half-dozen capsule proposals for strengthening the UN, including the FIRST brigade idea.[93] Press reports from the UN said the proposals were dismissed there as "simple partisan politics," but there is no doubt that the idea got much more publicity in this blatantly partisan setting than it ever did in its initial, more elaborate presentation.[94]

Thus advocacy of a U.S. standby commitment was monopolized, rhetorically at least, by the Republicans when they were in power at the end of the Eisenhower era and while they were out of power during most of the 1960s. It is hard to miss the conspicuous similarities between this interparty posturing and that in Britain during the same decade. Their advent to power in 1968 placed the Republicans in much the same situation as the Labour party just after its 1964 victory, of being the party that, having been identified with a prostandby position, was suddenly faced with the option of carrying it forward or abandoning it.

But until another course is selected, U.S. declaratory policy will remain more or less as stated during congressional hearings in the spring of 1968. Although the State Department took refuge behind "actively considering" and "studying" the question of U.S. earmarking, the Department of Defense seemed to have already made up its mind. Paul C. Warnke, an assistant secretary of defense for international security affairs, testified:

> We are not sure at the present time whether this is appropriate for a variety of reasons. I think one of them, of course, is the fact we do have available trained forces that could be utilized, for peacekeeping functions, in situations in which this might be acceptable to the nations concerned. The acceptability of the middle powers is, of course, much easier to establish under these circumstances.[95]

A few weeks after these Defense Department sentiments were voiced, the State Department tried out one more variant. A paper delivered to the Peacekeeping Committee at the UN contained this sentence: "Still other countries such as the United States and the United Kingdom have indicated a willingness to continue supplying logistic support as the future may require."[96] This, for UN consumption, is a rather agile kind of earmarker-by-association pairing of the United States with an avowed standby country, without enlarging or narrowing the operative U.S. commitment to be ready to supply logistical resources if appropriate.

Contrary to the impression perhaps given by repeated mention of Congress, Capitol Hill has not had much effect on U.S. government attitudes toward preparedness. The most that can be said is that in the second half of the 1960s Congress and the State Department at least initiated a little realistic dialogue on the relevant problems. Previously, mutual education had suffered as greatly as mutual insulation had thrived. In 1956–57, Congress—or really, a core group in each chamber —spent most of their energies paying lip service to sundry schemes for permanent UN armies, while the State Department (along with the secretariat and most member states) was doing its utmost to discourage this approach.[97]

The pendulum of congressional concern has swung in a familiar rhythm. Enthusiasm for UN peace forces during and immediately after major international crises has alternated with comparative lack of interest during intervening lulls. Washington legislators, of course, enjoy no exclusive claim on this conditioned-reflex behavior, but Congress's barometer has been unusually precise and predictable. The cant accompanying permanent peace force proposals has encompassed re-

curring themes. One such theme saw a UN force as a substitute for U.S·
military involvement around the world. On this count, the 1968 presidential campaign was not much different from that of 1958, after the
U.S. Marines landed in Lebanon. Campaigner Vice President Hubert
Humphrey could exhort the United States to cast off its "role of global
gendarme" and create an alternative at the UN and in regional organizations.[98] A decade earlier Senator Humphrey, voicing sentiments
expressed by many of his colleagues then, could say: "I have addressed
myself again and again to the need of the Government of the United
States assisting in the development of a United Nations police force, so
that we did not have to take upon ourselves the burden of policing huge
areas of the world."[99] Another theme appears with the cyclic response
to individual crises. When the first Senate resolution calling for "a force
of a similar character" to "be made a permanent arm" of the UN was
introduced, UNEF was not three months old;[100] and ONUC was just one
month old when essentially the same resolution was reintroduced, urging a permanent force modeled on UNEF *and* ONUC.[101] This pattern
has not changed much over the years. Resolutions urging permanent
peace forces have routinely had multiple sponsors and bipartisan support in both chambers, have been encouraged by various world peace
interest groups, and have been tabled against a backdrop of broad
though uncritical support from the public at large, support that even
outruns that polled in most countries that are regular suppliers of UN
soldiers.[102]

Deviations from this pattern are more interesting than the pattern itself. Substantive congressional hearings on UN preparedness have been
convened twice, once in the House in 1958 and again in the Senate in
1968.[103] Associated with both events are efforts by the State Department
to move Congress away from the permanent force idea and into directions that the executive branch has considered more feasible and more in
accord with U.S. interests. The House action came on the heels of the
Lebanon crisis, at which time both houses received resolutions on permanent forces essentially like one adopted a year earlier by the Senate.
On the basis of its version, the House held subcommittee hearings and,
after listening to the advice of State and Defense Department officials,
modified the proposed language by deleting references to permanent

"arm" or "instrument." The result—still, with the 1957 Senate action, the only concurrent resolutions on the subject ever adopted—asked the UN to consider the development "within its permanent structure, of such organization and procedures" as are needed to manage peacekeeping forces.[104]

At the hearings a decade later, the situation almost reproduced itself, except that the State Department's impact on the legislative drafting took place before rather than during or after public hearings. A subcommittee of the Senate Foreign Relations Committee heard two days of testimony in 1968 on a proposed resolution urging the government, "as an immediate objective," to "encourage and support" earmarking programs by UN members; to "be prepared" to make available logistical and other support assistance. Only as a matter of "long-range development" of the UN did the language refer, separately, to a permanent force.[105] The wording of the resolution appeared exactly as it did in a House resolution submitted in early 1967.[106] It was at this earlier juncture, apparently, that executive branch influence was felt. Before 1967 the congressmen who co-sponsored this resolution had been enthusiasts of the more traditional, permanent-peace-force approach. It seems that their preferences shifted after a series of consultations they had before putting together the 1967 draft. They met, reportedly, with State Department officials in Washington, U.S. Ambassador Arthur J. Goldberg and his staff, and several permanent representatives from other member states. By mid-1967 the proposal had acquired more than fifty additional sponsors and a public endorsement by the State Department, the first gesture of its kind.[107] At the Senate hearings, Joseph J. Sisco, the assistant secretary of state for international organization affairs, commended this "constructive" resolution, which "correctly places the problem in two time frames, what can and should be done now and what enlargement of effort may be possible in the future."[108] Clearly the department was satisfied that the language de-emphasized both permanent arrangements and a specific U.S. standby commitment.[109]

The concurrent resolutions submitted to both chambers in 1967, neither of which was ever voted on, provided a procedural basis for the spring 1968 public hearings and registered the personal concerns of those legislators especially interested in this subject. Among backers of the House bill was a handful of congressmen who also lent their weight to a related measure—the addition of a peacekeeping rider to the Foreign Assistance Act of 1967. The paragraph put Congress formally on record as being in full support of one of the three prongs of U.S. preparedness policy, the strengthening of standby programs. After expressing the sense of Congress that these are valuable, the rider requested the President "to explore" at the UN "both the means and the prospects" of establishing such arrangements and to submit a report "upon the outcome of his initiatives, together with such recommendations as he may deem appropriate."[110] Filed by Secretary of State Dean Rusk and unveiling neither initiatives nor recommendations, the report consisted of a terse survey of recent preparedness developments and a half-dozen appendixes containing U.S. speeches and papers presented in New York over the preceding several years. Unimpressed proponents of the rider have dismissed the executive response as "brief and undramatic."[111]

Indirectly the foreign aid bill rider was connected with the second of the troublesome issues produced by the triple U.S. preparedness design, namely, whether the United States can give material as well as political support to standby programs in potential supplier states. In many different formulations the United States has said that the "most practical way" to ensure availability of peacekeeping manpower "is to encourage and aid countries to earmark forces for UN service."[112] The question has been what the United States *itself* could do to demonstrate this conviction, what kind of "encouragement and aid" it could give. Suggestions from in and out of government have centered on one particular device: the U.S. military assistance program. Once again the basic line of policy had been set down by President Eisenhower in his 1960 speech to the Assembly: "I assure countries which now receive assistance from the United States that we favor the use of that assistance to help them maintain" standby contingents.[113]

This has not suffered the obscurity of the U.S. promise to earmark logistical services. Rather, it has reappeared often in official doctrine and in recommendations of expert private groups and individuals. Nearly always it is tied explicitly to existing provisions of the Foreign Assistance Act stipulating that military assistance may be furnished, among other reasons, to permit recipients to participate in collective or regional arrangements "consistent with" the UN Charter or collective measures "requested by" the UN.[114]

The sense of this language represents one of the many layers of purpose tacked onto military assistance legislation since the programs began during the late 1940s, initially in the emergency transfers to Greece, Turkey, and Iran, and later in the broader multinational allocations to signatories of the NATO treaty. The first comprehensive military aid law, the Mutual Defense Assistance Act of 1949, was in fact integral to the newly created alliance, and military assistance was a principal asset in the U.S. cold war arsenal.

The 1949 act restricted eligibility for assistance to states formally allied with the United States and a few others whose security was directly of interest to Washington. Aid giving to facilitate participation in UN collective action was not specifically mentioned as a possible end-use.[115] Only as a result of the Korean war did the United States appreciate the potential of the UN as a possible military check against communism, an awareness embodied, of course, in the Uniting for Peace Resolution. In line with this awareness the 1951 military assistance law extended possible uses of military aid to cover participation "in United Nations collective security arrangements and measures."[116] Successive but nonessential changes in this language found their way into the aid bill in 1961 and have been included annually since then.[117]

President Eisenhower's military assistance offer a year earlier presumably rested on these provisions, though he did not say so. Like his earmarking gesture, this offer's origin is uncertain but probably does not go back very far, since the 1958 congressional hearings show no mention of this proposal either. From its debut in the 1960 Assembly until the resurgence several years later of U.S. interest in standby ventures, this military assistance idea reposed in an official netherworld, though continuing to hold promise in the eyes of interested nongovernmental experts.[118] Never has the offer been wholeheartedly revived by the government. By the mid-1960s a diluted version of it had begun trickling into official policy statements, yet the follow-through has been more perfunctory than purposeful. The idea has not caught on even with potential recipients, and of late the State and Defense departments have shown that they have serious reservations about its practical utility. Neither appears willing to give it more than frankly passive acceptance at most.

At the UN the United States does not expressly refer anymore to U.S. "military assistance" but only to unspecified "aid." In the first official mention of the idea since the Eisenhower remarks, Ambassador Goldberg, late in November 1965, pointed out that some prospective standbys "may be unable to assume the full burdens of training and equipping" standby units; therefore, "aid to earmarking countries could be made available either through the UN or bilaterally."[119] Periodically, the United States "reaffirms its readiness to cooperate in practical plans to aid" earmarkers.[120] Goldberg's remarks were made at about the same time that recommendations were being drafted for a much-publicized 1965 year-end convocation of private citizens at a White House conference on international cooperation. Among the peacekeeping initiatives urged there was the use of U.S. military assistance to support standbys.[121] The Goldberg speech elicited scant attention, and the recommendation to the White House was buried among hundreds of others in the catalog of subjects. But even this slight exposure surpassed what previously had amounted only to an inconclusive, brief congressional questioning of the Pentagon's military assistance director by a House member sympathetic to the proposal, and to a speech in 1964 by a ranking State Department official in the UN Bureau, who indicated that the U.S. government was favorably disposed to the idea of directly assisting national programs that would increase UN peacekeeping capabilities.[122] At least nominally, over the next few years this Goldberg formulation became the standard version of the U.S. position. In 1966 and 1967, it also was the basis of new language added by the Department of Defense to the United Nations section of its annual appropriation statement. Secretary Robert S. McNamara said the United States was "prepared to explore the possibility" of equipping and helping to train peacekeeping personnel from other states in the hope that this "would provide tangible encouragement" for them to earmark.[123]

Then, in 1968, the entire issue got jumbled. The recently inserted language was deleted from the Defense Department statement in February.[124] In March, the private executive report on the Foreign As-

sistance Act rider announced that for the first time Latin American recipients of military assistance were being encouraged by U.S. Country
Teams to earmark UN units. In May, at the Senate hearings, the relevant
paragraph of this executive report was incorporated nearly verbatim
into the testimony of Joseph Sisco—*except* for the announcement about
Latin America, which was taken out entirely.[125] All that was left was an
assurance that possible uses of military assistance by earmarkers was
being studied. Thus only once has the government gone on record as
having decided to link UN standby needs to military assistance programs
in a specific geographic region of the world, and this instance was
promptly relegated to an obscure document that was never published,
though it remains on file at the Senate Foreign Relations Committee.
Instead of restating the instructions about Latin America to Country
Teams in open hearings, the State Department pointedly removed
them; instead of reexpressing willingness to aid standbys, the Defense
Department excised the language in 1968; and instead of adopting the
State Department's position that the matter was under study, a Defense
official said, not altogether comprehensibly, that the military assistance
authority "has been utilized in the past, and it will be utilized in the
future."[126] There is no evidence, in the public record at least, of any past
use. Top Defense and State officials have had opportunities to say
whether this authority has ever been used, and they have left the impression that it has not.[127] Nor has the annual statement prepared for
Congress by the Pentagon director of military assistance ever spoken of
use for this purpose.[128]

The tendency might be to blame sloppy bureaucratic coordination
or even, perhaps, to look for the same kinds of interdepartmental bick-
ering over basic policy that divided State and Defense two decades ago
when the United States was formulating a response to its own preparedness proposals in Uniting for Peace. But U.S. policy makers now see
themselves faced with a more fundamental, more structural difficulty:
central requirements for political impartiality impose limits on what and
how much the United States can do to support preparedness in other
countries. Reasonable men differ on where these limits are, but they do
exist and U.S. officials have referred to them when dealing with congressional or other critics who want the United States to do more to

help earmarkers, to do it more visibly, and to do it more aggressively. The answer—and a sensible one—from Sisco: "We have felt the best way to stimulate a number of these countries" to earmark "is for such initiatives to really come from what might be considered a much more impartial source, namely the U.N. itself."[129] Implied is the fear that the United States could politically, and mortally, smother preparedness with an embrace too vigorous, too lengthy, or too amorous. This dilemma, the need to give enough but not too much support, is different from the one in 1950, and helps explain the apparent inertia of the United States—its seeming inability to fashion concrete and constructive innovations out of its genuine support for expanded UN preparedness.

SEVEN

Perspectives on Preparedness

AMMARSKJÖLD's archetypal experiment at Suez attracted new converts to the idea of United Nations peacekeeping—even a few British ones. Among them was Barbara Ward, economist-author who treated an Amerian audience in 1958 to this bristling prose: "The West must push hard" for UN peacekeeping forces "as an effective containment of Soviets on the prowl" and as a way to "give anticommunism its chance to breathe in liberated, UN-policed areas."[1] Although this sentiment was markedly out of step with Western official thinking at the time, which tended to de-emphasize the older image of UN forces as cold-war weapons, it nevertheless was a common theme in hard-line private speechmaking of the period. More important, it conformed closely, probably exactly, to communist perceptions of why their cold-war adversaries professed such strong commitment to beefing up the military powers of a UN that Khrushchev was then deriding as "a branch of the U.S.A."[2] A decade later the Soviet UN delegation did what it never before had done; it gave its approval, by vote and voice, to a proposal designed to strengthen UN preparedness. Symbol far outweighed substance, for the proposal itself was of minor consequence, merely facilitating a study of past experience by politically agreed methods. Soviet acquiescence, however, especially on terms it regarded as something of a compromise, did represent one small but explicit step away from absolute Russian mistrust of UN preparedness programs. Soviet policy toward peacekeeping has not been overhauled, and Soviet preferences are still very nearly the opposite of American ones on major issues of principle and practice. But there has been some constructive preparedness action and joint superpower support for specific peacekeeping missions in the Mediterranean, in South Asia, and in the Middle East during the 1960s.

The mood has changed since the days when peacekeeping could be peddled as a defense against prowling Reds. The fundamental shifts that have occurred in superpower relations have generated occasions when both have seen fit to use UN peacekeepers as servants of their shared self-interest in damping down dangerous local conflicts, and in reciprocal abstention from direct involvement. But these convergent interests do not automatically guarantee one rather than another set of UN peacekeeping institutions. Nor do they point up what particular kind of preparedness is possible. Mutual awareness of these interests is only a precondition for genuine United States–Soviet bargaining on preparedness matters. Yet it is the essential precondition because it opens a door that was shut during most of the UN's first twenty years when a dialogue among the deaf pitted totally alien concepts of peace-keeping against each other. No longer is it assumed that significant progress on preparedness can be expected under similar conditions.

Superpowers may set boundaries, write broad ground rules, and perhaps even create moods for preparedness diplomacy at the UN, but the actual shape of preparedness is in the hands of other agents as well. Goals have to be chosen, priorities arranged, and methods selected; and how the structure looks at any given time, what kind of preparedness is available, depends on a complex interplay of three interests and outlooks: those of diplomatic negotiators dealing with preparedness questions, those of secretariat executives responsible for peacekeeping affairs, and those of technicians bent on alleviating stubborn nuts-and-bolts problems. These are the three shapers of preparedness. To some extent this triple classification is artificial. Real-life individuals cannot always be pigeonholed neatly into one or the other group. The categories are intended to represent perspectives rather than people. They are intended to isolate the three most important currents of thinking about preparedness and to emphasize the three sets of concerns that dominate the continuing debate, each with its own viewpoint about what is desirable or achievable. They are intended to identify the movers, the shakers, and the obstructors, who singly or in combination determine what gets done, what gets deferred, and what gets deleted from preparedness agendas.

In these agendas the topics divide into two comprehensive categories. The more important one covers rock-bottom principles: Who will exercise political responsibility for UN preparedness? At the center, at the UN, who controls, makes, refines, reviews, finances, and if necessary oversees execution of preparedness policies? And how is political responsibility to be shared between the center and the periphery, between the collective UN and its individual members? Second, there are less far-reaching though still critical questions of another kind, concerning how, precisely, preparedness resources are to be organized. National suppliers are the basic raw materials; and along with the other two preparedness components, logistical and managerial wherewithal, they need to be fitted into a readiness system that is operationally adequate and in line with diplomatic realities at the UN. These two categories—political responsibility and operational adequacy—mingle continually. They can seldom be separated, never when major preparedness issues are at stake. Arguments about how military staffing and planning should be done at the UN are ultimately about whose political responsibility these would be; the same is true of arguments about how to organize standby states into a call-up system or how to learn from past preparedness experience. From the point of view of the military practitioner or the standby planner, this experience naturally shows some approaches to be more efficient than others, but these criteria are decidedly secondary until the broader political understandings are thrashed out successfully.

Shapers of Preparedness and Their Interests

Each of the three shapers stands in a singular relationship to preparedness. Each wants a different end product, each is conditioned by a different history, and each concentrates on different priorities. Each would do things differently if it were in full control.

The diplomats generally pursue primarily national interests and bring with them primarily national outlooks on a preparedness diplomacy that has always been an intensely adversary process. Their objective is not to pursue some abstract notion of adequate preparedness; it is to create only those preparedness institutions that are consistent with their government's basic views on UN peacekeeping and over whose functioning they will have what they regard as adequate control. Therefore, on different grounds and in varying degrees, national representatives tend to attach greatest importance to questions in the category of political responsibility. "Who does it" is by all odds more important than "what needs to be done." Operational efficiency tends to mean efficiency only on one's own political terms. Soviet-American bargaining has its effect here, yet the list of other countries diplomatically involved also includes some of the main suppliers of peacekeeping personnel, whose concerns for preparedness are immediate and personal and whose grasp of relevant problems is solid. Their political influence is often commensurate.

Secretariat executives currently exercise such centralized responsibility as there is for preparedness. With international perspectives, they seek to defend this responsibility against attempts to restrict it or to transplant it elsewhere in the UN organizational structure. Likewise they resist efforts to enlarge this responsibility in ways that they think go beyond the political consensus in the diplomatic community, while also encouraging enlargement of that consensus. As political managers and administrators with a historically controversial role in peacekeeping, the secretariat executives are mainly concerned with the political-diplomatic half of the preparedness agenda. Thus their orientation is of a kind similar to that of the national representatives, except that the secretariat is caught in the middle of competing national preferences to which it somehow must be responsive. It is simultaneously being asked to do much more, and to do much less; to assert greater independence from diplomatic pressures, and to be immobilized by them; to play a more active role in preparedness initiatives, and to abandon dynamism in favor of excessive caution. These cross-pressures converge on the person of the secretary-general, who is forced to be more a secretary and less a general in preparedness affairs. He sees it as imperative, moreover, that he prevent his broader peacekeeping authority from being eroded to a point where he is reduced to what U Thant in a much-quoted remark of some years ago called "a glorified clerk."

It is no wonder the technicians feel that no one is listening to them, that they alone seem to care about the concrete problems involved in putting together peacekeeping missions. They see UN readiness and resources as woefully substandard, yet the diplomats and the secretariat seem negligently uninterested in doing anything about it. The technicians, whether civilians or military men, reverse the priorities: questions of political responsibility take second place to the definable, tangible, operational requirements for better military planning, smoother emergency procedures, greater standardization of equipment and training, and fatter or at least more stable budgets. Here, the outlook is functional and the interests are avowedly nonpolitical, weighted on the side of efficiency. If the international community expects peacekeepers to perform adequately, argue the technicians, the necessary advance preparations must be made and the widely recognized shortcomings of preparedness must be erased.

Naturally, there is some dissonance in the interaction of these three points of view. Wherever one stands, either too much or too little is being done, or being asked for. The state of preparedness is not so much the sum total of these three attitudes as it is the lowest common denominator among them. If preparedness problems and potential are ever to be sensibly understood, it will be essential to appreciate that this interplay is, in itself, more significant than any one of the individual elements. Perhaps the worst blind spot in conventional thinking about preparedness is its failure to see these interconnections and to take into account the processes involved in shaping UN capabilities.

Certain factors complicate the job of assessing this interplay. For one thing, the several perspectives may each change a good deal, and may reveal inconsistencies over time, or they may simply remain ambiguous, making it difficult to know for certain who really believes what. Nor is it always possible to determine which policy positions are adopted for tactical diplomatic reasons and which ones reflect more basic values or preferences and therefore are presumably less susceptible to rapid or substantial modification.

Negotiations in the Committee of Thirty-three

Diplomats and preparedness issues are still largely strangers to each
other. In UN political bodies, systematic and organized attempts to
tackle these issues are of relatively recent origin, dating only from the
mid-1960s. That these attempts were so late in starting is itself ample
testimony to the deeply controversial nature of the issues involved;
that progress has been so slow, indeed barely perceptible, in recent
years is additional indication of the intransigence of the obstacles to the
emergence of diplomatic consensus about preparedness.

During most of the decade after 1956, two things were certain. First,
the Soviet Union would resist any and all Western proposals for
strengthening preparedness in or outside the UN. Initiatives, particularly American ones, toward secretariat reform or creation of standby
forces were thoroughly odious to the Russians. Referring to the Eisenhower standby plan, the Russians used language that they would dust
off again and again, even in the late sixties, whenever they wished to
register credible opposition to preparedness programs. "I need hardly
point out," Gromyko told the Assembly in 1958, "how greatly support
for such plans would endanger the cause of peace and the United
Nations itself."[3] The West saw no need to adjust its terms in any way.
Hammarskjöld, and later Thant, quietly and informally involved the
secretariat in preparedness, though neither thought he could go as far
as the United States wanted. Repeatedly, for instance, Washington
made it clear that it believed the secretary-general's military staff could
be enlarged substantially without soliciting Soviet approval.

The second certainty was that preparedness would not be given
serious attention by the diplomats because their predominant concerns
were with the overriding constitutional and financial controversy
stirred by the United Nations Emergency Force (UNEF) and the
United Nations Congo Operation (ONUC). In their minds the
essential questions were how peacekeeping missions could be authorized, controlled, and paid for. Alleviation of preparedness problems
would probably come after agreement on these fundamentals, though
possibly at the same time. Establishing the respective authority of the

Council and the Assembly and the extent of collective financial responsibility for peacekeeping bills took precedence over how to create and sustain a preparedness system to do the peacekeeping jobs that might be agreed on.[4]

After the disposition of the Article 19 affair, it was apparent that the constitutional and financial principles espoused by the Russians and the Americans were going to remain far apart, too far to permit formal agreement. Article 19 also demonstrated, perhaps more unmistakably than any event in recent UN history, that neither superpower's concepts of peacekeeping would prevail at the UN unless the other capitulated. United States officials sum up the effects of this standoff succinctly: "Any common denominator on broad guidelines" for authorizing, financing, and running peacekeeping missions "could only be achieved at a level substantially below the actual practice in current operations."[5] In other words, tacit understandings about peacekeeping are more permissive than explicit consensus ever could be under present circumstances. Ambiguities will have to be tolerated because the price for eliminating them would be too high and might in fact damage rather than bolster peacekeeping capacities. The difference between what the USSR will actually allow peacekeeping institutions to do and what it will *say* they can do is not enormous, but it is large enough to be worth preserving until a more satisfactory solution is found.

One by-product of this impasse over principles has been a reorientation of diplomatic attention toward preparedness. The forum has been the Special Committee on Peacekeeping Operations, created in February 1965 by the General Assembly to find a way out of the Article 19 thicket that had produced the humiliating voteless Assembly the preceding autumn. Made up of thirty-three members with balanced political and geographical identities, it is empowered to explore "the whole question of peacekeeping operations in all their aspects."* The Special Committee is the only setting the great powers have ever used, even though sparingly, for joint discussion of peacekeeping readiness.

---

* GA Res. 2006 (XIX), Feb. 18, 1965. The national composition: six states from Africa, six from Asia, five from Eastern Europe, five from Latin America, five from Western Europe; and Australia, Canada, France, Britain, the USSR, and the United States.

When they finally got around to it, they delivered a worthwhile lesson in the politics of preparedness.

And it is politics. The Military Staff Committee had discovered twenty years earlier that there were no purely military, purely technical dimensions to centralized preparedness for collective security. This has now been emphatically reconfirmed for peacekeeping. Such glimmerings of accommodation and progress as there have been in the Special Committee are the result of hard political bargaining and the willingness of the United States *and* the USSR to settle for less than what they regard as optimal. They have not come about, as some think, because solutions to preparedness problems can somehow be sanitized, stripped of political implications, or made amenable to exclusively pragmatic manipulation. The first preparedness questions addressed by the committee concerned political responsibility, not organization of resources. Mutual compromise on the former paved a way for initial, modest efforts to deal with the latter.

The decisive tactic in the committee's work was to uncouple preparedness from authorization and financing issues, which happened after the 1966 General Assembly. At that session numerous resolutions on peacekeeping were under consideration. The crucial one, drafted by Canada, was a complicated and comprehensive package. It was consciously designed to be conciliatory to the USSR, and Ottawa had gone to some lengths to insert paragraphs perfectly consistent with Soviet views. But to the Russian delegation, these were just so many sops, because whatever the Soviet Union might have judged acceptable in the proposed language was outweighed by the resolution's failure to assert exclusive Security Council control over all peacekeeping matters. For instance, the proposed draft did not exclude the possibility—one doctrinally anathematic to the USSR—that the General Assembly could launch peacekeeping missions if the Security Council were veto-bound. In a committee of the Assembly where majority rule governs, the resolution was adopted and recommended to the plenary over communist negative votes. The Russians, with an assist from the French, then undertook a forceful diplomatic campaign to dissuade the membership from giving the proposal the needed two-thirds vote in the plenary. They succeeded, the draft resolution was deferred into oblivion, and nothing resembling this package has been heard of since.6 The reduction of the package to its component elements has been wrongly interpreted as depoliticizing preparedness. Instead, this more selective approach merely left the diplomats free to consider the technical *and* political aspects of preparedness, detached from the guaranteed controversy of the authorization issue.

The new tack received the Special Committee's approval in May 1967 when its members agreed to examine separately the suggestions already on record relating to "facilities, services, and personnel which Member States might voluntarily provide" for peacekeeping operations.7 One such suggestion had been made several years earlier when the secretary-general independently urged a study of the major preparedness problems involved in using standby forces that member states offer.8 Sweden, Canada, Japan, and others picked up this suggestion again during committee debates in 1966, but it got lost in the larger diplomatic shuffle. When brought up the following year, it became the focal point for preparedness politics. To the negotiators there was vital political significance in who would authorize such a study, who would actually do it, what it would contain, and, in sum, who would be politically responsible for it.

These questions were answered within the framework of a broader debate that had been going on for a number of years and that goes to the heart of Soviet and American positions on peacekeeping and preparedness. Ostensibly they both argue on bureaucratic and legal grounds; in reality they are interested in the locus of political control over the UN's international security policies.*

The main propositions for this debate in a preparedness context had been laid out in 1964 by the Soviet Union as part of its negotiating strategy during the Article 19 crisis. By the end of that year the USSR and a few Eastern European allies had outlined the view they were to explain more fully during the late 1960s. Its essence was that all preparedness activities be brought under the full and exclusive control of

* The positions and arguments of both sides are examined more fully on pp. 220 ff.

the Security Council. This had long been the Russians' position on all use of military personnel by the UN, for they say there is no constitutional difference whatever between the Council's jurisdiction in peacekeeping and in collective enforcement. What was new and apparently unexpected was the proposal that the Military Staff Committee be regenerated and Article 43 agreements be negotiated as soon as possible.[9] In part this move can and probably ought to be read as an attempt to counteract the then-growing tendency to work for a preparedness system outside the UN, beyond the orbit of direct Soviet control. So interpreted, the move was a reaction against thinking widely supported in the West and in many supplier states, and manifested most clearly in the activist ideas of Lester Pearson. Czechoslovakia implied this causal connection quite clearly in late 1964.[10]

Communist states and important noncommunist ones seem to be willing to consider the Soviet formulation, particularly as refined in 1967,[11] as potentially applicable to peacekeeping preparedness. They see special significance in Soviet exclusion of great-power military forces from any participation in the revised Article 43 system—a step that by definition would eliminate most possibilities for using the system for collective coercion as intended in 1945. The United States does not agree. Preparedness for peacekeeping and preparedness for Chapter VII enforcement, the United States says, are not incompatible, but they must be kept segregated, and if UN members wish to deal with both, separate procedures should be followed. The important political reasoning behind this U.S. position includes the contention that to adapt the Security Council–Article 43 system for peacekeeping would weaken the executive powers of the secretary-general in the peacekeeping sphere and would magnify the collegial responsibility of the Security Council at the expense of the secretariat's independent, unified authority; that it would, in short, upset the present balance of responsibilities between the Council and the secretary-general.

These two interpretations found their way in 1967 into negotiations about how to conduct the study urged by the secretary-general. The Special Committee had barely begun preparedness discussions when war broke out in the Middle East. By the time consideration was resumed in the fall Assembly, the secretary-general had repeated his call for a study, and this new impetus provoked a spate of resolutions almost as complicated as those of the year before.[12] Opinions polarized in predictable directions, each with its share of supporters and slight variations. The United States insisted that the secretary-general be fully responsible for the study, while a Russian counterproposal equally firmly insisted on the Military Staff Committee. Some, including the Scandinavians, cautioned against forcing the issue, and in the end both superpowers gave in a little by approving a plenary resolution that merely said a preparedness study "would be appropriate" for someone to undertake.[13]

In effect, details were left to the Special Committee to work out on the basis of understandings arrived at privately as well as those voiced during the Assembly debate. To begin with, a very thin line was drawn between what the members would agree on and what they would agree to disagree on. Oddly enough, they disagreed about the very purpose of the study, but their respective interpretations were mutually tolerated. The Russians needed to explain their compromise acceptance of a study by someone other than the Military Staff Committee. "Strictly speaking," they said, "all studies" should be done by the Security Council with the assistance of the Military Staff Committee. Therefore, and in this the French concurred, the Special Committee's study ought really to be thought of as "preliminary," because its "ultimate objective" would be to enlighten the Military Staff Committee and the Council.[14] The American delegation, of course, went on record as unable to accept any conclusions other than that the committee's mandate was "clearly to improve practical preparations for consent-type peacekeeping" and that the Military Staff Committee and the Security Council had altogether different purviews.[15]

Having done this posturing, having set out their "theologies," as one committee member said, the protagonists then agreed to carry out the study in a small working group composed of the four great powers plus Canada, Czechoslovakia, Egypt, and Mexico. The group confined the first stage of its work to an examination of observer missions authorized by the Security Council.[16] Factual materials were supplied by the secretariat, although the Americans and the Russians placed different interpretations on the secretariat's precise relation to the study. The United States tried to give the secretariat an enlarged substantive role while the Soviet Union sought to restrict it, even though it was obvious to everyone that the secretariat was the only source, anywhere, for the needed information. The Russians tried to prevent the United States from exploiting this point, but American representatives capitalized on opportunities to refer to "the observer study prepared by the Secretary General."[17] As far as the Soviet Union was concerned, he merely provided supplementary material and no analysis, because the Special Committee could "not transfer its functions to the Secretariat in any way."[18] The U.S. version was in fact fairly close to the truth. The diplomats exercised uncontested authority to review the report and ask for revisions. At the disposal of the working group also were papers solicited by the parent committee from countries that had established standby forces. These national communications, or rather the procedure by which they were delivered, constituted a tactical victory for the sponsors of the idea. For years the secretary-general had felt that he could not request such statements without express authority, so Canada in 1966 unilaterally and informally distributed a paper describing the training and organization of its standby units.[19] Although the paper was circulated rather widely, including to communist states that asked for it, no other standby followed Canada's example, and a formal proposal that they do so was defeated along with the other provisions of the Canadian resolution at the 1966 Assembly.[20]

  The first phase of this study was still in progress in early 1970.[21] It is expected to contain agreed, overall guidelines for preparing and conducting future UN observer missions and to present, through the information compiled by the secretariat, a composite historical picture of UN observation experiences. There are indications that a second phase of the study might similarly cover the bigger peacekeeping operations involving organized contingents such as the United Nations Force in Cyprus (UNFICYP). The United States not only strongly advocates this but also has tried to make it palatable to the Soviet Union by suggesting that only missions authorized by the Security Council would be surveyed initially.[22] But obstacles remain. Although the USSR has no serious qualms about the actual conduct and results of the Cyprus operation, it does have reservations in principle about the intrastate variety of peacekeeping; and the other major operation authorized by the Council, the Congo force, of course precipitated one of the Soviet Union's most bitter anti-UN campaigns. It was perhaps with this in mind that the Czechoslovakian delegation cautioned: "The importance of that first step forward should not be exaggerated, for there probably would be further differences of view in the future, especially in connection with discussions of other possible models" of peacekeeping to be studied.[23]

The most instructive feature of this initial plunge into concerted preparedness diplomacy is not the raw data generated or the modicum of Soviet and American good-faith bargaining that was in evidence; rather it is the demonstration, in microcosm, of the irrepressible influence of political values on seemingly unpolitical preparedness matters. This need not be permanent, but it is inescapable in the short run so long as there is no way to make progress without superpower consensus. From this viewpoint, one of the most revealing themes in the Special Committee was the tendency of the Russians, their allies, and the French to tie preparedness to political arguments rather than consider it strictly "technical" and "practical." When the United States and others demurred, claiming that preparedness steps need not prejudice political principles, the Russians said that these were "pious words" and that preparedness was not "an abstract scheme that would be equally appropriate for operations that were in accordance with the Charter and for those which were contrary to it."[24] Preparedness, in other words, was only as politically legitimate as the brand of peace-keeping for which it was intended. The attempt to depoliticize nego-tiating items is a sometimes useful tactic that permits a measure of flexibility: it may be easier to shift position on supposedly technical matters than on political ones. Yet the somewhat disingenuous prod-dings of the United States were most unlikely to be received favorably —at least no more favorably than if roles had been reversed and the Soviet Union had been requesting the United States to deal, under the Military Staff Committee, with the technical and practical aspects of preparedness only and to ignore the political ramifications of doing so.

The Thirty-eighth Floor and the Administrators

Knowing what diplomatic representatives purport to believe about preparedness is only moderately difficult. Identifying the more straightforward demands of the technicians is still easier. By comparison, the reasoning of the secretariat strikes many as opaque, private, and somewhat inconsistent over time.

This was Hammarskjöld speaking in 1958: "The UN Secretariat has by now had extensive experience in establishing and maintaining UN operations involving military personnel and, without improvising or augmenting unduly, can quickly provide operations of that nature" with the needed support personnel, services, and equipment.[25]

The year 1960 found him saying it is "a considerable weakness that the Secretariat has not in its ranks a highly qualified military expertise which is able, on a current basis, to maintain a state of preparedness" for peacekeeping chores. This "strengthening of the Secretariat on the military side" would help the UN itself "to have a state of preparedness with considerable flexibility and in the hands of a qualified staff which quickly and smoothly can adjust their plans to new situations and assist the Secretary General in the crucially important first stages" of a peacekeeping operation.[26]

U Thant in 1967: "It is often said, for example, that lack of military staff and lack of planning in the Secretariat are an important source of weakness." This assertion is "based on a misleading equation of United Nations peacekeeping operations—which are only semi-military in their functioning—with normal national military operations." It is "hard to see how a United Nations military staff, even if authorized by the competent organs, could justify its existence and actually improve very much the quality either of existing operations or of hypothetical future ones."[27]

A few years earlier, in 1964, a ranking member of the secretariat, speaking unofficially, sounded this alarm: "improvised" and "shoestring" peacekeeping management "is a feature in the Secretariat's work which worries me far more than any other, for, sooner or later, we will have a disaster which will be due to inadequate means, inadequate planning, inadequate preparations, and then we shall be in very serious trouble."[28]

This zigzagging has closely followed shifts in circumstances, political climates, and secretariat perceptions. The first Hammarskjöld pronouncement was made in the afterglow of relative successes in the Middle East; the second showed the strain of the unanticipated, staggering loads on the secretariat at the beginning of ONUC. The 1964 unofficial remarks reflect the frustrations of a bureaucracy overextended to a near-impossible degree. And finally, Thant's comment embodies the defensive, negative self-conception of a contemporary secretariat that sees itself spreadeagled by opposing pulls of the great powers. Hammarskjöld at the time of his 1960 statement was prepared to override Soviet opposition to preparedness measures he was contemplating, on the probably correct assumption that the membership would back him. But the Soviet vendetta after the summer of 1960, the accession of a mutually acceptable secretary-general, basic changes in membership and balance of influence within the UN, the constitutional crisis of 1964 and 1965—all these compelled new premises that would make preparedness dependent on a great-power consensus that was slim indeed. The result during the 1960s was a secretariat more passive, more uncertain, and more cautious in preparedness matters than nearly all peacekeeping supporters wished it to be or thought it needed to be.

The secretariat's position points up the inescapable dilemma confronting the architects of centralized preparedness: to find a way of marrying institutions identified with Soviet mistrust to new political approaches aimed at easing this same mistrust. The clouds of Soviet suspicion hang heaviest over the secretariat, and while most proponents of effective peacekeeping agree that these clouds must be lifted, there is substantial disagreement on how to go about doing this without jeopardizing the future of peacekeeping and diluting those international executive powers the Russians have challenged at every opportunity.

The principal source of Soviet antipathy was the Congo episode, and it quickly became an obsession. It is expressed today with only slightly less acrimony than it was when Patrice Lumumba and Russian maneuvering in central Africa were both checked, partly at the hands of the UN. Histrionics still alternate with calm indictments. Virulent personal attacks on secretariat officials modulate with bland constitutional arguments against secretariat prerogatives. In 1969, a Soviet national high-ranking in the secretariat could breach propriety by publishing an anti-Hammarskjöld article in an American magazine.[29] Two years before, the Soviet ambassador, in the midst of Security Council debate on the Arab-Israeli war, could unleash a gratuitous salvo of personalized criticism at Undersecretary Ralph Bunche, who was a ranking Congo adviser to Hammarskjöld and who has remained, under U Thant, in charge of all peacekeeping affairs. He is one implied target of such Soviet invective as that in the 1967 Assembly directed against the "Congo Club" of "American citizens who were high-placed functionaries" around Hammarskjöld.[30]

Soviet hostility is not a result of Congo policies or Congo personalities only. It is also based on the very structure of the secretary-generalship and the subordinate secretariat departments. In an important peacekeeping position paper in 1967 the Russians warned against secretariat-directed operations, adding pointedly, "quite regardless of the person who holds the office of Secretary General."[31] The organization and practices that had evolved since the late 1940s for the central management of peacekeeping both formally and informally neutralized Soviet influence. Exclusion of Soviet personnel from field missions during the first generation of preparedness operated to similar effect within the secretariat. But not all peacekeeping decision-making arrangements have been designed primarily for this end. Secretaries-general have acquired greater, more concentrated powers also in order to protect their independence from disruptive pressures for collegial direction or effective administrative vetoes, from whatever subdepartment or nationality.

In 1945 an important Soviet-American bargain was struck that gave the top job in the Department of Political and Security Council Affairs to a Russian national. His responsibilities were to include all matters relating to the use of UN armed forces on order of the Security Council. He was to be at the center of UN security policies. It would be extraordinary if more than two of the senior military officers who have served the UN over the years ever knew the name of the Soviet citizen who occupied this post during their stint as UN soldiers. In practice the bureaucratic history of the secretariat as peacekeeper is a lengthy and intricate effort to make sure that this department had little or nothing to do with peacekeeping.

Under three secretaries-general, titles have changed and formal duties have been redrafted, but through it all the isolation of this department has been nearly complete. As UN responsibilities for managing peacekeeping grew, "political affairs came to be regarded by many officials as the closely-held specialty of a small group, chosen personally by the Secretary General without regard to organizational niceties."[32] Usually this coterie was in the executive office of the secretary-general, or on the staffs of the two undersecretaries for special political affairs, both of whom are department heads without portfolio and available for flexible assignment by the secretary-general. Since the twin posts were created by Hammarskjöld early in his tenure, Bunche has always filled one and always been charged with running peacekeeping missions. An intimate, informal three-cornered relation joins the secretary-general and these two subordinates regardless of which of the latter carries the heavier peacekeeping loads at any particular time. Together they have been the executive hub of political-military decision making.

Well-intentioned proposals, now heard regularly from so many quarters, for a "strengthened" or "expanded" staff for the secretary-general conjure up the bitterest of Soviet memories. During the Korean war Lie set up a special section in the executive office to bypass the obstructive Soviet deputy, and ten years later Hammarskjöld achieved the same result during the Congo experience. In preparedness matters, suggestions that special secretariat components be set up to service standby units also remind the Soviet Union of a past event: to monitor the despised Uniting for Peace Resolution's preparedness provisions, Lie added to his executive office the Uniting for Peace Resolution Group, whose management fell to a military officer who was a close adviser and emissary for the secretary-general during the Korean war.

Throughout most of the 1960s the execution of peacekeeping has centered on the office of Undersecretary Bunche, though in recent times the other special undersecretary has given an occasional assist. Of all the professional posts in the United Nations system, something like 8 percent are filled by people engaged in political and security work.[33] Most of these are in the regular departments of the secretariat; they are not assigned to the undersecretaries for special political affairs and are not in any way concerned with peacekeeping. Beyond the peacekeeping duty, the two undersecretaries, with a total professional supporting staff of six (as of 1969 when the sixth was added), are responsible for a range of political, social, economic, and technical activities, as the secretary-general may direct. Three or four out of the six work with Bunche on peacekeeping, none probably on a full-time basis except in periods of crisis.

Until the end of 1968 when the military adviser's post was abolished, a senior officer, Indian Major General Indar Jit Rikhye, was attached directly to the executive office and worked closely with the undersecretary when necessary. The position of military adviser has had a checkered history. For a short time after UNEF was deployed, the executive office retained a general officer and three junior assistants to act as the secretary-general's "consultants." It had been disbanded by 1960 when Rikhye took the post then called Military Adviser for the Congo Operation. Never did his staff number more than four, and that was at the height of ONUC, whose budget then supported the staff.[34] After the launching of the Cyprus mission in which military advice was extremely valuable at headquarters, the staff dwindled abruptly, and so did its relevance. For all practical purposes it ceased to exist except for minor liaison and technical services. Rikhye himself spent less and less time at headquarters. He led a small team of UN observers to the Dominican Republic in early 1965—much as he had done several years earlier in West Irian—and when the India-Pakistan conflict broke out later that year Rikhye, as a citizen of one of the parties, had to keep his distance from the management of the UN observer corps set up to oversee the cease-fire. In 1966 he was off again to take over UNEF, whose chief of staff he had been in the 1950s. During most of the time after 1964 a lone Finnish officer, now a colonel, remained on the thirty-eighth floor as nominal assistant to a roving superior. He is still there, as part of the executive office, though retitled Military Liaison Officer to the Secretary-General.

Seventeen floors below is the administrative nerve center for peace-keeping, the Office of General Services, also headed by an American director ranked as an assistant secretary-general.* General Services is rightly called the housekeeping nucleus of the entire UN; it is responsible for procurement, transportation, communications, security, and other technical matters. Support of peacekeeping forces is for the most part bureaucratically undifferentiated; that is, all the subdepartment units perform other normal functions in addition to servicing peace-keeping missions. (There is only one secretariat official whose title bears the word "peacekeeping"—he is in charge of financial accounts.) Thus, all peacekeeping operations are touched at one time or another by the long-established secretariat channels—personnel, legal, public information, and related management and administration. But despite this diffusion, support responsibilities are concentrated heavily in the Field Operations Service, created by Lie in 1949, now part of General Services, and serving as the locus of day-to-day civilian administrative backup for military peacekeepers.[35]

Mistakenly, it is often thought that Field Service provides peace-keeping missions with all of their international civilian support personnel and that the total number of these may not exceed the 300-man limit imposed in 1949. In practice, the limit is circumvented by what is apparently a simple interpretive device: the ceiling is said to apply only to functions financed out of the regular budget. In 1967, therefore, no Field Service posts in Cyprus and UNEF counted against the limit because these were paid for out of special accounts.[36] When included in the tally of the 260 or so regularly budgeted, these two missions pushed the total number of active Field Service personnel above the 300 mark.[37] The professional civilians in every mission—legal, political, public information, and top administrative officers—are not part of Field Service; they are from elsewhere in the secretariat or are specially recruited. Field Service provides guards, mechanics, drivers, radio operators and technicians, clerks, some secretaries, and general-duty personnel.[38] Below them in the hierarchy are locally recruited staff. Each mission has needed a different general mixture of

---

* Titles used here conform to the top echelon reorganization of the secretariat that became effective in 1968. UN Doc. A/7359, Nov. 27, 1968.

civilian personnel: UNEF in its last years averaged around 100 internationals and ten times this many locals; UNFICYP runs on 50 or so internationals and about twice this many locals; the Middle East UNTSO (United Nations Truce Supervision Organization) observers have recently carried about 125 locals and some 210 internationals. At headquarters, 10 professionals currently take care of managing Field Service activities, peacekeeping and others as well, and they represent about one-sixth of all professionals in the Office of General Services.

In this organization of part-time peacekeepers, preparedness for future missions has never risen above the most rudimentary levels. Over the years in the secretariat, however, some preparedness ideas have been explored and some problems anticipated, though very little has been seen in official print or even gone beyond informal work by those concerned. In particular, many years of experience in centrally supporting UN missions inevitably has had a kind of spillover effect on civilian administrators, resulting in detailed and comprehensive paper-doctrine for virtually all major administrative tasks likely to be encountered. Standing operating procedures (SOPs) line their bookshelves in New York. Volume after volume of rules, regulations, and routine practices address hundreds of problem areas—worldwide procurement of diverse supplies and equipment, office management and civilian personnel guidelines for field headquarters, travel and maintenance arrangements for UN observers or civilians at mission sites, cost-accounting and finance systems, technical instructions for Field Service mechanics, communicators, security officers, and the like. From this general body of knowledge, basic administrative and logistical structures can be built for each new force.

The extent of involvement of civilian administrators in the field varies with the nature of each operation. A chief administrative officer (CAO) is always the top civilian administrator at mission headquarters, and though technically in the chain of military command, he is directly accountable to General Services in New York—a bisection of authority that has caused its share of difficulties. He is the head of the civilian staff, financial watchdog, and final reviewer of procurement policies. Since observer missions generally lack the military logistical appendages needed for supporting battalion-sized units in large operations, the civilians in the smaller missions must provide top-to-bottom logistical and administrative services, using as their bible a thick, all-inclusive Field Administration Handbook. The bigger operations have also produced dissimilar patterns of civilian involvement. Because of the massive British support to UNFICYP, the CAO in Cyprus has little to do beyond managing the money and acquiring minor supply items not available from British bases such as UN clothing and civilian cars. (In 1967 there were only three administrative professionals attached to UNFICYP.) But in the Congo and Egypt, administrative jobs were far more complex and demanding, requiring much larger staffs and more cooperation with military logisticians.

Contacts between secretariat administrators and national suppliers of units or observers is extensive, though with limited purposes. For observation missions nearly all personnel matters are handled on the twenty-first floor; the military adviser's office had only marginal responsibilities. Financial affairs for all types of missions bring suppliers and administrators into especially frequent contact. And because the controller's office handles negotiations for UN reimbursement, it must acquire familiarity with the practices and equipment of participating countries.

Financial constraints and lack of formal authority have prevented UN administrators from building up much reserve potential, either of people or of supplies. The little that has been created is largely a result of decisions made since the mid-1960s. When the Congo operation phased out in 1964, very little of its major equipment was retained by the UN, but in the years immediately afterward, a UN storage facility at Pisa (an aircraft hangar that the Italian government had been providing free of charge since 1957) was used to keep on hand assorted minor items such as clothing and other personal effects, typewriters, projectors, and other nonmilitary equipment. Headquarters of UNTSO in Jerusalem was a much more important reserve establishment. It has long been a training ground for Field Service personnel, and UNTSO civilian and military observer rosters were intentionally overstaffed, sometimes by 5 or 10 percent, to create a source of ready manpower in emergencies. It was used as such on several occasions. Until 1967, Jerusalem headquarters had been stocking and maintaining as well as it could small amounts of communications equipment, much of it backloaded from the recently terminated United Nations India-Pakistan Observation Mission (UNIPOM). Other UNIPOM radios and vehicles were sent to Pisa. In fact this mission's logistical difficulties stimulated the modest stockpiling of recent years. It was not a big operation, yet it was badly mishandled in the early stages. Communications problems were particularly glaring. United Nations radios initially brought down from nearby Kashmir were ill suited to UNIPOM conditions. New equipment, relatively unsophisticated Motorolas, had to be manufactured on an emergency schedule. Workable intramission communications were not available until a month after the operation began, and radio links between UNIPOM headquarters and all observer teams were not complete for nearly two months. After the Middle East war in 1967, radio stocks in Jerusalem were transferred to Pisa, as was some UNEF equipment, and the Pisa depot first began showing up in UN budget presentations after 1969. "Limited" and "minimum" reserves of radios, vehicles, and other equipment valued at only $1,000,000 is said to be stockpiled, and the depot is to backstop operations in the Middle East and Kashmir.[39]

Advance preparedness within the small office of the military adviser was never more than primitive, for it functioned mostly as a central servicing outfit for launching and maintaining operations.[40] No medium- and long-term planning was ever systematically undertaken, and even the routine services were limited by the size of the staff to top priority items. The office served more as a central clearinghouse than as a military-executive staff. It was, as a former UN commander has observed, rather like a military establishment without a general staff or a defense ministry, and with consequently greater burdens of detailed staff work at the field headquarters level.[41]

When there was time, when operations were not being set up or in a critical phase, the military adviser's office engaged in unofficial preparedness activities. The quiet work in the early sixties that helped design Scandinavian programs and channeled advice to other standbys is an important example. Later efforts were undertaken by the military adviser to draw upon his office's experience and to put in writing some of the most critically needed SOPs, guidelines, and handbooks, none of them with official status. Like the administrative guidelines, these were intended to produce general doctrine that would reduce improvisation where possible and be adaptable to military aspects of new missions, such as personnel, logistics, and air transport requirements. These were drafted over a period of several years with the advice of interested peacekeepers, and they were circulated to relevant sections of the secretariat. Completed before the adviser's post was terminated in 1968, they have never been released or given a UN imprimatur.

Neither the undersecretary's nor the military adviser's office was ever able to build up comprehensive dossiers on the organization, equipment, and readiness of standby countries. The information on file almost certainly is no more detailed, or useful for planning purposes, than the sketchy national data in the public domain. On the whole, the top political echelon of the secretariat continues to maintain the official aloofness toward standby programs that U Thant in 1964 said was necessary "in the absence of any authorizing action" by a political body. He had "welcomed the offers" from standbys but was "in no position to do much more" than this.[42] Usually he has responded with a short letter of acceptance to the standby government. The offer is treated as unilateral and conditional, and the secretary-general restates his own lack of formal authorization, making it understood that because the precise composition of every mission cannot be determined in advance, there is no assurance that offered units will be used.[43] Staff assistants in the military adviser's office once experimented briefly on paper with mobilization schemes and with what military planning jargon calls brick systems for deploying progressively larger and more complex UN forces, but these have had little to do with the actual standby offers received or with their size, and in any event were too abstract to be of much practical value.

Only once, shortly before Hammarskjöld's death, has the secretariat seriously considered joint in-service training for both civilian and military peacekeepers. After the Congo operation the need for such a program seemed obvious. The military adviser's office and General Services drew up detailed plans for a UN-sponsored course of instruction. Hammarskjöld was fully briefed on the proposal and decided to finance its initial cost of about $80,000 out of the Congo budget. His approval for going ahead with the program came just before he was killed and the idea has remained submerged since. It was to be an eight-week course for ten civilians and ten military officers, embracing study at the secretariat as well as field work for two weeks at either ONUC or UNEF. These men would then hold themselves on UN standby for a specified period of time. The basic concept was not new inside the secretariat. As long before as 1950, the Field Service budget programmed funds for in-service technical training, basic and advanced, which included instruction at field missions.[44]

Like the military staff, the political hierarchy at the secretariat has devoted most of its time to managing real peacekeeping missions rather than preparing for those yet to be. Daily affairs soak up most of the energies of the undersecretary for special political affairs and his minuscule staff: advice to the secretary-general, diplomatic contacts with national representatives at the UN, steady flows of cables, instructions, and reports to and from field headquarters, responses to new crises at mission sites, and coping with the countless routine details of central policy making and implementation. But if the thirty-eighth floor's preparedness achievements are inconsequential, its professed attitudes on the subject are not, for they set the tone of the UN approach to preparedness. Until not very long ago its views were masked by official silence and by the claimed lack of authority. This stance was maintained over the years despite responsible and not-so-responsible criticisms of the secretariat's underpreparedness and apparent unconcern about the consequences. Then on top of this came the collapse of UNEF, an event that produced wholesale skepticism about the soundness of the peacekeeping idea and the adequacy of its institutions. In the course of answering these doubts the secretariat chose also to unburden itself of some fundamental convictions about preparedness.

What came out was negative in the extreme, surprising even those secretariat-watchers conditioned to caution on the part of the thirty-eighth floor. Not only did the secretariat discount the utility of some of the reforms often urged upon it, it also conveyed the generally resigned tone typified by this paragraph from U Thant's annual report:

> The Secretariat at the present time has neither the authorization nor the budget to engage in widespread planning, staff work, recruitment or training activities such as are common to national military establishments; nor, indeed, in present circumstances would such activity have much practical utility. A plan for the training of officers for United Nations peacekeeping duties was elaborated in detail some years ago, but has never been implemented for lack of authorization and finance.[45]

This is curiously elliptical language. The reference, presumably, is to Hammarskjöld's training plan, but if it had practical value then, why not now? Moreover, authorization and financing for it were never explicitly sought from any political organ, at least so far as the public record shows, and decisions since then against reviving the plan have reportedly been made exclusively inside the secretariat. To say that staffing and planning would do no good under present circumstances begs the real question. Of course, prevailing conditions are restrictive. Acknowledging this is one thing, and probably correct as far as it goes. But it is quite another thing to conclude—as does companion language in the same statement (see page 198 above)—that such measures would have little value even for "hypothetical future" operations. This proposition reflects a tendency evident in the secretariat to portray ad hoc, improvised procedures as unchangeable facts of life for the UN and to insist that it is only within the power of national military establishments to undertake adequate planning measures.

Exceptional motives suggest themselves as explanations for this attitude on the part of the secretariat. It may have wanted to shift the blame for substandard preparedness onto the impasse reached by political organs, onto the diplomats whose disagreements were really decisive. Too, this was a way of answering the implied criticisms of secretariat underpreparedness in Special Committee debates, where frequent calls were heard for enlarged and more efficient staffing on the thirty-eighth floor. The secretariat also seemed to be saying, and with solid justification, that its own longer-range interests would not be served if it were to take preparedness initiatives that went much beyond great power political tolerances, which were all too measurable by Soviet and French reactions to the 1966 Canadian resolution. Before their last-minute campaign to defeat the proposal in the Assembly, there were some indications that the secretary-general had been considering strengthening his military staff and giving it permanent status. One justification for this would have been the short paragraph of the draft resolution inviting member states to give the UN information on national units and facilities that could be used in peacekeeping missions. A small staff group at headquarters could have been detailed to process and analyze these data, but the fate of the resolution suggested that a unilateral step of this sort by the secretary-general would have encountered prohibitive resistance. The 1966 debacle left the military adviser's office with a most unpromising future, and the eventual decision to scrap it altogether was not difficult to forecast.[46]

The Pragmatists and Problem Solvers

This category contains diverse types of people. Peacekeeping practitioners, outside experts, generalists and specialists, military men and civilians—all have applied their knowledge to what they consider the outstanding preparedness problems. All have tried to chip away at least some of the excess costs, the frequent operational and administrative inefficiencies, the endless logistical difficulties, and the confusions that invariably occur within multinational field formations thrown together under emergency conditions. To say that technicians concentrate their efforts on making peacekeepers perform more effectively is not to suggest that they are necessarily insensitive to political implications, though some are. It is only to distinguish their priorities from those held by diplomats and international executives.

The technicians have, as they must, different preoccupations, biases, and outlooks. It is a telling commentary on their predicament that they find themselves talking mainly to each other, largely in the political vacuum created by the diplomatic impasse over peacekeeping. Even more revealing is that the exasperated problem-solvers repeat the same things again and again. This is less because the vacuum induces a stale inbreeding of ideas than because many of their solutions are sensible and constructive, no less so in frequent repetition. Their collective output is buried in national archives, voluminous conference records, task force recommendations, and countless position papers, mostly products of the 1960s.

Midway in the decade a peacekeeping conference generated a profusion of technical papers and dialogue. Expectedly, this outpouring, mainly in 1964-65, coincided exactly with the increase in interest among standbys and with the strong though short-lived appeal of getting around the stalemate inside the UN by concerting preparedness efforts outside.

The most useful exercise technically was the Ottawa meeting in 1964. It stands as the only real "working conference" ever to be convened on preparedness. As such it had the necessary paraphernalia of hard effort—study groups with tightly defined subject assignments, well-ordered and precise agendas for each group, detailed background papers for every item discussed, definite guidelines for channeling discussion, and so on. Though the overall results would have been more satisfactory with fewer delegations, more time, and a better distribution of expertise, the documentation is a one-of-a-kind compilation of raw materials on technical problems and possible remedies, and it represents enormous efforts by the Canadian Department of National Defence to distill its own vast experience and commit it to paper.[47]

Numerous other conferences have been oriented to less thoroughly technical concerns. Their formats were designed for general unofficial exchanges of information and recommendations on political and military issues, rather than for staff-level problem solving. Such meetings have been convened in Scandinavia, Britain, Canada, and the United States; many have drawn multinational civilian and military attendance, though all with the heaviest concentration from the host country or the region involved.[48] In addition to individual papers presented at various conferences, private studies have been conducted by experts on the myriad technical problems facing peacekeepers.[49] Some experienced UN military officers have prepared exceptionally useful reports on their service, a few written for publication in professional or specialized journals. Technical recommendations also have been submitted to the Committee of Thirty-three by Canada, the

United States, and the United Kingdom.[50] And finally, a few of the more prominent scholarly "grand designs" for organizing UN peacekeeping resources have combined political analysis with technical suggestions for anticipating, training, and supporting field operations.[51]

There has been a single, unsuccessful attempt to institutionalize technical preparedness cooperation internationally on a private basis, under no official, national umbrella. Lester Pearson had hoped to achieve this same result intergovernmentally outside the UN, but with continuity and regular machinery for nations interested in preparedness—not just a study group here, a conference there, and a book or article somewhere else. To provide an alternative to this lack of coherence, the World Veterans Federation, encouraged by an endorsement from U Thant, established in 1966 the International Information Center on Peace-Keeping Operations (IPKO). Operating out of Paris, staffed by two professionals, financed mostly by private donations, IPKO aimed at exploring prospects for "cooperative action on the nongovernmental level on the technical aspects of these operations which might be considered relatively non-controversial." As a start in providing its services IPKO was "to collect documentation, issue publications, undertake and encourage research and liaison, and possibly hold one or more meetings."[52] The organization folded in less than two years, after having initiated modest information and research activities. Extensive IPKO canvassing turned up only meager interest either in using this kind of informal cooperative mechanism or in giving it adequate political backing, documents, advice, and money (only Canada and Norway contributed). The fatal flaw was that as a private channel IPKO depended ultimately on these uninterested governments in vital ways. The experiment showed once again the futility, so evident elsewhere, of trying to depoliticize such an intensely political subject. The same pressures that have militated against intergovernmental preparedness cooperation undermined IPKO's appeal. This private venture failed, in short, because preparedness is not essentially a private matter.

The entire spectrum of technical activity since 1956 warrants several observations of a general nature. The secretariat has been marginal to the process. The military adviser attended two of the major international conferences and a deputy to Undersecretary Bunche attended another. That is about all. Surprisingly enough, the branch of the secretariat closest to technical and administrative affairs, General Services, does not seem to have had any contact whatever with these outside programs. Nor is there any partnership with existing training. The Nordic staff course assigns an important amount of time to non-military aspects of UN staff work, yet UN civilian administrators, who in practice are responsible for many of these very aspects, have had no contact with the curriculum. This mutual isolation, however caused, merely serves to exaggerate the built-in differences in viewpoint.

Far too many of the technical blueprints and suggestions evoke a nagging sense of abstractness, rather like ticking off prescriptions from an elementary textbook on military practice and organization. Missing are standards of performance applicable specifically to the UN, to its sources of military wherewithal, to its institutional constraints, to its peculiar kind of multinationality. Needed is sensitivity to the experiences of other heterogeneous military planning systems in modern times. To use a mundane example, even the most sophisticated military alliances have not been able to reach the level of equipment standardization or commonality of procedures that is often blithely demanded of the UN. It is equally shortsighted to err in the opposite direction, as the secretariat has been prone to do, by saying that because the UN is not equivalent to a national military establishment no preplanning of any importance is possible. The readiness system of the UN cannot be as foolproof as many technicians would wish, nor as haphazard and helpless as the secretariat has recently said it has to be.

Close technical cooperation across national boundaries will never be easy to bring about even with optimum political consensus in the UN. The problems themselves are often inherently stubborn, and before some of them can be solved, the governments involved will have to overcome a deep reluctance to expose their shortcomings to their colleagues from other peacekeeping countries. The multilateral preparedness contacts to date, despite their limited horizons, have revealed considerable national self-protectiveness, jealousy, and the prideful pretension that will crop up in the future—especially if more and more diverse military establishments take part in preparedness programs. Matters of comparative military preparedness, know-how, or efficiency, and particularly the prospect of invidious comparisons, frequently touch sensitive nerve endings even among the friendliest states. The situation brings to mind an uppish reply once made to a pollster who had queried his interviewee on the desirable conduct of international cooperation: "The other countries should cooperate with us. We shouldn't cooperate with them."

Three Generations of Preparedness

To look back over the unfolding of the several major perspectives on preparedness and of the various national readiness programs is to be struck as much by the distinctions among the generational cycles through which UN preparedness has passed as by their similarities. Progression from one generation to another has been marked by discontinuities no less than by continuities, by abrupt, sharp turns as well as by slight shifts in tempo or direction. A synoptic comparison of these periods—1945 to 1955, 1956 to about 1965, and the mid-1960s to the present—conveys their main accents and significance.

It is the first generation that probably deserves to be set apart most clearly from the others, for its remoteness was one of both content and tone. The failure of the United Nations to create preparedness institutions, either for collective enforcement or for consensual peace-keeping purposes, reflected the immobilism of the organization during the severest years of the cold war, when it could neither mitigate nor escape the divisive effects of that confrontation. This was a generation dominated, as no later one was, by a preoccupation with collective security, yet there was never a consensus to sustain this preoccupation: the giants were deadlocked in the Military Staff Committee; the American proponents of the move to create sanctions capabilities that could operate in spite of Soviet wishes to the contrary demonstrated their own vacillation by reneging on the military provisions of the Uniting for Peace Resolution; and the members of the UN who had seen at the outset of the Korean experience a vindication of the organization and of the collective security idea became thoroughly disillusioned with the role, particularly after China's intervention made it clear that collective security could slide the UN into conflict with great powers.

This was also the only generation without a peacekeeping constituency at the UN, at least not an adequate, consistent one, that could serve as a foundation for preparedness diplomacy and institutions. Persistent disagreement among the Big Five over the establishment of military capabilities for collective sanctions limited prospects for effective peacekeeping institutions, as seen in the Soviet Union's insistence that all efforts to bolster nonsanctions capabilities were really attempts to establish, through the back door, the kinds of military forces on which the Military Staff Committee had recently been unable to agree. Moreover, the basic concept of peacekeeping had not yet been articulated as a rallying cry for an organizational commitment by UN members. Nor did the small-scale observer missions, mostly of very restricted composition, leave much incentive for member governments to undertake any serious self-examination of their potential as peacekeepers. Indeed, in an organization saturated by the bipolar rhetoric of the external environment, the likelihood of a regular UN vocation as an intermediary appeared slim. The first secretary-general's preparedness diplomacy showed all the effects of having been carried out without this peacekeeping constituency. His ambitious proposal for a UN Guard drew support from no quarter, not from medium-sized and small powers with a variety of reservations, not from the predictably hostile Soviet Union, and not even from the United States.

This first generation, furthermore, is the only one about which it can be said that UN-Soviet relations were carried on in a state of fundamental antagonism, despite some isolated ambivalence in Soviet behavior in the organization. Besides the structural disadvantages the Russians experienced as the parliamentary and political minority, Moscow was progressively embittered by a succession of specific events during this generation. On a number of occasions Western powers had succeeded in excluding Soviet participants from UN field missions and in neutralizing Soviet vetoes by transferring certain issues to the Assembly. As early as 1947 an attempt was made to institutionalize procedures for regularly escaping the Soviet veto. This was the so-called Little Assembly, set up under a Soviet boycott as an alternate forum to the Council; although it had little practical significance, it did in some ways foreshadow the Uniting for Peace move. For the Russians and the UN, the low points came during and just after 1949–50. A renegade Yugoslavia was elected to replace the Ukraine as the communist nonpermanent member of the Security Council. The new government of mainland China was excluded from the organization, although Lie, to the strong displeasure of Washington, vigorously advocated its inclusion. The Korean action was voted through while the USSR was absent from the Council and the much-derided Uniting for Peace Resolution was approved by the Assembly over communist opposition. The Assembly also extended, illegally in the Soviet view, the term of the secretary-general, whose reappointment was being strenuously opposed by Moscow for his part in the Korean episode; and Lie subsequently proceeded to praise the Uniting for Peace Resolution rather lavishly and to set up within his own staff a specially constituted section to help implement its military preparedness provisions.

In this first generation, as again in later ones, major preparedness proposals were frequently linked to the particular diplomatic circumstances that motivated their sponsorship, colored reactions to them, or affected their prospects for success or failure. A representative list might begin with Lie's Guard initiative, which became entangled, especially in Russian arguments, with the current situation in Palestine. Similarly, the Uniting for Peace Resolution needs to be understood not only in terms of the immediate needs of the Korean operation, but also, and this is more important, in terms of the broader changes in U.S. worldwide containment strategy that coincided with its origin. North Korea's crossing of the 38th parallel had profound repercussions on the Truman administration's thinking about the defense needs for Europe. During the same months that Washington was drafting and pressing the resolution, and on the assumption that communist aggressive designs might well not remain confined to Asia, the United States was making far-reaching decisions to revamp the structure of the NATO alliance: by committing substantial numbers of American troops to the Continent, by creating an integrated military command there, by encouraging Europeans to beef up their own contributions, and by taking the first steps that eventually would lead to a rearmed Germany within the alliance. Some of the few states that did respond positively to the resolution's standby provisions assigned their forces doubly—that is, either to the UN or to the bolstered NATO—and Washington later tried to persuade Latin American allies to provide, under the terms of the resolution, troops for the Korean war. Moscow, knowing that any military capabilities put together under the resolution's preparedness paragraphs would be controlled by a UN majority usually responsive to the United States, accordingly regarded the so-called Acheson Plan as negatively as it viewed all Western attempts to erect military alliances as counters to Soviet power.[53]

The list of subsequent associations acquired by preparedness proposals would also include, during the second generation, President Eisenhower's proposal for a UN standby force, which encountered resistance partly because of its connection with the United States' intervention in Lebanon. And it would include, at the juncture between the second and third generations, Lester Pearson's major effort to encourage creation of preparedness institutions outside formal UN channels and the Soviet Union's revised Article 43 proposals; both of these were closely tied to the Article 19 crisis, which contributed to the failure of the Canadian initiative and which seems to have triggered the Soviet one.

Two events in 1953—the death of Stalin and the accession of Dag Hammarskjöld to the secretary-generalship—formed the background for the years of transition into the second generation of peacekeeping preparedness. The new Soviet leadership combined greater flexibility in external policies with occasional glimmers of comparative amiability, and the effect was soon felt at the UN. The cold war was to be waged, if not with duller weapons, at least in a somewhat softer style, a strategy soon to be embodied in the "peaceful coexistence" slogan. For his part, the new secretary-general was to guide and adapt the organization into a peacekeeping role appropriate to the changing and more complex international milieu of the mid-1950s. United Nations membership was beginning a phenomenal expansion that would last a decade, the system of mutual deterrence between the superpowers began to stabilize, and it was becoming apparent that workable conceptions of how the UN fitted into this pattern of change would copy neither the rigid canons of the early cold war nor the rosy expectations of San Francisco.

Soviet foreign policy reappraisals between 1953 and the end of 1955 bore directly as well as indirectly on Moscow's behavior and attitudes toward the UN.[54] The USSR joined with the other permanent members of the Council in agreeing on Hammarskjöld as a compromise candidate for the top UN post, a step now cited as a beginning in the Soviet "thaw," and Moscow seemed satisfied that the new secretary-general's actions during his first years in office showed an attempt to avoid the partisan stances on East-West issues that his predecessor had adopted. The scrapping of antiquated Soviet theories of a "two-camp" world—a step that had been foreshadowed even in the final years of Stalin's rule—prompted Moscow to court the support and favor of leading Third World states and simultaneously to exploit more aggressively the anticolonialist sentiments and issues in UN political bodies. Some receptivity toward multilateral disarmament negotiations being conducted within the UN was also evident. Furthermore, in 1955 both superpowers reversed their policies of "competitive exclusion" that barred admission of prospective UN members favored by the other side, and the sixteen-member package deal was sealed late that year.

Individual states that were eventually to become closely identified with UN peacekeeping or preparedness were affected by shifts in Soviet external policies during these same years. More conciliatory relations were established with Finland, Yugoslavia, and India. Moscow's decision to sign the Austrian State Treaty without an accompanying German settlement paved the way for full restoration of Austrian sovereignty, for withdrawal of all Allied occupation troops from the country, and for the entry of Austria—plus two other subsequent peacekeepers, Ireland and Finland—into the UN as part of the 1955 package. Of the various countries whose bilateral relations with the USSR took a markedly favorable turn during these years, several were shortly to be major participants in UNEF, notably India, Yugoslavia, and Finland. There is no evidence for any direct causal connection here, but it does not seem unreasonable to believe that this factor may have contributed to the selection of these countries as participants and may have been one of the ingredients, though admittedly a lesser one, that added to the Soviet Union's continuing willingness to acquiesce in this peacekeeping operation, whose establishment Moscow did not oppose (it abstained on the enabling resolution in the Assembly) and whose political purposes were not inconsistent with Moscow's own preferences and interests. However this aspect of bilateral relations entered the general peacekeeping picture, it most definitely has been a factor in the decision of states like Finland and Austria to engage themselves in a peacekeeping career. Finland's case is particularly illustrative. The government's interest in peacekeeping in the second half of the 1950s was unmistakably spurred by the recent improvement in relations with its huge neighbor, as well as by the definite conversion of the UN by 1956 from collective sanctions concerns to consensual, impartial peacekeeping.[55] Had there been any real prospect of adverse reactions from Moscow, Finland certainly would not have provided a UNEF unit, given Hammarskjöld his first military adviser, or taken part in the observer mission in Lebanon, all within its first three years as a UN member.

The second generation of preparedness was the only one to open with some relatively promising signs. The Military Staff Committee's failure began the first, and the massively demoralizing UN constitutional and financial crisis of 1964–65 ushered in the third. The second generation was in many respects the most active and the one in which the UN's peacekeeping responsibilities were undertaken with the greatest vigor, all three of the major operations having been launched during this decade. It was the generation that saw the clearest development of the peacekeeping concept and the emergence of a constituency behind peacekeeping preparedness. There was some enlargement of features that had made their initial appearance in the first generation, such as the increasing activity of an impartial secretariat. But unlike the earlier generation, the second assumed that no great power could now participate as actively in peacekeeping as the United States and a few other permanent members of the Security

Council had done in the years immediately after the war, or as the great powers of the League era had done.

Among the most instructive differences between the first two preparedness generations are those relating to the preparedness diplomacy of the two secretaries-general with whose names they are associated. At first glance, attention focuses on dramatic similarities: both generations began with a UN chief executive accepted by the superpowers, both ended with a complete and stormy rejection of him by the Soviet Union, and both cases turned largely on issues connected with UN military forces, in Korea and in the Congo. In Lie's case, the breakdown of confidence left his office and the UN enfeebled and ineffective; in Hammarskjöld's, had his death not intervened, the results in all probability would have been the same unless he had relinquished his position. In both cases, even Soviet polemics were at times hauntingly alike: about Lie, "He is unobjective, two-faced, and we will have no truck with him"; about his successor, "We do not, and cannot, place confidence in Mr. Hammarskjold. . . . If he himself cannot muster the courage to resign in, let us say, a chivalrous way, we shall draw the inevitable conclusions from the situation."[56]

From the standpoint of preparedness diplomacy, however, what is more important is the sequence that brought each secretary-general to this terminus. The differences are striking and important, and Hammarskjöld's preparedness generation was a marked departure from Lie's. The latter's early preparedness proposals had had no support from either superpower or from a membership constituency of any kind, and his association with the preparedness aspects of Uniting for Peace came after his relations with the Russians had totally deteriorated. Hammarskjöld, on the other hand, not only had a middle power constituency—and in part helped to solidify it—but also the strong backing, for preparedness, of the United States, and many of his preparedness initiatives came before his confrontation with Moscow. What Hammarskjöld managed to accomplish, and the momentum that he started, was therefore a product of those years when his credit with the Soviet Union still had some value.

Only speculation is possible on just how good the second secretary-general might have thought his prospects were for at least persuading the Soviet Union to tolerate some preparedness steps by the organization. While it is comfortable in retrospect to simply conclude that he had been far too optimistic, at the time the situation may well have seemed less clear. For one thing, there had always been, even in the first generation, a certain ambiguity in the Soviet position on actual peacekeeping operations. While rhetoric in opposition was often strong and while the creation of enduring preparedness institutions was held in routine disfavor, in specific situations "such as the Palestine and the Kashmir cases, there was a degree of Soviet cooperation with the peacekeeping aims of the majority; this included, in some cases, voting with the United States and the majority or, at least, acquiescing in the decisions reached. Soviet tolerance was further tested during this period by the universal practice of excluding Soviet participation in UN bodies sent to the field while other permanent members of the Security Council were not excluded."[57]

This pattern of Soviet tolerance became even more visible in the second half of the 1950s, in the cases of both UNEF and Lebanon, when Hammarskjöld was developing his ideas about preparedness. Even though the Russians did not help pay for these operations, and even though periodic, low-key warnings were issued by them about the growing independence of the office of secretary-general, Hammarskjöld may have felt some confidence that peacekeeping functions were being viewed a bit more sympathetically by Moscow. And he may well have taken notice of the apparent, though unstated, convictions of those countries—again, an example is Finland—that had to be reassured of Soviet attitudes before agreeing to participate as peacekeepers. It is questionable whether Hammarskjöld, given the style and record of his first few years as secretary-general, would have put forward the preparedness proposals that were elaborated in his Summary Study of UNEF if he had anticipated the possibility that they would be received as negatively as they were, a reception that was partly because of the controversy created by the General Assembly's consideration of the Middle East crisis at the time the Study was submitted to it. When the Study was being drafted just after UNEF had been established, Hammarskjöld's "good standing" was widely taken for granted. In 1957 all the permanent members of the Council had recommended him for a second term and the Assembly had reelected him without dissent, the president of that body dubbing him "surely our supreme international civil servant." And the same month found the Soviet delegate himself expressing "appreciation" for Hammarskjöld's "devotion to our Organization" and for the "scope of his activities and endeavors."[58] Hammarskjöld soon began enunciating, in bolder terms than ever before, a broad and activist conception of the secretary-generalship. Along with this he elaborated, also with increased conviction and evident satisfaction that he was not overstepping any critical boundaries, an equally bold concept of the place that peacekeeping could have in the work of the organization. A remarkably strong statement to this effect was delivered in 1959.[59] It does not seem implausible, therefore, to regard his preparedness diplomacy of these years as a by-product of this overall mood of self-confidence. Whether fully justified or not, it certainly was buttressed on occasion by hints of Soviet approbation of his general handling of the job—such as Moscow's 1958 proposal that he participate in a summit conference on Middle East issues under UN auspices—and by the conviction that he enjoyed the strong backing of the UN membership as a whole. This makes less surprising his decision in 1959 to go forward with the preparedness letter to the twenty-three peacekeeping countries despite the recent shelving of the Summary Study by the Assembly.

But even if there had been reason to expect some successes with these preparedness designs before 1960, the Congo experience eroded it almost completely. The remainder of this second preparedness generation was dominated first by the vehement Soviet attacks on the office of secretary-general and on the very structure of the secretariat itself, and second by the growing constitutional and financial crisis that engrossed the membership until mid-decade. Especially in the core group of potential peacekeeping countries interested in preparedness programs, activity on the national level was sustained by the momentum that had been building since the beginning of the generation. But no official UN measures to increase peacekeeping preparedness, except U Thant's cautious call in 1964 for a study of relevant problems, were considered possible in the face of one of the most fundamental confrontations between superpowers in the organization's history, a collision provoked by their opposing views on peacekeeping purposes and institutions. In one sense the final years of this second generation gave explicit confirmation to the failure of the kind of preparedness diplomacy Hammarskjöld had set in motion. The confession of failure was the decision reached by Lester Pearson, who had been associated with Hammarskjöld's preparedness initiatives since 1956, that the only hope of progress was in going outside the formal UN framework in order to place preparedness on a solid footing. Only in the second generation of preparedness was this strategy adopted, paradoxically at a time when it was least likely to succeed.

The transition from the second to the third generation—a transition punctuated by the collapse of the Pearson effort and by the trauma of Article 19—was a reorientation from one prevailing mentality to another. The contrast can be portrayed as between a generation that tried primarily to probe and expand the limits of an ambiguous consensus and one (the present one) that seeks primarily to establish and clarify the area of consensus before recommitting itself to the goal of substantially improved preparedness activities.

The crisis that beset the UN in 1964–65 was therefore both an attitudinal and a chronological divide in the development of preparedness. Preceding it, the peacekeeping constituency and the secretary-general who urged it along were in the center of the stage; following it, they remained in the wings. They were aware, as a result of Article 19 and the reluctance of the 1966 Assembly to take a stand on the peacekeeping package tendered by Canada but strongly resisted by the Russians, that preparedness institutions could not be significantly refined unless both superpowers, as a minimum permissive condition, were recognizably in favor of doing so. No longer is there any serious talk of dealing with these matters outside the UN, beyond the reach of Soviet influence. That Soviet-American negotiations on preparedness issues have been taking place is distinctly characteristic of the third generation. In a symbolic sense at least, this constitutes a kind of reversion to the first generation, the only other time that the great powers together sat around a conference table to discuss the question of creating UN military institutions, though it was then of course in the context of collective security rather than consensual peacekeeping. Much has been written, in the 1960s especially, about the "return to the Security Council as the forum preferred by both super powers for launching peacekeeping operations." The trend has been clear, and its logical implication—that preparedness also depends on superpower consensus —has been accepted in the substance of the recent negotiations in the Committee of Thirty-three.

What ought to be evident from this short survey of the three preparedness generations is that each has been the product of a specific set of factors and their interrelations. To single out any factor from its generational context is to risk distortion. To take one example, it is tempting but probably erroneous to attribute the overall variations among the periods solely to the differences among the three men who have occupied the office of secretary-general. Each has indeed behaved in characteristic ways, each has made individual contributions, each has made his own mistakes. What seems more important, however, is to appreciate that not only did they have dissimilar intellectual orientations and diplomatic manners but also each functioned in a somewhat different United Nations. U Thant's preparedness diplomacy has been undeniably more passive than Hammarskjöld's, but in the second half of the 1950s there had been no Article 19 and no Congo. Hammarskjöld was far more successful than Lie in creating at least the nucleus of a preparedness constituency, but he had the advantages of a more favorably distributed membership after 1955 and of the "demonstration effect" of UNEF.

To know how the components of preparedness have evolved, to have a sense of the forces that have molded them, and to be aware of the diverse perspectives on preparedness are essential for an understanding of how UN preparedness got from 1945 to the present. They are no less essential as background for projections about the future of preparedness diplomacy and institutions.

EIGHT

The Shape of Future Preparedness

T HIS current, third generation of preparedness, marked as it is by diffusion, experimentation, unilateralism, and informality, must pass into a fourth if the United Nations is to be ready for major peacekeeping responsibilities in the next decades. It has not been a wasted generation by any count, and it may well turn out to have been indispensable for an understanding of what needs to be done next, and what can be done. Marginal refinements will not help very much, nor will isolated though reasonable attacks against soft spots in the present system of preparedness. Each of its components must undergo quantum improvements, and the shapers of preparedness must be careful and creative, tough and pliable, all at the same time.

What should the fourth generation be like? Or the fifth? What kind of preparedness ought there to be by, say, the beginning of the 1890s? What has to happen along the way? What, in particular, needs to be learned from the uneven experiences in supplier countries and in New York? Which lessons can be discarded as circumstantial? Which are essential and therefore need to be woven into the fabric of future preparedness?

A Ten-Point Strategy

How to construct another model for future preparedness—for how many men, in what stage of readiness, in how many countries, with how much central military planning, and with what skills and equipment—

is an important question. But it is even more imperative to erect an outer shell, a mosaic of assumptions, propositions, and intuitions that will give perspective and dimension to the model-building, and that above all will give it the relevance so frequently missing. What has to be molded is a strategy for preparedness, one looking both forward and backward, one as conscious of objectives as it is of constraints. Consider, as starters, this decalogue.

1. The United States and the USSR, as the decisive protagonists in preparedness diplomacy, must actively and comprehensively engage each other about items in the first half of the preparedness agenda: those issues underlying the exercise of broad political responsibility for preparedness. Until this happens, significant progress cannot occur. The situation may not get worse; but it will not improve without attention to these fundamental questions. However closely present-day preparedness diplomacy sees itself wedded, or perhaps chained, to ad hoc problem solving—and for the 1960s this probably has been the most reasonable alternative—future generations need not be circumscribed by the tendencies to avoid rather than address the basic questions of political responsibility for preparedness. Without identifiable superpower consensus on these matters, which could be shown either in explicit arrangements or in the more likely implicit understandings, the effective limits of "ad hoc-ery" will be reached all too rapidly. There is no riskless course in such comprehensive engagement, no guarantee that it would be productive. There are only signs that it might. The present standoff—relieved only by painstaking, oblique, and very modest progress in the Special Committee—is frustrating in its uncertainty and minimal in its results. If there is to be broad forward movement, future trade-offs cannot be avoided by either side. Both concepts of peacekeeping must suffer some dilution. The desirable end result in this bargaining, easier to postulate than it will be to negotiate, should be parity of superpower noncontrol over the preparedness system. Like arguments about half-empty or half-full tumblers, this might as easily be called parity of control, and in reality it may be just that. Yet preferably the emphasis ought to be on the superpowers' distance and detachment from the preparedness system rather than on their crude, direct domination of it.

2. If both superpowers are to be encouraged to accept such parity, political responsibility in New York will have to be shared more widely than it presently is. Preparedness, if it is to receive significant Soviet backing, must cease to be the exclusive responsibility of institutional arrangements fashioned historically to exclude all Soviet influence. Foresighted advice written ten years ago about superpower relations at the UN is still eminently sensible in a preparedness context: "It may be that [the United States] should relinquish some of the symbolic manifestations of Western proprietorship of the United Nations, and concede in some measure to [the Soviet] demand for greater assurance that the organization will not act against their will."[1] The paramount implication for preparedness is that the secretary-general's immediate and nondepartmental staff in the executive and the undersecretary's office will have to loosen its hold over such preparedness programs as can be devised with superpower support. Taking this step need not mean the setting in motion of an inexorable process that can only end in a secretary-general divested of his prerogatives in preparedness matters.

3. Relative superpower disengagement requires a concomitant increase of involvement by suppliers and medium-sized or small powers that are potential peacekeepers. The purpose should be not merely to provide them with the proportional voice they deserve in affairs that concern them but also to induce them to act directly as insurers of the adequate preparedness capabilities they strongly favor out of self-interest. These countries ought to become the visible initiators of central preparedness programs. The history of preparedness diplomacy can be recorded as an unvarying pattern of action and reaction by the superpowers on virtually every important readiness proposal made at the UN. Everyone else, or nearly so, has been silenced by this bipolar locking of horns. This third force of qualified and interested peacekeepers must now be encouraged to play a continually active role, one that would be made much easier by a measure of superpower disengagement. Ideally, fewer and fewer debates on preparedness items should be transformed into "taking sides" with the Russians or the Americans.

4. Except perhaps for rhetorical purposes, the myth of collective responsibility for preparedness ought to be discarded. Just as there is no longer any purpose served by insisting on mandatory collective assess-

ment as a necessary mode for financing peacekeeping, it is by now accepted, reluctantly but correctly, that keeping the peace is infinitely more important than keeping it collectively, however desirable that may be. The same conclusion applies to preparedness. It is more important to construct an effective preparedness system than to establish one that is broadly collective but less effective. Probably a combination of the two will be impossible. Because the UN will lack resources to invest in preparedness, the alternatives are not simply theoretical ones. Choices will involve where to allocate money, where to channel diplomatic energies, where to solicit participants for readiness schemes, and even who to train and how intensively. To date, some states have borne disproportionate burdens of leadership and material sacrifice. They will have to be willing to continue doing this. Preparedness responsibilities will be selective rather than collective. This nucleus group needs modest expansion, but probably to no more than about two dozen states, which would include many of the currently most active standbys, some Eastern European countries, and a handful of Third World states with sufficient interest and resources. In sum, the core states, the main purveyors of national preparedness, must represent a political, racial, and geographic cross section of UN members. But this is not to say that a majority or even a near-majority of them can or should be involved in preparedness with equal intensity. This is neither possible for the UN to manage nor necessary for significantly increased efficiency. It will be better to design a preparedness system in which the level and quality of national outputs can be representationally envisaged as a series of concentric circles. The enlarged nucleus would be at the center, while other countries associated with the system in progressively lesser ways would be in the outer circles.

5. A predominantly centralized system of preparedness will not and need not come about in the near future. Between the UN and its interested members a division of labor must evolve. Politically acceptable boundaries for such a division must be marked out. Greater centralization of preparedness is desirable and the maturation of UN institutions for this purpose is a worthwhile objective, but less ambitious approaches can also be productive. Nordic ventures since the late 1950s demonstrate that it helps to pursue joint preparedness activities where a coop-

erative habit already exists and where shared political interests have generated at least some common multinational machinery and policies. Perhaps even more important, they show that the Soviet Union is not automatically hostile to all cooperation beyond the formal UN framework. From this viewpoint it is remarkable that the Nordic states have gone some distance, though very cautiously, toward realizing the outside-the-UN interchange so strongly advocated by Lester Pearson in 1964 and so loudly opposed then by the Russians. What is now in order is a thorough exploration of the possibilities for further enlarging the scope and membership of the existing Nordic programs, developing supplemental ones, linking them fruitfully with New York, and structuring them in ways and at times least likely to be politically provocative or to discourage confident participation by target countries. The next generation of preparedness will still be widely decentralized, but it must be better ordered and more purposefully synchronized than its predecessors.

6. So long as preparedness relies mainly on national military establishments for manpower, skills, and equipment, more must be known about what has to happen inside these establishments if UN commitments are to be made and met. This requirement seems self-evident and hardly worth mentioning. But the record suggests otherwise. All too casually, architects of widespread national readiness programs emphasize the whole while ignoring the individual pieces, or they concentrate more on getting countries to make preliminary commitments to preparedness than on determining how or even if they can be fulfilled. Often this translates into calls for immediate declarations of interest, as when Eisenhower in 1960 urged "all" UN members to earmark forces, emphasizing "the time to do it is now—at this session of the General Assembly."[2] This impatience is by no means monopolized by Americans or by official spokesmen, and it shows up in the kind of bandwagon approach that marked the 1963–64 period. The experience of New Zealand and Iran shows how brief the bandwagon ride can be, and the more active Nordic programs underline the complex and serious problems of making substantial readiness program arrangements effective, even in relatively sophisticated military establishments responsible to governments enthusiastically loyal to the UN. The conclusion is not

that efforts to enlist broader participation in preparedness should cease; it is rather that there must also be a fuller appreciation of what is involved at the national level and of how it affects the possible design of the overall system. Repeatedly, expert and logical proposals for mobilizing suppliers, jointly training them, or sustaining their readiness over time are drawn up with scant regard for the differences among the participating national military establishments. It is not just a matter of their size. Within them are found, in bewildering variety, different patterns of internal organization, legal rules and procedures, recruitment, military traditions, inbred habits, distribution of missions, task orientations, degrees of professionalism, and socially based attitudes about military service and its purposes. Whether fifteen or fifty countries are eventually welded into a comprehensive preparedness arrangement, these and many other individual characteristics will have to be taken into account in shaping it and creating expectations about how it should perform.

7. In coming generations, preparedness diplomacy will be required not only to avoid particularly troublesome features of past hassles over legal-constitutional issues, but also to anticipate the eventual complications that almost certainly will accompany the seating of mainland China on the Security Council. A substantially improved preparedness system must be achieved without reviving the confrontation between opposing superpowers on the issue of General Assembly versus Security Council authority to launch peacekeeping operations, a confrontation both sides now seem willing to avoid. To try to take politics out of preparedness is illusory, but it would be wise to keep preparedness separated from this particular constitutional impasse and to shift the diplomatic battleground to its correct locus: the questions where political responsibility for preparedness rests and what division of operational responsibility should exist between the Security Council and the secretary-general in the conduct of operations. Not too long ago it could reasonably be argued that improved preparedness would be acceptable to the Soviet Union only if the United States relinquished its longstanding insistence on residual peacekeeping prerogatives for the Assembly. Now this conclusion needs to be refined, for both superpowers seem to be able to live with the constitutional situation much as it was at the close of the 1960s. Even while they differ over the proper powers of

the secretary-general, both in fact grant the Council rather than the Assembly a predominant peacekeeping responsibility, and both conceivably would prefer to keep the Assembly's options tacitly open for a day when Communist China's veto could immobilize a Security Council otherwise in agreement to act. As for China's potential impact on preparedness activities, a sensible approach in advance of Chinese membership on the Council would be to establish preparedness institutions and practices that implement the strategy identified above as seeking parity of noncontrol over preparedness by *all* permanent members of the Council, the strategy that would result in their relative disengagement from preparedness affairs and would reduce opportunities for their direct influence on the preparedness system. There can be no ironclad guarantees against an obstructionist China, just as there can be none against any permanent member determined to make its weight felt. The objective cannot be to insulate preparedness from the inevitable influence of any of the great powers, but to make the system as resistant as possible to the buffeting of disruptive pressures. At a minimum, therefore, the elements of a comprehensive preparedness system should be in place before China joins the Council. The system should be able to function effectively without constant intervention by the permanent members; the third force of peacekeeping countries should have a role that is both conspicuous and institutionalized; and the secretariat should have a relatively independent part to play in the functioning of the preparedness system.

8. During the next stage in the development of preparedness, it will be essential to provide the United Nations with adequate resources for centralized preparedness planning and for dissemination of relevant specialized information to interested member governments. The system that is established to perform these functions must blend technical competence and political responsiveness; it must be able to draw upon both military and civilian experts, to assess the accumulated preparedness experience of the secretariat, and to enjoy the continuing confidence of supplier states. The system should be geared to the concerns of states already involved in the preparedness system, as well as to those with an interest in participating but lacking sufficient awareness of what this might entail.

9. The clearer the intent to construct a system of preparedness for noncoercive, voluntary peacekeeping, the better the odds favoring gradual emergence of a viable system in the next generation. Collective enforcement schemes modeled on the original Article 43 punitive framework or on the Uniting for Peace Resolution are simply not feasible for the foreseeable future, nor is the omnipotent international army promised in the U.S. draft treaty on general and complete disarmament.[3] The preparedness diplomacy of the past twenty-five years conveys this important lesson: establishment of a preparedness system is more likely to follow rather than precede political understandings concerning its future uses. Preparedness has never been politically viable in the abstract; its apparent purposes must not be unacceptable to the major actors whose voices are decisive and must not be too open-ended or ambiguous to elicit their sustained approval. Peacekeeping is the only faintly visible area of sufficient consensus. The United States, the Soviet Union, the peacekeepers, the would-be suppliers, the secretariat—none show evidence of wanting to set up a preparedness system for purposes beyond peacekeeping. To reach higher might well endanger even this uncertain prospect.

10. It has been said that what peacekeeping needs is not a permanent army but a set of permanent concepts. This remains the essence of a constructive, realistic approach to preparedness institutions in the decades immediately ahead. Improvisation and uncertainty must be reduced, and this will require introducing more permanence and centralization into the system than now exist. But such modest results as these would be light years away from a standing, internationally recruited and controlled peacekeeping force able to be dispatched on the UN's own authority to trouble spots around the world. The fact remains that holders of the power, responsibility, and influence needed to bring such a permanent force into being unreservedly do not want one —and these include the UN and all of its important members. Barring radical shifts in international values and fundamental reordering of the world's political and military capital, peacekeeping chores will be most effectively performed by agents who function more on behalf of the UN than as an integral and permanent component of it.

Reconsidering Article 43 and the Military Staff Committee

Application of this longer-range strategy will require redistribution of political responsibility for preparedness. Unless this occurs, the preparedness system will continue to stagnate and will lack political consensus and the necessary concentration of efforts. The most promising approach for bringing about such redistribution seems to be to link peacekeeping preparedness to a modernized Article 43 framework, which would include the Military Staff Committee. This appears to be the organizational solution that can be made suitable and acceptable, if not optimal, to both superpowers as well as to a wide range of interested and directly affected member states.

Two sets of issues have to be kept in mind when evaluating the relevance, for peacekeeping, of Article 43 and the Military Staff Committee. The first set requires an assessment of recent indications, manifested in the Committee of Thirty-three, that the Soviet Union is willing to consider at least some preparedness arrangements apart from this Charter-based framework. This evidence raises the questions whether, in time, the Soviet Union could be persuaded to relinquish its customary position in effect if not in word, and whether, therefore, it would be wise or necessary to reintroduce Article 43 into a dialogue that seems to be making some progress without it. These inferences are plausible but as yet not very compelling. About all that can be said is that they are probably premature. The outcome of current negotiations is still unknown. There is certainly no sign in the public record that the Soviet Union is disposed to forget about Article 43 or the Military Staff Committee; in fact, as mentioned in the previous chapter, the USSR insisted in principle that the preparedness "study" was being conducted on behalf of the latter body. At the very least—and this leads to the second set of issues—how an Article 43 system might function in a peacekeeping context seems worth exploring. It seems important to examine the objections to it that have been lodged by the United States and others and to inquire whether that system could conceivably be used to produce preparedness arrangements that are desirable and politically responsive. As a matter of diplomatic tactics it may or may not be advisable to reintroduce Article 43 into the debate under present circumstances; but as a matter of substantive analysis, it seems essential to look beyond those circumstances and to assume that the question of Article 43 and the Military Staff Committee will have to be confronted by the superpowers and others as well.

The most significant feature of the Article 43 framework *as far as preparedness negotiations are concerned* is that it is a relatively clean slate devoid of objective content and settled functions. The system and its Charter-based procedures can be structured to mean or to do just about anything that contemporary negotiators wish and can mutually agree on. There is a straightforward explanation for this fluidity: no constitutional guidelines or historical precedents exist for the reactivation, in a peace-keeping context, of Article 43 and its appurtenances—the Military Staff Committee and the agreements. The system's original postwar objectives and methods had nothing to do with the conflict-control mechanisms evolved since then by the UN; nor does there seem to be any historical obstacle to a future linkup between Article 43 and peacekeeping.

There is no magic in Article 43. It is not the key to all the closed doors. Precisely because it has no intrinsic or a priori relevance to peace-keeping, the assertion that it has to be used for peacekeeping preparedness is as arbitrary as the claim that it cannot be used. It is merely a convenient rubric for superpower understandings that would have to be reached whether or not Article 43 had ever been written. It is already part of a treaty, the United Nations Charter, accepted by all UN members. Above all, Article 43 is malleable, and there are good reasons for believing that the United States and the USSR may be able to adapt it to their purposes more easily than they could create entirely new machinery. The very dormancy of Article 43 has distinct advantages. Were it associated with past peacekeeping controversies or were its possible uses confined to avenues utterly unacceptable to one of the superpowers, its reactivation would be most unlikely. As it stands, however, it is flexible enough to allow each to explore the other's intentions and demands, and it is expansive enough to leave room for the reciprocal concessions that undoubtedly will have to be made.

It is not inconsistent to argue that as a matter of general strategy the great powers ought to be relatively disengaged from preparedness and at the same time to posit an Article 43 solution that gives these same powers a key role in the preparedness system. The explanation is that antinomies are built into the situation: on the one hand great powers will trust a solution only if they have what they consider adequate controls over it, while on the other hand the system must be independent enough from the regular intervention of the great powers to have a pulse and momentum of its own. These competing claims cannot be ignored; they must be faced. To argue that a modernized Article 43 provides a credible and desirable solution is to make the judgment that it best straddles the dilemma posed by these dual objectives. An appreciation of the pliability of Article 43 requires, first, some observations on contemporary diplomacy and then some historical comparisons.

THE SOVIET POSITION

Today there exist no suggestions, proposals, or negotiating offers that indicate clearly how anyone wants to use Article 43 for peacekeeping purposes. The 1964–65 proposals by the Soviet Union and its allies—because they were not comprehensive projections but quick tactical reactions to prevailing Western approaches to peacekeeping preparedness—were really little more than vague prescriptions drawn from Charter language, dosed with polemics and occasional sweeteners, and throughout emphatic that participation in UN security operations be open to member states of all political persuasions.

In 1964, Soviet comments took several lines.[4] The Security Council must be solely responsible for all matters concerning the preparation and use of UN military personnel, literally from beginning to end. The secretary-general would have a dependent role. As chief administrative officer of the UN, which is the way he is described in the Charter, he would bring all his resources to bear in executing the decisions of the Council. Specific UN forces should contain contingents from Western, neutral, and communist states, though no strictly proportional formula was mentioned at the time. Communist countries would participate in the command of UN forces. It would be inadvisable for any permanent member of the Council to send units. The Security Council's military advice and assistance, all of it, would come from the Military Staff

Committee, which would also draft model Article 43 agreements on the basis of which the Council would enter into negotiations with supplier states willing to hold units in readiness for UN action, much as foreseen by the language of the Charter. Two Eastern European states, Czechoslovakia and Bulgaria, expressly offered to enter into Article 43 agreements on the conditions outlined by the Soviet Union.[5]

The year 1965 brought elaborations in the course of oral statements to the Committee of Thirty-three. The Czechoslovakians asked for contributions to forces by equal shares, in a formal, evenly balanced troika fashion.[6] Since then, however the Soviet Union and Czechoslovakia have dropped this insistence on crude equality, substituting a more flexible call for participation by states belonging, as the phrase goes, to different social and economic systems.[7] Soviet statements that year aroused somewhat more curiosity.[8] Earlier ambiguous comments about command were clarified. There would be no troika at the top of military hierarchies in the field, a complete departure from the Soviet version of the general disarmament treaty, which demands a tripartite command and control of an international police force in a disarmed world. For peacekeeping operations one commander would be in charge, appointed by the Council after consultations with the concerned governments, including suppliers. Participating countries would be given responsible posts on the commander's staff. (The Czechoslovakians said at one point that he should be chosen from a country not belonging to major military alliances.) The Russians, rectifying a conspicuous oversight in their 1964 language, made clear that supplier states would not be voiceless in Council decisions on peacekeeping. Reverting to a provision of the Charter inserted in 1945 at the behest of medium-sized powers, the Soviet delegate invited all potential suppliers to participate in the Military Staff Committee's work.* Since 1965 Soviet remarks on this point occasionally have been transparent blandishments, though scarcely conceded as such, to Third World states, assuring the newly independent nations that they too could play

---

* Article 47(2) includes this sentence: "Any Member of the United Nations not permanently represented on the Committee shall be invited by the Committee to be associated with it when the efficient discharge of the Committee's responsibilities requires the participation of that Member in its work."

a part. But there also has been the straightforward justification to would-be contributors that they would have a say in matters affecting them directly.

One of the now-standard sticking points in discussions of Article 43, and one of the certain banes of future negotiations, is the disagreement on what is meant by Charter language giving the Military Staff Committee responsibility, under the Council, for "strategic direction" of all UN forces. Western diplomats argue that this would be one of the provisions that would be used by the Soviet Union to undercut the executive authority of the secretary-general. Given the centricity this point has acquired, it is curious indeed that in their 1964 memorandum the Russians did not mention this phrase but referred only to overall Security Council authority. The Soviet Union did not raise the issue until 1965, and then only in a secondary way while referring to the associative status of would-be suppliers, promising them participation in the strategic direction of forces.[9] Here, too, subsequent statements on what this promise means have been sometimes more, sometimes less inflated, depending, it seems, on the enticements intended for the Third World audience.[10] A play for African support is obvious in the USSR's unearthing of another forgotten Charter provision, this one calling for the use of regional subcommittees responsible to the parent Military Staff. Urging that this be done for peacekeeping, the Soviet Union explicitly cites the Organization of African Unity (OAU) as a possible regional candidate.[11]

THE AMERICAN RESERVATIONS

For several years the United States chose to ignore these largely Soviet proposals, and most other countries, if they have said anything, have merely taken sides on whether or not to talk about them. No one has delved even slightly below the surface of the Soviet language. With a few curt references, the United States has downplayed it by saying, in essence, that to try negotiating Article 43 arrangements again might be acceptable but that these would have nothing to do with peacekeeping. They would deal with the mandatory collective sanctions envisaged in Chapter VII. Since prospects for sanctions forces are no brighter now than they were in the 1940s, continues the U.S. argument, concentration on peacekeeping rather than on enforcement would obviously be more constructive. This clever sidestepping has visibly irritated the USSR, inasmuch as its entire position on UN security forces rests on the claim that there is no distinction between the two, and that they are separated artificially by the United States only to allow missions called "peacekeeping" to be handled outside the Article 43 framework.[12]

In reality, U.S. tactics mask apprehension about three issues.[13] Other countries, key peacekeepers among them, share all or some of these concerns with the United States. Probably most important is the view that an operative Article 43 system would erode and inexorably destroy the executive powers of the secretary-general, whose function and stature would be reduced and who would end up completely subservient to the Military Staff Committee and the Council. A second objection is that, because of the ties between Article 43 and mandatory enforcement and because of Soviet refusal to admit any difference between peacekeeping and coercive operations, the line separating the two concepts would be so blurred that most member states would decide not to put units at the UN's disposal for fear of becoming entangled in sanctions or combat forces. A third implication of Article 43 arrangements is said to be that accepting them would be tantamount to acknowledging exclusive peacekeeping powers for the Security Council, because the Assembly has no jurisdiction over Article 43 and the Military Staff Committee.

"STRATEGIC DIRECTION": THEN AND NOW

Hidden in these contemporary arguments and counterarguments are historical anomalies that in themselves are more revealing than the recent probings and ideas about bringing Article 43 back to life.

The Military Staff Committee is being convoluted beyond recognition. Originally it was to do for UN collective security forces what the Combined Chiefs of Staff did for the Anglo-American allies during World War II, and broadly speaking, the Security Council was to be to the Military Staff Committee what Roosevelt and Churchill had been to the Combined Chiefs. In practice the Combined Chiefs had two jurisdictions.[14] One was executive. The Chiefs exercised what was then called "grand strategic direction" over all combat theaters in which

British and American troops were located. Operational strategy and command in each area fell to either country or, in some cases, to both jointly. The Chiefs' other function was to provide continuing military advice to their political superiors in Washington and London. The San Francisco proposals that eventually became part of the Charter were British in origin and intentionally patterned on the wartime experiences of the two alliance partners. But instead of two, there would now be five. Each permanent member of the Council would designate his chiefs of staff or their representatives to sit on the Military Staff Committee. (This provision for representatives was also based on the earlier alliance machinery: both national chiefs of staff were quite naturally too engaged in running the war to be able to meet centrally, so they set up in Washington a Joint Staff Mission to stand in their place.) Thus, had there ever been a Charter-version collective security operation, the Military Staff Committee would have been the supreme military authority over contingents of the Big Five, whose forces, through Article 43 agreements, were to have been the bulwarks of every sanctions operation. Single or joint field commanders, nationals of the permanent members, would have been responsible to the committee.[15]

Now, a quarter of a century later, the Soviet Union proposes, and all supporters of a revived Article 43 system agree, that great-power contingents are not to be included in UN forces. This radically alters justifications for the Military Staff Committee and wipes out its raison d'être as a supreme military council. The committee was to have permitted the Big Five to control, closely and directly, mainly *their own* armies in the field, led by *their own* commanders, conducting military action immediately and concretely affecting *their own* security interests, and involving *their own* material resources under temporary UN control. The committee's full executive authority, therefore, was largely self-directed, self-imposed, self-regulatory, and self-executing. Its jurisdiction would probably have been far-reaching if the scope of the Combined Chiefs had been used as a precedent, for it had been empowered to plan, act, and issue commands on all military matters from resource allocation to global strategic policy. The working structure of today's Military Staff Committee, its theoretically tight controls, its grandiose province of strategic direction, its basically oligarchic executive powers at the top, all are predicated on the assumption that the great powers are the decision makers *and* the doers. With that assumption now cast aside by general agreement, the committee's military-executive potential is anachronistic and irrelevant. If it is to have contemporary uses, they can only be nonexecutive ones, consistent not only with the actual distribution of peacekeeping operational responsibilities away from the permanent members but also with their possession of effective alternate political controls in the Security Council, which need not be disturbed or diluted.*

These changes, wrought in once-plain meanings and settled contexts, carry important implications for prospective negotiations. If the Article 43 deadlock is to be broken, the Russians must concede that the Military Staff Committee enjoys no basis whatever for exercising over peacekeeping the controls it would have had over collective security armies. Practically, this means that the committee cannot intrude on the unified chain of operational command that emanates from the secretary-general. Within the controlling political instructions he must be allowed to exercise effective and independent executive authority over the conduct of operations. He did not usurp it from the committee, as the Russians imply. The committee never had it. The origin, rationale, and content of that body's unused executive powers are totally unrelated to the institutions that have grown up around the secretary-general as peacekeeper over more than twenty years. The United States, on the other hand, must acknowledge that the Article 43 system can be given nonexecutive responsibilities in matters of peacekeeping preparedness. The United States is on record as saying that the Military Staff Committee's "realm is enforcement action. The provision for consent-type peacekeeping is another matter."[16] Washington has not always believed this. Someday other comments may turn up like those in 1949 of Dean Rusk, then assistant secretary of state, who stated unequivocally in con-

---

* In 1969, a prestigious group of American private citizens endorsed a proposal, formulated by the United Nations Association of the United States of America, for a revitalized and expanded Military Staff Committee that would act as a purely advisory body to the Security Council. For the proposal, see United Nations Association of the United States of America, National Policy Panel on Multilateral Alternatives to Unilateral Intervention, *Controlling Conflicts in the 1970's* (UNA-USA, 1969), p. 44.

gressional testimony that if the Article 43 system had ever been implemented these same forces would have been used for noncoercive peacekeeping.[17]

Medium-sized and small potential suppliers must prod the superpowers in these directions and must at the same time make clear that they, as likely participants, are willing to take on active responsibilities in preparedness under Article 43. Among the noncommunist governments that have already indicated, in the Committee of Thirty-three, some mild interest in explorations of Article 43–Military Staff Committee possibilities are Canada, the Netherlands, Mexico, Japan, and France; Sweden has merely said that any national data on peacekeeping preparedness submitted to the committee might also be valuable to the Security Council should it decide to reconsider the Article 43 question.[18] India's general position on peacekeeping would also imply some interest in Article 43 prospects. Beyond these any measure of overall membership support is mostly guesswork, because the UN members have never been asked to debate or vote on the merits of the issue. As part of its 1966 peacekeeping resolution, Canada included a section recommending efforts to negotiate Article 43 agreements, and a separate vote on this paragraph produced fifty-four in favor, twelve against, and thirty-eight abstentions.[19] This vote, however, reveals very little of any consequence, for the affirmative bloc undoubtedly contained not only states with radically different concepts of what an Article 43 system should entail but also a probably much larger group with no definite notions on the subject.

It is essential to be clear about what points are not at issue, or do not seem to be. No matter what nonexecutive role is given the Military Staff Committee, the secretariat's civilian administrative structure for supporting and running peacekeeping missions will not be affected. The Russians have consistently said that the secretary-general, "as the chief administrative officer of the United Nations, should contribute by all means at his disposal to the execution of the relevant decisions of the Security Council."[20] This would naturally require the necessary technical support resources inside the Office of General Services. In addition, formal troikas are not a contentious item. The Soviet Union and its allies do not insist either on a three-headed command structure or on neatly balanced ratios of troop and unit contributions.

An Article 43 system also would apparently not endanger the established pattern of voluntary, noncoercive peacekeeping, even though the Soviet Union has professed to believe that "any use whatsoever of United Nations armed forces constituted enforcement action and had therefore to be governed by the relevant provisions of Chapter VII."[21] In practice this rigid formulation has been softened in recent years, and significantly so. The operative words in this phraseology carry not only the conventional connotation (that is, sanctions) but also another one evident in recent Soviet syntax: the operation in Cyprus, said the Russian ambassador in the Committee of Thirty-three, "had been undertaken and was continuing on the basis of Security Council decisions adopted under Chapter VII of the Charter."[22] This is not yet a standard formulation in the Soviet diplomatic repertory. But if it conveys their thinking accurately, it suggests areas of common understanding behind the semantic differences. It suggests that what the United States and almost everyone else call peacekeeping and what the Soviet Union refers to as Chapter VII or enforcement action can refer to one and the same phenomenon, as in Cyprus. By excluding the great powers from troop contributions in an Article 43 system the Russians seem to have been going still further to encourage this conclusion, because militarily the likelihood of UN sanctions without great-power involvement can be discounted as being very remote. This makes it possible to envision an Article 43 system capable of preparing for what has so far gone by the name peacekeeping, having nothing to do with collective sanctions. Finally, there seems to be no problem with preserving the voluntary nature of supplier participation. A Czechoslovakian memorandum quite explicitly says that units offered under Article 43 cannot be employed unless the supplier agrees.[23]

The preparedness questions that are certain to provoke serious dispute divide into several categories. Most fundamental is how to apportion preparedness jurisdiction among the UN bureaucracy and political organs. The next is what provisions should be written into Article 43 agreements; and a third is what range of preparedness duties should be given to a regenerated Military Staff Committee.

PROPOSAL: A PREPAREDNESS REVIEW GROUP

A bureaucratic distribution of responsibilities must meet some minimum essential requirements, most of which are not being adequately met by existing machinery for preparedness diplomacy. It has to encompass the principal holders of functions related to preparedness. It must be politically responsible as well as inclusive of technical expertise. It must create institutionalized practices and habits for addressing and resolving major problems of preparedness policy. It must reinforce civilian control of UN military policy and preparedness, while still reflecting the political-military nature of preparedness problems. It must be manageable and flexible, and still be consistent with established procedural rules, precedents, and practices applicable to UN organs. Above all, it must open up opportunities for progress presently blocked by technical or political impediments.

A restructured Article 43 system, if it is to take these multiple objectives into account, will have to be a product of a cooperative effort by the permanent members of the Security Council, the secretary-general, and key peacekeepers. A number of approaches conceivably could be useful. One that seems to have special advantages as a preliminary step would be the establishment of a new forum with an exclusive mandate for preparedness. It would be the first of its kind for peacekeeping, and it need not be another self-perpetuating box on the UN organization chart. It could be called the Special United Nations Preparedness Review Group. Its composition and character would reflect the dispersion of preparedness responsibilities in New York and accordingly would not be the legal creature of any single source of authority. Instead it would be a composite body, small and selective, with components from the Security Council, the secretariat, and the General Assembly's Committee of Thirty-three.

The Security Council's contribution to the review group would be a specially created subsidiary body. Over the years, the Council has set up standing committees that in general practice have been committees of the entire Council membership; it has also established field missions; and it has created a series of smaller, single-purpose subcommittees composed of only some Council members.[24] This third mode could be used to appoint a Council delegation to the review group consisting of the permanent members.* Strictly speaking, there is no foursquare precedent for creating an ad hoc Council subcommittee to participate as one element in a standing forum with wider membership. But a strong partial precedent can be found in an early Council subcommission that was put together for the sole purpose of negotiating with a counterpart committee from another UN organ, the Trusteeship Council.25

The second element of the review group would be a delegation appointed by the secretary-general and consisting of one representative each from the offices of the two secretariat officials closest to preparedness, the undersecretary for special political affairs and the director of General Services. The third component would be selected by the Committee of Thirty-three from among its membership. It too might be made up of four delegates, preferably chosen from those with substantial peacekeeping experience, with active standby programs, or with an expressed and serious interest in participating in future operations. As an outgrowth of its recent preparedness work, the committee might well be the proper agency to recommend that the Assembly urge the secretariat and the Council to join it in creating the review group components.

All representatives to the review group would participate coequally. The group would function by consensus rather than normal voting. Following a practice employed long ago by the Security Council, the chairman of the Military Staff Committee could be invited to sit in on the sessions, but not as a full representative.26 The secretary-general should have a military adviser on his staff at the time, and he could be accorded similar observer status.

The group, appropriately staffed, would be empowered to call for statements or written materials from any UN member and should have access to all relevant secretariat files. Its agenda ought to include four priority items. The first should be to compile and present a comprehensive report to the UN members on the current state of peacekeeping preparedness. The group should then draft model Article 43 agreements, with a view to recommending that the Security Council invite

* The Big Four served together in a similar capacity as half of the eight-member working group that was in charge of the Committee of Thirty-three study.

bilateral negotiations with potential suppliers.[27] A next step would be to design, also for conveyance by the Security Council, an initial program of work for the Military Staff Committee, one that reflects the findings in the state-of-preparedness report as well as the prospects for starting work quickly on some of the outstanding, and solvable, preparedness problems. Finally, the review group should set its sights on a longer and more challenging target: a thorough assessment of the needs for the next generation of preparedness, the problems they will raise, and the resource implications that follow. The ultimate aim of their assessment should be recommendations for an orchestration of national and international preparedness policies. As part of this review, the group should evaluate its own future, if any, as a continuing forum for concerted negotiation and exchange among the key actors. The review group, or something like it, may be helpful in breaking up the diplomatic logjam of the early 1970s, but the institutional changes that would inevitably attend important preparedness progress may reduce the continuing utility of such a makeshift collaborative device.

ARTICLE 43 AGREEMENTS MODERNIZED

Any Article 43 agreements probably could not extend the legal responsibilities or obligations of suppliers beyond what present standbys have undertaken unilaterally. Essentially they would amount to a firm moral and political commitment, a declaration of intent to participate. It would be, therefore, a vastly different kind of commitment, a far more permissive one, than the original Article 43 agreements would have embodied. In one of the contested articles of the 1947 report of the Military Staff Committee, China and France wanted explicit assurances that their offered forces could be employed if needed for self-defense or national emergency. A rare consensus among the other three delegations was their refusal to accept an explicit provision to this effect. The United States and the United Kingdom considered such a clause a loophole that would allow the contracting government to escape Article 43 obligations and to refuse to send the agreed forces without even consulting the Council. Obviously, in a vitally important sense, these were to have been *the Council's* forces.[28]

New agreements for peacekeeping would probably be split into two parts, the first defining conditions and understandings of the offer, the second giving details on size, organization, readiness, and other technical aspects. The first section should stipulate that the offer is voluntary and assumes noncoercive and consensual uses. If a broader sanctions framework becomes acceptable later, then another set of agreements could be drawn up. They need not raise constitutional questions. By definition in the Charter, Article 43 agreements are for the use of the Council. Only this much need be said, and an Assembly role should be neither foreclosed nor insisted on. An express understanding should be reached to the effect that the Council enters into the agreement on behalf of the United Nations as a whole, and accordingly will deposit copies with the secretary-general, whose responsibility would continue to be to execute the peacekeeping decisions of the Council and to assume effective direction and control of proffered forces.

The second, technical portion of the agreements should not be construed merely as a way to funnel information to the UN, though this will be an important function. In addition, it should be consciously thought of as the underpinning for an eventually extensive corpus of officially promulgated readiness standards with central inspection and evaluation of national programs. Standbys have repeatedly cried for UN guidelines and models, but at the same time they have not seemed to appreciate that a logical reciprocity would be involved and that they must be willing to accept UN ascertainment of compliance with these standards. The Article 43 system should move progressively closer to this end. In practice, this probably would mean that an Article 43 agreement would not be simply one document or one transaction between the Council and each possible supplier. Rather, an agreement might begin as a general statement of national preparedness, actual or planned, and this could be followed by supplemental annexes detailing specific programs or target preparedness levels and spelling out terms of UN review and supervision.

THE MILITARY STAFF COMMITTEE MODERNIZED

It will be easier to lay out work assignments for the Military Staff Committee than to reach diplomatic understandings on the committee's lines of responsibility upward to political superiors. So far the USSR has drawn one line, in one direction only. Its terminus, of course, is the Security Council. For the kinds of detailed, technical staff work that might be undertaken by the committee during the next preparedness generation, this line alone would be functionally pointless: the Council would not use the results of such work, probably would have very little interest in it, and could not digest it anyway. Plainly, the committee must establish close and regular contact with the secretariat's twenty-first and thirty-eighth floors.

Such collaboration, it seems, would not be entirely unprecedented, despite the mutual insulation implied in Soviet interpretations. In fact the first and only report of the Military Staff Committee was initially sent directly to the secretary-general. He, in turn, was asked by the chairman of the committee to forward the findings to the Security Council and to call its attention to certain considerations raised by the report's scope.[29] The secretary-general, earlier in the committee's life, also had a hand in developing its rules of procedure and its statute.[30] In view of this early practice, it would be in order for the present-day Military Staff Committee to maintain dual responsibilities to and communications with the Council and the secretariat. It could routinely report to the Council on its activities, could provide it with specially requested military advice, and could thereby recognize the Council's ultimate political authority. At the same time, it could work directly with the secretariat in a host of conceivable ways.

In broad terms, the committee, or more properly the peacekeeping countries associated with it, should start doing the preparedness staff work and studies previously beyond the technical and political competence of the secretariat. The permanent members of the committee, with some exceptions, would be the general directors, overseers, and coordinators of this activity. For the substantive inputs, subcommittees should be created and be staffed largely by military officers from states signing Article 43 agreements. Their mandates should direct them, in cooperation with secretariat civilian administrators, to prepare for release the needed standing operating procedures, to develop training standards, to engage in preplanning of military logistics and support services, and to formulate operational doctrine for peacekeeping.

Besides the obvious advantage of accomplishing some of these things within what presumably would be a politically acceptable framework, the committee's involvement in these problems would have beneficial side effects. (It also, curiously enough, would finally be a partial re-creation of the paragon, the Combined Chiefs of Staff, which similarly maintained a system of subgroups for war-related technical problems and which brought together both civilians and military men when necessary.) The secretary-general would have solid reasons for re-establishing a military adviser's office to provide continuing liaison with the committee's system, to help interpret the thirty-eighth floor's military experience to the subgroup planners, and to constitute, as in the past, an advisory and service section immediately available to the secretary-general in managing field operations. Another positive result would be the creation of an incentive for all potential supplier governments to assign military attachés to their diplomatic missions in New York. Very few do this now; even standby states such as Norway, Denmark, and the Netherlands do not. These attachés would be participants in the committee's staff groups or would be on hand to provide them with information, and would have to keep abreast of their efforts in order to report to their UN ambassador as well as to their home defense ministry.

If an acceptable, effective military planning and information circuit can be established along these lines at the UN, it would make good sense to try to go forward with complementary centralized preparedness programs that are not strictly in the military vein but that have been circulating in the idea mills for some time now. Among the foremost of these is the suggestion that work related to peacekeeping be undertaken by the United Nations Institute for Training and Research (UNITAR), a semiautonomous organization in the UN system financed by private and governmental sources.[31] Certainly this would be fully consistent with UNITAR's statute, but its officers would still have to be confident that the secretariat and key member states would support its efforts in this area—and signals on this score until now have been thought much too negative. The in-service training program designed by Hammarskjöld in the early 1960s doubtless should be activated, probably under UNITAR's auspices. The organization already has established programs for combined training of national and international officials engaged in nonmilitary field missions as part of the UN Development Program. And UNITAR works intimately with the secretariat and is uniquely placed to conduct research on top-level political-military problems of peacekeeping. Modest seminars for civilian officials assigned to UN missions are now run by UNITAR, and a similar effort could be directed at military attachés, or at more senior officers (attachés are usually colonels) sent by their governments to New York for this purpose. Manuals covering specialized subjects such as UN technical assistance activities have been produced by UNITAR;[32] peacekeeping subjects could be given similar treatment. Another possibility would arise from UNITAR's acknowledged intention to associate itself with other national or international institutions with common interests. Conceivably, information and training personnel could be exchanged with national preparedness staffs focusing on peacekeeping training and orientation. Basic longer-range peacekeeping research on a cooperative basis might also be programmed by UNITAR and the Department of Political and Security Council Affairs, which contains an inactive section whose formal instructions say that it "undertakes studies and prepares papers on problems" pertaining to the UN's peace and security responsibilities.[33]

Restructuring the Standby System

The second half of the preparedness agenda is bound closely with the fate of the first. Whether basic understandings can be reached about the distribution and exercise of political responsibility for preparedness will determine in large measure whether secretariat capabilities can be bolstered and national programs broadened. States considering the possibility of starting readiness programs will be acutely sensitive to the firmness of the diplomatic foundations underlying the entire preparedness system.

The 1960s witnessed a succession of miscalculations about what conditions might spur more member governments to come forward with advance preparedness offers, either earmarked units or other resources. Errors were usually made because of an unexplainable optimistic feeling that if only some conspicuous hurdle could be overcome or if some organizational invention could be devised, then things would begin falling into place. For a time it seemed that systematizing preparedness outside the UN framework might be the answer. Great importance was thus attached to Pearson's initiatives, which were equivalent to an institutional escape from the impasse in New York—a detour designed to persuade potential suppliers that despite the frozen diplomatic situation a workable way could be found to collaborate for better preparedness through specially created informal arrangements beyond regular UN channels. Pearson had hoped, on behalf of the organization, to stimulate wide involvement that eventually would have included, as he once remarked, representatives from all continents. Another much-advertised culprit was the Article 19 crisis. If only *it* could be resolved satisfactorily, went the argument, then a flood of volunteers, eager to set aside personnel for UN duty, would ensue. A third variant was to blame the lack of military staff within the secretariat to plan the employment of earmarked forces, to dispense advice and training guidelines, and to coordinate efforts across national boundaries.[34] But as things turned out, Pearson's ideas enjoyed a very brief vogue, the Article 19 showdown was averted, and the secretariat grew less rather than more inclined toward internal military staffing and planning. So when the decade closed, the overall scope of national preparedness had changed little since the initial spurts of activity between 1963 and 1965.

In coming generations, even an adequate consensus about political responsibility for preparedness will not suffice to pave the way for enlarged national readiness. New, more flexible approaches to member state programs will be required too. Experiences of standby and supplier countries during previous generations will need to be culled for problems likely to recur elsewhere. Diversity within military establishments must be taken into account, and governments with relatively limited resources must be provided with avenues by which they can make some contribution, however minimal.

In creating a reservoir of peacekeeping talents, preparedness planners will have to keep in view two complementary objectives: it must contain both operational competence and political versatility. Some candidates must possess military skills of a high order and bring with them a presumption of political acceptability as intermediaries in most disputes —twin credentials that a handful of peacekeepers have already displayed by the very frequency of their participation in past missions. Still other potential suppliers must be on hand mainly to meet the subjective requirements for impartiality that invariably influence determinations of who peacekeepers are to be in each new operation. Because impartiality involves, to a degree, a balancing of apparent national biases, the UN occasionally will need to be able to draw upon varying ideological identifications, regional affiliations, skin tones, and political reputations. A preparedness edifice capable of accommodating these two purposes will not be erected quickly or easily, and aiming for dramatic breakthroughs will only retard the patient groundwork that must precede durable results.

NEW CALL-UP ARRANGEMENTS

Structural renovation of the existing UN call-up system should be a priority order of business under a modernized Article 43. The finished product ought to be such that member states could associate themselves with the new arrangement in a variety of ways. Alternative forms of participation, each with its own Article 43 format, performance standards, and procedures, should be designed for the main types of readiness offers that are called for. At a minimum these would cover, separately, advance provision of full military units and related support facilities; logistical services; observers, staff, and other military specialists; and civilian policemen or civilian technicians such as those that have already been offered for disaster and relief work.

By now it should be obvious from the preparedness activities of the past dozen years that the first of these categories—availability of infantry-type peacekeeping formations—is going to pose some formidable difficulties. The United Nations will remain in the odd position of being a shopper in a military marketplace whose goods it cannot readily refuse and whose quality is largely beyond UN controls. It must take what it can get from members' national establishments, or it gets nothing at all. It must accept offers from conscript armies as well as professional ones, crack units as well as sorely undertrained or underequipped ones, battalions that have existed for many years as well as one-time-only outfits with minimal preparation. It furthermore has to suffer the complications that heterogeneous military structures have always faced—differences in language, habit, procedure, and outlook. Yet even with this overload of handicaps, the UN must somehow acquire the modest, reliable mobilization capability that some member states have already tried to give it, though with generally spotty success. The organization still needs standby plans that work, standbys that are standing by and deployable quickly enough to cope with short lead times in unexpected crises.

Just how quickly the UN must be prepared to act militarily is hard to specify in the abstract. The machinery for making the necessary political decisions is itself none too well oiled, and delays in sending new missions to the field may have less to do with inadequate military readiness than with the political clearances that have to be first obtained. In New York formal authorization of an operation can entail lengthy public debate and slow private diplomacy—one side effect of which, however, is to alert possible suppliers and the secretariat to the wisdom of quiet preparations even in anticipation of an official go signal. Negotiations over mission composition may engage the secretary-general and interested states in protracted bargaining, while chosen participants must take time-consuming internal steps that usually include decisions by or consultations with cabinets, legislatures, and military chiefs. Altogether this may span days or, as in the Cyprus dispute, several weeks. Short of the still distant prospect of a diplomatic consensus strong enough to give the secretary-general internationalized standing forces that could be dispatched to trouble spots on his authority alone,[35] this extended mobilization process can only be reduced, not eliminated. Thus, even though a call-up seldom has to be reckoned in hours, even though the organization does not need what military contingency planners refer to as instant-reaction forces, it nonetheless has to have on hand a reliable emergency potential—an ability to muster military units at least as rapidly as all enabling decisions can be completed, which in practice may often be a week or less, a timetable that few standbys now plan for.

Quite obviously this prescription could be filled with great ease if all countries offering peacekeeping contingents in advance were to have fully volunteer, professional armies and no reluctance to draw formed units from them for UN peacekeeping service. But this is not the case, and is not going to be. Furthermore, many of those countries that do have professional military establishments are unwilling to order even regulars abroad, and those with conscript systems either are characteristically hesitant to do so or flatly rule it out in all circumstances not directly involving national security. In a very real sense, then, the practices so far employed by the Canadians, Indians, or Dutch marines will be the exception, and Nordic, Irish, or Brazilian methods the rule. Many, probably most, member states providing peacekeepers will prefer to use some type of voluntary recruiting, and the delays that are inevitably generated must be counteracted if the UN is to have a workable emergency call-up system.

AGREED PERFORMANCE STANDARDS

An essential step, one that would be greatly facilitated by a more central management of overall preparedness arrangements, will be to establish agreed performance targets governing the mobilization speed and general readiness of national units to be raised for peacekeeping. By definition, these guidelines would apply to genuine first-use emergency units able to go anywhere anytime and not to ordinary rotation contingents for ongoing missions. The UN must set these standards even if it cannot enforce them, and it must encourage would-be suppliers to meet them even if they cannot be penalized for failing to do so.

The existence of such standards, along with the evolution of fairly widespread seriousness about measuring up to them, will have different impacts in different countries, depending on the type of military establishment and the choice of methods for fulfilling UN commitments. On the whole, however, the standby concept should be able eventually to take on a common, more or less consistent meaning, whereas up to now definitions of "standby" have proliferated almost in equal proportion to the number of countries announcing standby programs. Some minimum uniformity is necessary not just for reasons of satisfying logical or conceptual purity, but mainly because it is a prerequisite for sound military planning. Planners, and certainly political decision makers, must know accurately what resources are at their disposal, how heavy the demands put on them can be, and how they will operate in practice.[36]

A TWO-TIERED MOBILIZATION PROCEDURE

Agreed standards, if they embody a judicious mixture of stringency and realism, could elicit maximum effort from participating countries, some of which ought to be persuaded to set up, if necessary, a double-tiered internal system for mobilizing UN contingents, the first to be activated for rapid response in emergencies, the second to be used for slower call-up or for rotation battalions. Naturally, in countries that intend to keep fully formed and specially prepared professional units on standby, such a system probably would not be needed. Nor would it be necessary in states raising volunteer units—whether volunteers come from regular military regiments as in Ireland, or largely from civilian life as in the Nordic states, or from both as in Austria—so long as these volunteer forces are truly *effective* within prevailing standards. If they are not, then the best alternative would be a two-tiered process, under which a nonvolunteer system would be used for raising the initial rapid-response units—but only for these. In other words, a complete formation from the regular military establishment would be dispatched for quick-action standby purposes; as soon as it could be brought home, a replacement unit recruited from volunteers would be sent to replace it; and this second-tier method would be used for all subsequent rotations. In a narrowly procedural sense, this suggested system is similar to the two-phase method used by the Norwegian medical corps in anticipating UN emergency callup.[37]

Countries disinclined to send abroad conscripts or nonvolunteer professionals are not going to reverse their attitude 180 degrees for the sake of the UN. Nordic governments, for example, are not about to employ their regular-mobilization armies for all UN battalions from the beginning to the end of a peacekeeping mission, as some experts have urged them to do. Nor will states with larger, standing conscript establishments meet all UN commitments with units containing draftees. Few politicians in such countries would have the temerity to urge such a course, and few governments would accept it. Yet it is not so far-fetched to conceive of 30-degree shifts to systems that would use regular national forces to meet the need for initial-response units only when voluntary procedures could not work quickly enough. It would be far more palatable politically for a government to back this more modest approach.

The option of using for UN purposes national service personnel or nonvolunteer regular soldiers has already found some favor in the Nordic area as well as elsewhere. It is entirely possible that this could gain wider official acceptance if it were strictly confined to first-use standby forces and if general confidence in the UN preparedness system increased and there were correspondingly stronger incentives to match higher standards.

Several important advantages would accrue to preparedness overall. The quick-response capability of the UN would be increased. Since ordinary national contingents are usually more competent military formations than one-time-only volunteer units, the UN would be able to field more highly skilled forces at that demanding time when they would pay the most dividends, in the often dangerous and uncertain early phase of a new peacekeeping operation. Wherever it might be used, a double-tiered procedure would also bring the incidental benefit of compelling a country that might not otherwise do so to expose wider segments of its regular military community to peacekeeping orientation and training, particularly at the critically important officer levels.

WIDER PARTICIPATION IN PREPAREDNESS

Expansion of the geographic and political base of a revamped UN call-up structure will be influenced not only by the availability of several alternative forms of participation but also by the pace and degree of political consensus that emerges. Clearer understandings about political responsibility will be a prerequisite for fresh stirrings of interest in standby efforts, both among past suppliers who have hesitated to make standby offers and among Eastern European and noncommunist member states that have shown a disposition to explore Article 43 possibilities. Altogether, if standby offers already announced are counted, a total of between twenty and twenty-five countries willing to volunteer full military units could be listed safely, if speculatively. In addition, the opportunity to designate contributions of lesser magnitude, either of observers or civilian policemen, could lengthen the list of potential suppliers. In either case, minimum numbers of qualified persons for either duty would suffice as an offer. The roster of smaller countries that have seen their way to supplying UN observers in past missions is impressively long and representative. Though standby efforts in both categories would not be trivial in scope—able officers, like able policemen, are scarce in these states—such offers would of course weigh much less heavily than infantry-type contributions.

Moreover, these options for graduated, progressively more demanding contributions to preparedness will enable governments that prefer to increase their participation step-by-step to do so in an orderly sequence. Two examples that come to mind immediately—no doubt there are others—are Japan and Switzerland.

In the complicated web that is Japan's internal debate over defense and security policy, one of the minor strands has been whether the government could or should contribute to peacekeeping forces under a United Nations that enjoys overwhelming national popularity. Officially the answer has been a firm negative. The ground most often cited is that Japan's pacifist constitution prohibits use of its 250,000-man "Self-Defense Forces" outside the country's borders. This is not a mandatory interpretation of the constitution, but one dictated, for the present at least, by domestic political constraints.[38] Behind this aloofness have been murmurs of interest. At the UN Japanese delegates have regularly favored discussion and study of the problems of raising standby forces—scrupulously avoiding on the one hand any hint that Japan would do so while admitting on the other that it is a subject of special interest to the government. Privately the Japanese have not concealed their curiosity about the details of existing standby programs, especially the constitutional implications and organizational practices of those in the Nordic area. Beyond this, officials have explicitly acknowledged that Japan is especially alert to possible civilian roles in peacekeeping.[39] And in 1969 Prime Minister Naotake Sato reportedly offered to contribute civilian personnel, facilities, and funds to an international commission for supervising a settlement of the Vietnam war.[40] All this suggests the possibility that Japan might well consider, as an experimental step within a new UN preparedness arrangement, the earmarking of a contingent of civilian policemen, especially since Japan has been one of the governments receptive to further exploration of prospects for using Article 43 as a peacekeeping framework.

Switzerland's situation is remarkable in several respects. Though not a member of the UN, Switzerland has provided both money and logistical services to peacekeeping missions. The question of seeking UN membership is under active, official study, and the UN policies of Sweden and Austria are watched closely by the neutral Swiss. In recent years they have discussed standby problems in some detail with Swedish officials and have sent a few students to the joint Nordic training courses. At one point in the mid-1960s it was announced that the government was examining the possibility of contributing to peacekeeping missions even *before* applying for UN membership.[41] Again, the availability within a new preparedness system of alternative types and levels of commitment would be conducive to the cautious, neutrality-preserving approach to peacekeeping participation that the Swiss can be expected to adopt eventually.

To complete this refurbishment of preparedness, the four great powers in the Security Council should be encouraged to offer logistical services on a formal advance basis. This step would carry far more political than technical significance, and in all likelihood it would not come until late in the process, more as a signal of common diplomatic ratification of the overall preparedness structure than as a carefully honed, joint technical undertaking. (However, its practical utility should not be underrated; with centralized planning and consultative machinery in New York, much more constructive advance work could be accomplished among potential suppliers, the secretariat, and logistical supporters, whether great powers or not.) In 1968 the United States issued what was in effect an invitation to France and the Soviet Union, urging them to join in a four-sided logistical offer.[42] While this was largely a tactical gesture in the Committee of Thirty-three—after all, the U.S. government was still a long way from such a move, and it fully appreciated how scant were the chances that the two invitees would agree, given the diplomatic stalemate over peacekeeping—the incident does hint that the United States may be willing to begin shedding its generally negative stance against Soviet involvement of this kind in support of peacekeeping missions.

If the greater portion of these various structural renovations materialize, an important step will have been taken toward the transformation of peacekeeping preparedness from a random patchwork of policies and activities into a purposefully designed system consonant with political tolerances in the United Nations. A stable, expandable framework will have been constructed within which well-circulated and detailed proposals for readiness refinements—ideas now thoroughly familiar to practitioners—could be realistically evaluated and fitted to prevailing requirements.

Certain favorite remedies that have been widely urged during preceding preparedness generations will probably cease to be germane, while others could take on fresh promise. For instance, any possible value in using U.S. military assistance to stimulate UN earmarking has been largely eclipsed by drastic and rather widespread cutbacks in the absolute levels and kinds of U.S. grant assistance and in the number of recipients since this idea was first tried, at a time when most potential peacekeepers received substantial amounts.[43] In any event, this approach is of doubtful effect on the handful of potential peacekeepers that already receive large quantities of U.S. military aid and could bear the burden of standby commitments without additional grants of hardware or training.[44]

A more productive route probably would be a campaign with two objectives. The first is to concentrate on creating reliable methods for financing peacekeeping budgets at the UN so that suppliers can be adequately and promptly reimbursed for extraordinary costs, which is often the financial factor they are most concerned about. The second is to centralize as far as possible the management and execution of selective assistance programs for standbys, to channel both through the UN, and to place operational training responsibility primarily in the hands of experienced middle power peacekeepers within a comprehensive preparedness system. It should not be necessary to discount, however, the possibility of exploiting natural or established organizations not part of the UN but politically acceptable for preparedness purposes, once it is clear that these are supplements to UN-controlled programs, not substitutes for them. Nordic programs might be expanded in membership and curricula, perhaps with financial help from the United Nations. Advantage could be taken of the quite extensive military interchange among members of the Commonwealth, many of which have been the backbone of past UN operations and are certain to be important participants in future ones.[45]

A Postscript

In the closing weeks of 1969, an ambassador to the UN representing a medium-sized country habitually at the forefront of preparedness activities offered an off-the-cuff retrospective judgment to his colleagues: More had been accomplished on preparedness during the previous six months, he was convinced, than during the preceding twenty years.

His remark invites reflection, for history has value both as a yardstick and as a teacher. In a narrow comparative context, the recent forward movement evident in the Committee of Thirty-three as a result of changing superpower approaches and attitudes toward preparedness diplomacy does indeed stand out as historically without precedent. But in a broader sense, the past twenty years have not been barren—not for the key middle powers that must constitute the backbone of preparedness, not for the secretariat executives who must give it central direction, and not for the contemporary analyst or policy maker who must try to comprehend the past and project into the future.

The desiderata outlined in the preceding pages of this chapter attempt to distill some of the principal insights from three generations of preparedness diplomacy and institution building. The ten-point agenda of preparedness objectives and the suggestions for specific preparedness policies should not be regarded as a package proposal that must stand or fall as a whole. The broad objectives, to the extent they are consistent with the past and responsive to future needs, could conceivably lead to a variety of other policy prescriptions. Similarly, the more detailed recommendations about Article 43, the Military Staff Committee, the proposed Preparedness Review Group, and the reconstituted standby system are by no means the necessary or inevitable by-products of the stated objectives. What is clear about the present state of UN preparedness is that it is inadequate. What is doubtful is whether incremental remedies will suffice to produce qualitative improvements. What is conceivable is a design for the future that is bold enough to vault the present impasse, yet realistic enough to protect and to further the interests of both superpowers as well as the middle power peace-keepers and the UN membership as a whole. What demands recognition about preparedness is not what has been accomplished recently, but the enormous distance yet to be covered.

Synopsis of United Nations Peacekeeping Missions

OF THE TWELVE PEACEKEEPING MISSIONS authorized since 1945 by the UN Security Council or the General Assembly (presented below in chronological order), the only ones currently operational are those in Cyprus, Kashmir, and the Middle East.

GREECE

The United Nations' first peacekeeping venture was a response to complaints to the Security Council in December 1946 by Greece that its northern borders were being violated by neighboring Albania, Bulgaria, and Yugoslavia, each of which was allegedly assisting guerrillas in Greece. Within thirty days a commission, authorized by the Security Council, began on-the-scene investigations. United Nations action on the commission's recommendations was prevented, however, by a series of Soviet vetoes in the Security Council.

At U.S. insistence the issue was brought before the veto-free General Assembly. In October 1947, the Assembly established a United Nations Special Committee on the Balkans (UNSCOB) empowered not only to investigate and report on the border situation but also to provide the parties with mediation assistance.

In 1952 Greece's northern borders became relatively quiet, and UNSCOB was replaced by a subcommission of the Peace Observation Commission that the General Assembly had established earlier under the Uniting for Peace Resolution. The UN presence in Greece was terminated in August 1954.

PALESTINE

During the twelve months preceding the expiration of the British Mandate for Palestine in May 1948, various UN bodies, commissions, and authorized individuals sought to facilitate a Jewish-Arab settlement concerning the future of Palestine. All attempts failed, and within hours of the declaration of independence by the provisional government of Israel on May 15, neighboring Arab states invaded Palestine.

After the failure of one brief cease-fire in July, the Security Council ordered another, this time under Chapter VII of the Charter. Under UN auspices negotiations between Israel and each of its four Arab neighbors—Egypt, Jordan, Lebanon, and Syria—commenced early in 1949. By July of the same year, each of these states had concluded an armistice with Israel. Included in the implementation machinery for each agreement and in Security Council resolutions was a United Nations Truce Supervision Organization (UNTSO), which had authority to report on observance of cease-fires and armistice agreements.

Initially UNTSO supplied UN observers to all of Israel's borders except that with Egypt. After the war in 1956, UNTSO's functions on this border were taken over by the United Nations Emergency Force (UNEF), which was located in Gaza and Sinai until 1967.

INDONESIA

Disagreements between the Netherlands and the Republic of Indonesia over the implementation of the Indonesian independence agreement formally signed by the two parties in March 1947 led to military hostilities in the early summer of that year. In August, at the request of Indonesia, the Security Council called for a cease-fire and established a Good Offices Committee to assist in carrying it out. The committee was aided by a small group of military observers from the staffs of the foreign consuls general in Indonesia (there were no embassies). After the cease-fire broke down several times, a truce agreement was negotiated with UN assistance in January 1948. This too failed to hold, and hostilities were resumed during the final weeks of 1948.

In January 1949, the Security Council again requested a cessation of the fighting and reconstituted the earlier committee as the United Nations Commission for Indonesia (UNCI), also with a complement of military observers. Agreements embodying a Dutch transfer of sovereignty to Indonesia were reached in November 1949. After completing its tasks connected with the carrying out of the transfer agreement, the UN mission was disbanded in early 1951.

KASHMIR

When India and Pakistan became independent shortly after the Second World War, they divided between them some five hundred princely states formerly under British sovereignty. One of these, Kashmir, has been a source of bitter dispute ever since 1947, when its Hindu leader opted for attaching his predominantly Moslem state to India.

In January 1948, India accused Pakistan in the Security Council of sponsoring raids on Kashmir. The Council acted by establishing a United Nations Commission for India and Pakistan (UNCIP), whose authorization included investigating and reporting as well as assisting mediation efforts.

By January 1949, the parties had reached agreements that permitted a cease-fire. To assist UNCIP in overseeing the cease-fire, a group of military observers became operational almost immediately. They have come to be known as the United Nations Military Observer Group in India and Pakistan (UNMOGIP), which today has responsibility for maintaining the truce in Kashmir.

EGYPT

In late October 1956, Israel, France, and Great Britain, provoked by President Nasser's earlier nationalization of the Suez Canal, launched concerted attacks against

Egypt. Security Council action to restore peace and to secure troop withdrawals was prevented by French and British vetoes. Consequently, with U.S. and Soviet acquiescence, Yugoslavia invoked the provisions of the Uniting for Peace Resolution and transferred the issue to the General Assembly.

During the first week of November, the Assembly adopted a cease-fire resolution and authorized Secretary-General Hammarskjöld to plan a peace force. The parties agreed, a cease-fire went into effect, and the Assembly created the United Nations Emergency Force (UNEF). Ten countries voluntarily provided troops, which numbered as many as 6,000 at one point—the first example of UN peacekeeping by a comparatively large-scale military force. These nonfighting units patrolled within Egypt along the Israeli borders in the Gaza Strip and the Sinai desert until May 1967, when Egypt requested their withdrawal.

LEBANON

In May 1958, Lebanon went before the Security Council to charge the United Arab Republic with massive intervention in its internal affairs, with infiltrating men and arms, and with conspiring by financial and other means against the Lebanese government. The Security Council waited to see whether the League of Arab States would be able to ease tensions. It could not, so the Council acted in early July to dispatch the United Nations Observer Group in Lebanon (UNOGIL) to ensure that no infiltration was occurring.

Middle East tensions increased in mid-July with the overthrow of the king of Iraq. Lebanon and Jordan immediately called for and received military support from the United States and Great Britain, respectively.

Great-power differences thwarted the Security Council, and an emergency session of the Assembly was convened. The United States and Great Britain agreed to withdraw their troops. By November the withdrawals were completed, elections had stabilized Lebanon's internal situation, and the borders were quiet. In mid-December UNOGIL terminated operations.

THE CONGO

The largest, costliest, and most complex UN peacekeeping operation was a product of the chaos that followed the Congo's attainment of independence at the end of June 1960. Within two weeks the army mutinied, law and order broke down completely, Katanga seceded, and the central government requested help from the United Nations. Secretary-General Hammarskjöld requested the Security Council to act swiftly. It responded by authorizing the United Nations Congo Operation (ONUC), with the United States and the Soviet Union voting affirmatively.

Utilizing civilian as well as military components, ONUC was authorized during the next four years to maintain law, order, and essential services throughout the Congo. Eventually, ONUC was granted authority by the Security Council to use force if necessary to perform its functions.

At its peak ONUC consisted of almost 20,000 military and specialized personnel contributed by thirty-four countries. ONUC cost the United Nations approximately $402 million. It was partly for financial reasons that ONUC was forced to withdraw completely in the summer of 1964.

The main problem left unresolved by the Indonesian accession to independence in 1949 was the status of the territory of West New Guinea (West Irian). The Dutch continued to administer the area despite Indonesian claims that it was an integral part of Indonesia. After more than a decade of political wrangling, Indonesians and Dutch clashed in minor military episodes during late 1961 and early 1962.

Negotiations in and outside the UN brought an agreement in August 1962 governing the terms of an immediate relinquishment of Dutch sovereignty, an interim period of control by the UN, and an eventual transfer of administrative authority to Indonesia, to be retained until a subsequent plebiscite.

Even before the UN formally acted to implement the agreement, the secretary-general's military adviser and a small observer unit arrived in West New Guinea to assist in the immediate tasks of implementation. One month later, in September 1962, the General Assembly authorized the establishment of the United Nations Temporary Executive Authority (UNTEA), which, with its military arm, the United Nations Security Force (UNSF), maintained local security and, under the ultimate authority of the secretary-general, fully administered West New Guinea until Indonesia took over in May 1963. With a core of UN officials, UNTEA was comprised mainly of a security force of some 1,500 Pakistani troops, and local military personnel temporarily placed under UNTEA's command.

YEMEN

Throughout 1962, Yemen was caught up in a civil war between royalist and republican factions actively supported by Saudi Arabia and the UAR, respectively. Diplomatic missions from the United Nations and the United States managed early in 1963 to arrange a disengagement agreement under which the warring parties and their supporters would cease military activity and undertake a phased withdrawal of forces.

To supervise the disengagement and to police demilitarized zones, the Security Council created the United Nations Yemen Observation Mission (UNYOM). The enabling resolution was adopted in June 1962, and observers arrived in Yemen within a few weeks with authority to ascertain whether or not the parties were complying with the agreement. Despite the limitations imposed by extremely difficult geographic and operating conditions, they were able to report that compliance, particularly on the part of the UAR, was minimal. Without the authority to enforce a solution on the parties, UNYOM's functions could not be performed. Accordingly it was withdrawn in September 1964.

CYPRUS

Greek and Turkish Cypriot communities entered a period of fragile, irregular cooperation following Cypriot independence in 1960. Age-old hatreds between the preponderant Greeks and the minority Turks erupted into violent fighting during Christmas week of 1963.

The immediate tasks of maintaining peace fell to the British, whose troops were already in Cyprus by treaty right. After attempts to reach agreement on a NATO peacekeeping force failed during the early months of 1964, largely because of resistance by Cypriot President Archbishop Makarios, the UN acted in March. Without objection by any of the great powers, the Security Council authorized the formation of a United Nations Force in Cyprus (UNFICYP), which became operational in late March. Since then, the Security Council has regularly extended UNFICYP's mandate to remain on the island.

Nine countries have provided military units or small contingents of civilian police, which at their peak numbered nearly 7,000. These forces are responsible for assisting in the maintenance of law and order and for normalizing conditions on the island.

INDIA AND PAKISTAN

War broke out between India and Pakistan in August 1965, and the matter was soon brought before the Security Council for action. After the parties had ignored its call for a cease-fire in the first week of September, the Council used exceptionally strong language and, with the consent of the United States and the Soviet Union, demanded a cease-fire and a subsequent withdrawal of military forces. Three days later a cease-fire formally went into effect.

The Council delegated to the secretary-general the responsibility for assisting in the supervision of the cease-fire agreement. He strengthened the existing UN observers in Kashmir (UNMOGIP) and created a new group to patrol the border between India and Pakistan, for which UNMOGIP had no responsibility. The new machinery was called the United Nations India-Pakistan Observation Mission (UNIPOM).

UNIPOM commenced operations in late September 1965 and remained on the scene until its functions were completed in March 1966, when it was disbanded. UNMOGIP has continued its role in Kashmir.

SUEZ CANAL

In the wake of the third Arab-Israeli war in June 1967, tensions and military incidents persisted in the Suez Canal sector. In early July the Security Council met to deal with violations of its recently ordered cease-fire and unanimously decided to authorize the secretary-general to station military observers at the Canal to supervise cease-fire arrangements. The new mission became operational in mid-July and is commanded by UNTSO headquarters in Jerusalem.

⇶ APPENDIX B ⇷

National Participants in Peacekeeping Missions

Countries	UNCI	ONUC	UNEF	UNFICYP[a]	UNIPOM	UNMOGIP	UNOGIL	UNSCOB	UNTEA-UNSF[b]	UNTSO	UNTSO, Suez Canal	UNYOM[c]	Total
Afghanistan	—	—	—	—	—	—	x	—	—	—	—	—	1
Argentina	—	x	—	—	—	—	x	—	—	x	x	—	4
Australia	x	—	—	x	x	x	—	—	—	x	—	—	5
Austria	—	x	—	x	—	—	—	—	—	x	x	—	4
Belgium	x	—	—	—	x	x	—	x	—	x	—	—	5
Brazil	—	x	x	—	x	—	—	x	[x]	—	—	—	5
Burma	—	x	—	—	x	—	x	—	—	x	x	—	5
Canada	—	x	x	x	x	x	x	—	x	x	—	x	9
Ceylon	—	x	—	—	x	—	x	—	[x]	—	—	—	4
Chile	—	—	—	—	x	x	x	—	—	x	x	—	5
China	x	—	x	—	—	—	—	x	—	—	—	—	2
Colombia	—	—	x	—	—	—	—	—	—	—	—	—	1
Congo	—	x	—	—	—	—	—	—	—	—	—	—	1
Denmark	—	x	x	x	x	x	x	—	—	x	—	x	8
Ecuador	—	x	—	—	x	x	x	—	—	—	—	—	3
Ethiopia	—	x	—	x	x	x	x	—	—	—	—	—	2
Finland	—	—	x	x	x	x	x	—	—	x	x	—	7

France	x	—	—	—	—	—	—	x	—	x	x	—	4
Ghana	—	x	—	—	—	—	—	—	—	—	—	x	2
Greece	—	x	—	—	—	—	—	—	—	—	—	—	1
Guinea	—	x	—	—	—	—	—	—	—	—	—	—	1
India	—	x	x	x	—	—	x	—	[x]	—	—	x	6
Indonesia	—	x	x	—	—	—	x	—	—	—	—	—	3
Iran	—	x	—	—	—	—	—	—	—	—	—	—	1
Ireland	—	x	—	x	x	—	x	—	[x]	x	x	—	7
Italy	—	x	—	—	x	x	x	—	—	x	—	x	6
Liberia	—	x	—	—	—	—	—	—	—	—	—	—	1
Malaya	—	x	—	—	—	—	—	—	—	—	—	—	1
Mali	—	x	—	—	—	—	—	—	—	—	—	—	1
Mexico	—	—	—	—	—	x	—	x	—	—	—	—	2
Morocco	—	x	—	—	—	—	—	—	—	—	—	—	1
Nepal	—	—	—	—	x	—	x	—	—	—	—	—	2
Netherlands	—	x	—	—	x	—	x	x	—	x	—	x	6
New Zealand	—	x	—	x	x	x	x	—	—	x	—	—	6
Nigeria	—	x	—	—	x	—	—	—	[x]	—	—	—	3
Norway	—	x	x	—	x	x	x	—	—	x	—	x	7
Pakistan	—	x	—	—	—	—	—	—	x	—	—	x	3
Peru	—	—	—	—	—	—	x	—	—	—	—	—	1
Philippines	—	x	—	—	—	—	—	—	—	—	—	—	1
Portugal	—	—	—	—	—	—	x	—	—	—	—	—	1
Sierra Leone	—	x	—	—	—	—	—	—	—	—	—	—	1
Sudan	—	x	—	—	—	—	—	—	—	—	—	—	1
Sweden	—	x	x	x	x	x	x	—	[x]	x	x	x	10
Thailand	—	—	—	—	—	—	x	—	—	—	—	—	1
Tunisia	—	x	—	—	—	—	—	—	—	—	—	—	1

National Participants in Peacekeeping Missions (continued)

Countries	Missions												
	UNCI	ONUC	UNEF	UNFICYP[a]	UNIPOM	UNMOGIP	UNOGIL	UNSCOB	UNTEA-UNSF[b]	UNTSO	UNTSO, Suez Canal	UNYOM[c]	Total
U.A.R.	—	x	—	—	—	—	—	—	—	—	—	—	1
U.K.	x	—	—	x	—	—	—	x	—	—	—	—	3
Uruguay	—	—	—	—	x	x	—	—	—	—	—	—	2
U.S.	x	—	—	—	—	x	—	x	x	x	—	—	5
Venezuela	—	—	—	—	x	—	—	—	—	—	—	—	1
Yugoslavia	—	x	x	—	—	—	—	—	—	—	—	x	3
Total	6	34	10	10	20	14	21	8	9	17	8	10	

Source: This chart is a slightly simplified and amended version of one found in Albert Legault, *The Authorization of Peace-Keeping Operations in Terms of the Nature of the Conflict*, IPKO Monograph 8 (Paris: International Information Center on Peace-Keeping Operations, 1967), pp. 42–43.

a. India has contributed command personnel.

b. The six countries whose participation is shown in brackets provided 21 observers to supervise the cease-fire arrangements before the arrival of UNTEA-UNSF in West Irian. The bulk of UNSF was made up of Pakistani soldiers totaling approximately 1,500. Also included in UNSF were some 16 officers and men of the Royal Canadian Air Force (RCAF) and a detachment of approximately 60 United States Air Force personnel.

c. UNYOM was provided with one reconnaissance unit and one air unit. The reconnaissance unit consisted of 114 Yugoslav officers and other ranks who were transferred from the Yugoslav contingent serving with UNEF. The air unit of about 50 officers and other ranks had been provided by the RCAF. From early December 1963, the Yugoslav ground patrol had been withdrawn and the group was restricted to 25 military observers from the other countries indicated. They were supported by a Canadian air transport unit.

Selected Readings

A USEFUL SPECIALIZED BIBLIOGRAPHY on United Nations peacekeeping is: International Information Center on Peace-Keeping Operations, *Peace-Keeping Operations: Bibliography*, prepared by Albert Legault (Paris: IPKO, 1967). The selected entries below are intended only to identify the more important general introductory works.

Bloomfield, Lincoln P. *The United Nations and U.S. Foreign Policy: A New Look at the National Interest.* Rev. ed. Boston: Little, Brown, 1967.

———, and Amelia C. Leiss. *Controlling Small Wars: A Strategy for the 1970's.* New York: Knopf, 1969.

———, and others. *International Military Forces: The Question of Peacekeeping in an Armed and Disarming World.* Boston: Little, Brown, 1964.

Bowett, D. W. *United Nations Forces.* New York: Praeger, 1964.

Browne and Shaw International Studies Division. "The United States and UN Peacekeeping: A View Toward the 1970s." Prepared for the Office of the Assistant Secretary of Defense, International Security Affairs. Processed. 1968.

Burns, Arthur L., and Nina Heathcote. *Peace-keeping by UN Forces from Suez to the Congo.* New York: Praeger, 1963.

Canadian Institute of International Affairs. *Peacekeeping: International Challenge and Canadian Response.* Toronto: CIIA, 1968.

Claude, Inis L., Jr. *The Changing United Nations.* New York: Random House, 1967.

———. *Power and International Relations.* New York: Random House, 1962.

Cox, Arthur M. *Prospects for Peacekeeping.* Washington: Brookings Institution, 1967.

Finkelstein, Lawrence S. (ed.). *The United States and International Organization: The Changing Setting.* Cambridge: M.I.T. Press, 1969.

Frydenberg, Per. *Peace-Keeping: Experience and Evaluation.* Oslo: Norwegian Institute of International Affairs, 1964.

Frye, William R. *A United Nations Peace Force.* New York: Oceana Publications, 1957.

Goodrich, Leland M., and Anne P. Simons. *The United Nations and the Maintenance of International Peace and Security.* Washington: Brookings Institution, 1955.

Gordenker, Leon. *The UN Secretary-General and the Maintenance of Peace.* New York: Columbia University Press, 1967.

Gordon, J. King (ed.). *Canada's Role as a Middle Power.* Toronto: Canadian Institute of International Affairs, 1966.

Haekkerup, Per. "Scandinavia's Peace-Keeping Forces for UN," *Foreign Affairs*, Vol. 42 (July 1964).

Holmes, John W. "The Political and Philosophical Aspects of UN Security Forces," *International Journal*, Vol. 19 (Summer 1964).

James, Alan. *The Politics of Peace-Keeping*. New York: Praeger, 1969.

Lefever, Ernest W. *Uncertain Mandate*. Baltimore: Johns Hopkins Press, 1967.

————, and Wynfred Joshua. *United Nations Peacekeeping in the Congo: 1960–1964; An Analysis of Political, Executive, and Military Control*. Prepared for the U.S. Arms Control and Disarmament Agency. Washington: Brookings Institution, 1966.

Padelford, Norman J., and Leland M. Goodrich. *The United Nations in the Balance: Accomplishments and Prospects*. New York: Praeger, 1965.

Pearson, Lester B. "Force for the U.N.," *Foreign Affairs*, Vol. 35 (April 1957).

————. "Keeping the Peace," in Andrew W. Cordier and Wilder Foote (eds.), *The Quest for Peace*. New York: Columbia University Press, 1965.

Rikhye, I. J. *Preparation and Training of United Nations Peace-keeping Forces*. Adelphi Paper 9. London: Institute for Strategic Studies, 1964.

Rosner, Gabriella. *The United Nations Emergency Force*. New York: Columbia University Press, 1963.

Royal Institute of International Affairs, Institute for Strategic Studies. *Résumé of the Joint Conference on United Nations Security Operations*. Ditchley Park, Oxfordshire: RIIA, 1965.

Russell, Ruth B. *The United Nations and United States Security Policy*. Washington: Brookings Institution, 1968.

————. "United Nations Experience with Military Forces: Political and Legal Aspects." Processed. Washington: Brookings Institution, 1964.

Simons, Anne P. *The United States and the United Nations: The Search for International Peace and Security*. New York: Manhattan Publishing Co., 1967.

Stegenga, James A. *The United Nations Force in Cyprus*. Columbus: Ohio State University Press, 1968.

United Nations Association of the United States of America, National Policy Panel on Multilateral Alternatives to Unilateral Intervention. *Controlling Conflicts in the 1970's*. New York: UNA-USA, 1969.

Wainhouse, David W., and others. *International Peace Observation*. Baltimore: Johns Hopkins Press, 1966.

Wehberg, Hans. *Theory and Practice of International Policing*. London: Constable, 1935.

Young, Oran R. *The Intermediaries: Third Parties in International Crises*. Princeton: Princeton University Press, 1967.

Notes

CHAPTER 1

1. Inis L. Claude, Jr., "The United Nations, the United States, and the Maintenance of Peace," in Lawrence S. Finkelstein (ed.), *The United States and International Organization: The Changing Setting* (M.I.T. Press, 1969), p. 73.

2. The pledges and a companion Security Council resolution are reprinted in U.S. Department of State *Bulletin*, Vol. 59 (July 8, 1968), p. 56.

3. Inis L. Claude, Jr., "The Security Council," in Evan Luard (ed.), *The Evolution of International Organizations* (Praeger, 1966), p. 78.

4. See Edward T. Rowe, "Changing Patterns in the Voting Success of Member States in the United Nations General Assembly: 1945–1966," *International Organization*, Vol. 23 (Spring 1969), pp. 231–53.

5. American and Russian behavior is analyzed, especially from the viewpoint of their majority and minority positions at the UN, in John G. Stoessinger, *The United Nations and the Superpowers* (Random House, 1965); see also Inis L. Claude, Jr., *The Changing United Nations* (Random House, 1967), Chap. 2.

6. Quoted in Andrew Boyd, *United Nations: Piety, Myth, and Truth* (Penguin Books, 1964), p. 48.

7. Quoted in Alexander Dallin, *The Soviet Union at the United Nations* (Praeger, 1962), p. 137.

CHAPTER 2

1. Quoted in Alfred Vagts, *A History of Militarism* (rev. ed., Free Press, 1967), p. 35.

2. The draft is Document 10 in Ray S. Baker, *Woodrow Wilson and World Settlement* (Doubleday, 1922), Article X, p. 92.

3. Ruth B. Russell, *A History of the United Nations Charter: The Role of the United States 1940–1945* (Brookings Institution, 1958), pp. 96–98.

4. Examples are plentiful. The 1968 presidential campaign found Hubert Humphrey proclaiming that "the alternative to American peacekeeping cannot be no peacekeeping" but "must be peacekeeping by the United Nations or by regional agencies" (San Francisco address, "A New Strategy for Peace," reprinted in the *Washington Post*, Sept. 27, 1968). Early in 1969 the private United Nations Association of the United States released a study panel's report echoing this notion in its opening sentences, urging stronger UN peacekeeping because "means must be found, promptly,

for a larger number of countries to share more fully the responsibility for international peacekeeping. It would be a mistake for the United States to continue carrying, or attempting to carry, so much of the responsibility alone" (United Nations Association of the United States of America, National Policy Panel on Multilateral Alternatives to Unilateral Intervention, *Controlling Conflicts in the 1970's* [UNA-USA, 1969], p. 7.

5. Lincoln P. Bloomfield, Amelia C. Leiss, and others, *The Control of Local Conflict: A Design Study on Arms Control and Limited War in the Developing Areas. Summary Report,* prepared for the U.S. Arms Control and Disarmament Agency (Center for International Studies, Massachusetts Institute of Technology, 1967), Vol. 2, p. 12. See also Bloomfield and Leiss, *Controlling Small Wars: A Strategy for the 1970's* (Knopf, 1969).

6. Appendix A provides a synopsis of all UN peacekeeping missions. For more detailed discussions, see Alan James, *The Politics of Peace-Keeping* (Praeger, 1969); Lincoln P. Bloomfield and others, *International Military Forces: The Question of Peacekeeping in an Armed and Disarming World* (Little, Brown, 1964); Arthur M. Cox, *Prospects for Peacekeeping* (Brookings Institution, 1967); David W. Wainhouse and others, *International Peace Observation* (Johns Hopkins Press, 1966); and D. W. Bowett, *United Nations Forces* (Praeger, 1964).

7. See pp. 31–32 for some indication of how civilian specialists, especially civilian policemen, supplement the activities of UN military peacekeepers in Cyprus.

8. Thomas M. Franck, *The Structure of Impartiality* (Macmillan, 1968), pp. 261, 307. This analysis is devoted mainly to lawmaking functions of impartial actors, but the theoretical insights are intended to apply as well to all third-party international decision makers.

9. Inis L. Claude, Jr., *Power and International Relations* (Random House, 1962), p. 110.

10. For the larger operations, these regularly take the form of Status of Forces Agreements. Those for Egypt, the Congo, and Cyprus are reprinted in *IPKO Documentation,* No. 22 (July 1967). See also Bowett, *United Nations Forces,* Chap. 13.

11. Appendix B charts data on the participation of the fifty-one countries that have served in the twelve UN operations.

12. The UN vessels were from Belgium, Denmark, West Germany, Italy, the Netherlands, Sweden, and Yugoslavia. Joseph P. Lash, *Dag Hammarskjold: Custodian of the Brushfire Peace* (Doubleday, 1961), pp. 95–97.

13. These two cases are reviewed in Wainhouse and others, *International Peace Observation,* pp. 323–57, 489–525.

14. Bruce F. Macdonald, "A Canadian Serviceman Looks at United Nations Peace-Keeping Operations" (paper prepared as a speech script; processed), pp. 5–6.

15. Kjell Goldmann, *Peace-keeping and Self-Defence,* IPKO Monograph 7 (Paris: International Information Center on Peace-Keeping Operations, 1968).

16. See ibid., and James A. Stegenga, *The United Nations Force in Cyprus* (Ohio State University Press, 1968), pp. 126–38.

17. A. J. Wilson, *Some Principles for Peace-Keeping Operations: A Guide for Senior Officers,* IPKO Monograph 2 (Paris: International Information Center on Peace-Keeping Operations, 1967), p. 6.

18. E. L. M. Burns, "Disarmament, Peace-keeping and the Middle East," *Disarmament* (Paris), No. 16 (December 1967), p. 7.

19. In purely tactical terms, these priorities, these gradations of minimum necessary pressure, are not unique to peacekeepers. The control of violence in other environments has also put high premiums on minimum coercion and maximum cooperation from the community being controlled. The most conspicuous examples—all displaying some parallelisms to peacekeeping in organizational methods, operational assumptions, and control objectives—are the activities of American policemen in volatile metropolitan areas across the nation, U.S. military governments after World War II, and British colonial internal security doctrines.

20. This is of course in addition to any broader mediation that might be conducted at top political levels by special diplomatic representatives of the secretary-general.

21. One thoughtful civilian expert who has seen the Cyprus operation at close range has drawn from it this most important general lesson: "UN doctrines for assisting in the maintenance of law and order . . . may be evolving in a direction where the rigid distinction between impotence on the one hand and outright control on the other" are meaningless. The Cyprus force has "confounded" the "gloomy belief" that impartiality is to be equated with impotence, that "the conciliatory method is a recipe for failure," and that "impartiality only invites the man with the big stick to beat the fellow with the little one." Anthony Verrier, "Guyana and Cyprus: Techniques of Peace-keeping," *Royal United Service Institution Journal,* Vol. 3 (November 1966), pp. 298, 303.

22. "Introduction to the Annual Report of the Secretary General on the Work of the Organization," *UN Monthly Chronicle,* Vol. 4 (October 1967), p. 101.

23. C. W. C. Oman, *The Art of War in the Middle Ages: 378–1515,* rev. and ed. by John H. Beeler (Cornell University Press, 1953).

24. Gabriella Rosner, *The United Nations Emergency Force* (Columbia University Press, 1963); Ernest W. Lefever, *Uncertain Mandate* (Johns Hopkins Press, 1967); Stegenga, *United Nations Force in Cyprus.*

CHAPTER 3

1. William R. Frye, *A United Nations Peace Force* (Oceana Publications, 1957), p. 46.

2. Gabriella Rosner, *The United Nations Emergency Force* (Columbia University Press, 1963), p. 207.

3. F. H. Hinsley, *Power and the Pursuit of Peace* (Cambridge University Press, 1967), p. 13.

4. Quoted in Stefan T. Possony, "Peace Enforcement," *Yale Law Journal,* Vol. 55, No. 5 (1946), pp. 916–17.

5. Inis L. Claude, Jr., *Power and International Relations* (Random House, 1962), p. 103.

6. Case studies are found in Méir Ydit, *International Territories* (Leiden: A. W. Sijthoff, 1961), pp. 95–184. Also see D. W. Bowett, *United Nations Forces* (Praeger, 1964), p. 4; and Hans Wehberg, *Theory and Practice of International Policing* (London: Constable, 1935), pp. 11–14.

7. Wehberg, *International Policing*, pp. 19–20.

8. Bowett, *United Nations Forces*, p. 11.

9. F. P. Walters, *A History of the League of Nations* (Oxford University Press, 1952), Vol. 2, p. 598.

10. See, for instance, the controversy inside Sweden on League issues. Swedish Institute of International Affairs, Special Study Group, *Sweden and the United Nations: Report . . .*, National Studies on International Organization, prepared for the Carnegie Endowment for International Peace (Manhattan Publishing Co., 1956), pp. 16–22.

11. Walters, *History of the League of Nations*, Vol. 1, p. 107.

12. Initial logistical plans for the Vilna force are summarized in a special report to the Council, reprinted in Sarah Wambaugh, *Plebiscites Since the World War* (Carnegie Endowment for International Peace, 1933), Vol. 2, p. 270.

13. Ibid., pp. 272–73.

14. This was the language of the League Council's authorizing resolution, reprinted in *League of Nations Official Journal* (December 1934), p. 1762.

15. J. Brind, "League of Nations: Report by the Commander in Chief, International Force in the Saar . . . 26 October 1935," *IPKO Documentation*, No. 29 (February 1968).

16. *League of Nations Official Journal* (September 1934), p. 1144.

17. Royal Institute of International affairs, *The Saar Plebiscite*, Information Department Papers, 14 (London: RIIA, 1934).

18. This, though, was not his optimum choice. He proposed early in 1934 that a small international force, apparently composed of military units, be sent to the Saar. German opposition blocked the proposal at the time. *League of Nations Official Journal* (December 1934), p. 1708.

19. *League of Nations Official Journal* (September 1934), p. 1141.

20. The commander's report mentions that one way the civil authorities in the Saar were able to request assistance from the force was to consult "one of the few neutral police officers whom it had been necessary to introduce a few months previously" (Brind, "League of Nations," p. 5). This is the only mention of the police in the report.

21. *League of Nations Official Journal* (December 1934), p. 1729.

22. Ibid., p. 1707.

23. Brind, "League of Nations," p. 17.

24. Brind reported that "the friendly but correct relations which the troops were able to establish with all sections of the population . . . contributed very largely towards the absence of disorder" (ibid., p. 6).

25. Ibid., p. 4.

26. Anthony Verrier, "Guyana and Cyprus: Techniques of Peacekeeping," *Royal United Service Institution Journal*, Vol. 3 (November 1966), pp. 298–306.

27. *League of Nations Official Journal* (December 1934), p. 1762.

28. Brind, "League of Nations," pp. 6–13.

29. Ibid., p. 1.

30. See Egon F. Raushofen-Wertheimer, *The International Secretariat* (Carnegie Endowment for International Peace, 1945), Chap. 1 and pp. 239–40.

31. "League of Nations," p. 5.

32. In the 1933 Leticia dispute between Colombia and Peru, an ad hoc League commission set up to administer the contested territory was empowered to "call on military forces of its own selection to assist in maintaining order," but opposition to foreign intervention—especially strong among Latin Americans—forced the League to use regular Colombian soldiers under international command, sanitized by League armbands and flags. Wehberg, *International Policing*, p. 17.

33. These cases are summarized in David W. Wainhouse and others, *International Peace Observation* (Johns Hopkins Press, 1966), Pt. 1.

CHAPTER 4

1. This term is found in UN Security Council, *Official Records* (SCOR), 1st year, 23d Mtg. (Feb. 16, 1946), p. 369; see also UN Doc. S/268/Rev. 1, Feb. 13, 1947.

2. *In the Cause of Peace: Seven Years with the United Nations* (Macmillan, 1954), p. 98.

3. The French plan is reprinted in Ray S. Baker, *Woodrow Wilson and World Settlement* (Doubleday, Page, 1922), Vol. 3, pp. 152–62.

4. League of Nations Covenant, Article 16.

5. The Protocol (officially called "Protocol for the Pacific Settlement of International Disputes") is an important document in the intellectual history of the interwar years. E. H. Carr, in his classic realist critique, indicts it as one of the products of the "dangerous path" of abstract rationalism that led to utopian "efforts to perfect the [League] machinery, to standardize the procedure, to close the 'gaps' in the Covenant . . . and to make the application of sanctions 'automatic' " (*The Twenty Years' Crisis, 1919–1939* [Harper Torchbooks, 1964], p. 29).

6. Article 13 of the Geneva Protocol.

7. Donald C. Blaisdell, *Arms for the United Nations*, U.S. Department of State Publication 3203 (June 1948), p. 144.

8. Inis L. Claude, Jr., *Power and International Relations* (Random House, 1962), p. 190. The *Report of the Military Staff Committee* documents U.S.-Soviet differences as well as those among the four Western powers (SCOR, 2d year, Spec. Suppl. 1, April 30, 1947).

9. See Article 3 of the Military Staff Committee *Report*, p. 1.

10. See Ruth B. Russell, *A History of the United Nations Charter: The Role of the United States 1940–1945* (Brookings Institution, 1958), pp. 234–37, 257–58, and 467. A

prominent private study, at first given only confidential and limited circulation, was prepared early in 1944 by the Council on Foreign Relations (*Some Problems of International Policing* [New York: CFR, 1944]). While it analyzed defects in each method, the report's conclusions were weighty against an internationalized force from the standpoint of U.S. political and military interests. Contributors included Hamilton Fish Armstrong, Allen Dulles, Grayson Kirk, Hanson Baldwin, and Henry Wriston.

A massive peace prospectus of interwar vintage that covered each alternative is in David Davies, *An International Police Force: An Abridged Edition of "The Problem of the Twentieth Century"* (London: Ernest Benn, 1932), p. 368.

11. Lie recalled that he, Ralph Bunche, and others prepared a plan that "assumed," on grounds not altogether clear, that even though Article 43 negotiations were unsuccessful "a sufficient degree of agreement had been reached for the establishment of a United Nations land force—an emergency force [for Palestine] composed of those minimum units which the Big Five were committed to place at the Security Council's disposal" (*In the Cause of Peace*, p. 166). At an earlier stage of negotiations he is said to have "sounded out" Belgium, Sweden, the Netherlands, Norway, Brazil, and Mexico as to their willingness to send troops to Palestine. Stephen M. Schwebel, *The Secretary-General of the United Nations: His Political Powers and Practice* (Harvard University Press, 1952), p. 140. In a legal memorandum prepared by the secretariat—a document that provoked much controversy for Lie because of its interpretations of Security Council authority—it is vaguely implied that forces somehow related to Article 43 could be dispatched to Palestine; SCOR, 3d Year, Suppl. (January–March 1948), p. 14. In any case, during the months immediately preceding the Israeli declaration of independence and the outbreak of war, the United States finally decided that it was not prepared to send American troops to enforce partition and that it would be out of the question to have Soviet troops in Palestine. See Lawrence D. Weiler and Anne P. Simons, *The United States and the United Nations: The Search for International Peace and Security*, prepared for the Carnegie Endowment for International Peace (Manhattan Publishing Co., 1967), pp. 207–13.

12. Lie's own account of his talks on the plan is in *In the Cause of Peace*, Chap. 16. Aside from any structural defects in his ambitious program, Lie was simply not able to convince Stalin that it was not all a U.S. scheme, and he could not persuade a very uninterested Truman or Acheson that the plan had worth or sensibility in the increasingly harsh cold war atmosphere.

13. GA Res. 377A (V), Nov. 3, 1950. The text is in *Review of the United Nations Charter: A Collection of Documents*, S. Doc. 87, 83 Cong. 2 sess. (1954), p. 557.

14. Institutionally the substitution was supposed to work this way: "Instead of commitments through Article 43 agreements, the Member governments were unilaterally to designate forces for United Nations use on call of the appropriate political organ. Instead of the Military Staff Committee, professional advice would come from the panel of experts" (Ruth B. Russell, *The United Nations and United States Security Policy* [Brookings Institution, 1968], p. 131).

15. The commission was an anomaly in several respects, most notably in that it was the only part of the Uniting for Peace Resolution that the Soviet bloc showed any disposition to view favorably, at least at first. Both the Soviet Union and Czechoslovakia initially agreed to serve on the body. But in 1952, over Soviet objections, the commission was given certain observation duties in Greece by the General Assembly. The commission functioned in this case (it was never again used) through a five-member subgroup on which communist members of the parent body naturally were not represented, and the subgroup's reporting procedure seems not to have depended on review by the full commission. See David W. Wainhouse and others, *International Peace Observation* (Johns Hopkins Press, 1966), pp. 226–27, 236–37; and Leland M. Goodrich and Anne P. Simons, *The United Nations and the Maintenance of International Peace and Security* (Brookings Institution, 1955), pp. 175, 351–52.

16. Alexander Dallin, *The Soviet Union at the United Nations* (Praeger, 1962), p. 31.

17. See Oran R. Young, *The Intermediaries: Third Parties in International Crises* (Princeton University Press, 1967), pp. 126–35, for an excellent theoretical analysis of the resolution, its relation to American interests, and its dependence on assumptions of Western control of UN political processes and of Western capabilities for mustering the needed collective military strength.

18. Julius Stone, *Legal Controls of International Conflict* (rev. ed., London: Stevens and Sons, 1959), p. 275. The Assembly seems to have been sufficiently concerned about the Soviet reaction to this U.S. initiative to include, as a sop, in a less-often-cited penultimate section of the Uniting for Peace Resolution, Soviet-sponsored language calling on the Security Council to "devise measures for the earliest application" of the Article 43 system. See GA Res. 377B (V), Nov. 3, 1950.

19. UN General Assembly, *Official Records* (GAOR), 6th sess., Suppl. 13 (1951), Annex 2.

20. Weiler and Simons, *The United States and the United Nations*, p. 295. The authors argue: "Not only was [this] . . . concept compatible with the American estimate of priorities in developing the free world's defenses, it was also the principal vehicle through which forces could be created. Aside from those nations which were associated with the United States through either regional security arrangements or bilateral programs, there was little interest in building up forces for collective action through the United Nations" (p. 296).

21. Quoted in David Cox, "Canada's Interest in Peacekeeping: Some Political and Military Considerations," in Canadian Institute of International Affairs, *Peacekeeping: International Challenge and Canadian Response* (Toronto: CIIA, 1968), p. 44.

22. Swedish Institute of International Affairs, Special Study Group, *Sweden and the United Nations: Report . . .*, National Studies on International Organization, prepared for the Carnegie Endowment for International Peace (Manhattan Publishing Co., 1956), pp. 109–17. See, for instance, the account of debates inside Sweden: "Discussion concerning the implications to Sweden . . . centered around . . . how such obligations

would affect Sweden's efforts to avoid becoming involved in conflicts between the great powers" (p. 110).

23. Alfred G. Katzen, "Collective Security: The Work of the Collective Measures Committee," in Clyde Eagleton and Richard N. Swift (eds.), *Annual Review of United Nations Affairs, 1952* (New York University Press, 1953), p. 207.

24. One American expert illustrated this connection with early sanctions planning by pointing out that Harding Bancroft, who had been brought into the State Department in 1945 chiefly to work on problems of economic sanctions, had been appointed U.S. representative on the Collective Measures Committee. This same expert believed the secretariat should have been studying political and economic sanctions in 1946–47 while the Military Staff Committee was concentrating on the military side. Joseph Johnson, "The Uniting for Peace Resolution," in Clyde Eagleton and Richard N. Swift (eds.), *Annual Review of United Nations Affairs, 1951* (New York University Press, 1952), p. 241.

25. Stephen M. Schwebel, "A United Nations 'Guard' and a United Nations 'Legion,'" Appendix in William R. Frye, *A United Nations Peace Force* (Oceana Publications, 1957), p. 216.

26. Ole Karup Pederson, "Scandinavia and the UN 'Stand-by Forces,'" *Cooperation and Conflict*, No. 1 (1967), p. 39.

27. Case studies can be found in Wainhouse and others, *International Peace Observation*, pp. 221–323.

28. Brian E. Urquhart, "A UN Perspective," in Lincoln Bloomfield and others, *International Military Forces: The Question of Peacekeeping in an Armed and Disarming World* (Little, Brown, 1964), p. 129.

29. UNTSO once had some seven hundred military observers, while neither UNMOGIP nor UNCI ever exceeded seventy-five. Naval vessels were used for observation and surveillance in UNTSO. A ship off shore served as a communications center for UNCI. Fairly sophisticated radio-monitoring equipment was used in UNSCOB. In UNSCOB and UNCI, military observers often carried sidearms or carbines, while in UNMOGIP and UNTSO most of them were unarmed. UNMOGIP deployment was uncomplicated: teams with a few military observers and a radio operator were stationed at specific geographic points on either side of a demarcation line. In Palestine, observer coverage was complex and shifting. Observers were assigned not only to Arab and Israeli army units but to convoys and at harbors, coasts, and airports. In Indonesia, observers were sprinkled throughout the territory, interposed between hostile forces, stationed at assembly areas for disengaged troops, and posted in mobile teams to the higher military headquarters of the opposing armies.

30. Sylvain Lourié, "The United Nations Military Observer Group in India and Pakistan," *International Organization*, Vol. 9 (February 1955), pp. 21–22; Paul Mohn, "Problems of Truce Supervision," *International Conciliation*, No. 478 (February 1952), p. 67.

31. Excerpts from the handbook are found in GAOR, 4th sess., Suppl. 8 (1949), p. 22.

32. Quoted remarks are from *To Amend the United Nations Participation Act of 1945,* Hearings before the House Committee on Foreign Affairs, 81 Cong. 1 sess. (1949), pp. 61, 62, and 79. Americanization of peacekeeping was evident throughout testimony at this time. Congress was reassured that U.S. control over UN operations was firm, that participation by American personnel was vital to U.S. security objectives, and that their intelligence-gathering potential could immediately benefit the United States. For domestic reasons these reassurances had to be strong and persuasive if Congress was to be convinced that the world organization deserved full U.S. support.

33. Weiler and Simons, *The United States and the United Nations,* p. 223.

34. The episode is summarized in David Brook, *Preface to Peace: The United Nations and the Arab-Israel Armistice System* (Public Affairs Press, 1964), pp. 93–97.

35. Folke Bernadotte, *To Jerusalem* (London: Hodder and Stoughton, 1951), p. 45. See also SCOR, 3d year, Suppl. for July (1948), p. 52.

36. The Council dialogue is recorded in SCOR, 3d year, 320th Mtg. (June 15, 1948), pp. 7, 9.

37. Logistics data are drawn from: a State Department compilation presented to Congress in 1949 and appended to *Amendment of the United Nations Participation Act of 1945,* H. Rept. 591, 81 Cong. 1 sess. (1949), pp. 7–8; Wainhouse and others, *International Peace Observation,* passim; for UNTSO, GAOR, 3d sess., 5th Cttee, Annexes (1948), pp. 104–05; and for Indonesia, SCOR, 4th year, Special Suppl. 5 (Feb. 15, 1950), p. 29.

38. This has often been the only expedient practice at the outset of operations, even recent ones like that in India and Pakistan in 1965; and it is not confined to the UN. When the newly created International Control Commissions began functioning in 1954 in Indochina, French logistics support was essential.

39. Samples of tables can be found in these sources: for UNSCOB in 1949, GAOR, 4th sess., 5th Cttee, Annex, Vol. 1, Agenda item 21 (1949), p. 13; for the Palestine mission during the same year, ibid., p. 3; for the Kashmir mission in 1950, GAOR, 5th sess., Annexes, Agenda item 39 (1950), p. 40; for the Indonesian mission in 1950, ibid., p. 37. For summary descriptions of civilian staffing at the outset of these missions, consult Wainhouse and others, *International Peace Observation,* passim. A table listing administrative staff after UNEF's first year of duty is found in GAOR, 12th sess., Annexes, Agenda item 65 (1957), p. 16.

40. The paper is "United Nations Special Committee on the Balkans: Observation Group Policy," reprinted in GAOR, 3d sess., 1st Cttee, Annexes (1948), pp. 50–55.

41. A brief description of prevailing financial practices in 1949 is found in *To Amend the United Nations Participation Act of 1945,* pp. 39–40.

42. A thorough description of Lie's blueprint and an analysis of member-state reactions is found in Schwebel, "A United Nations 'Guard' and a United Nations 'Le-

gion.' " The original documents prepared by the secretary-general are in GAOR, 3d sess., Annexes, Pt. 2 (1948), pp. 6–15, and GAOR, 4th sess., Suppl. 13 (1949).

43. Schwebel, "A United Nations 'Guard,' " p. 202.

44. GAOR, 4th sess., Suppl. 13 (1949), p. 2.

45. Lie, *In the Cause of Peace*, p. 193.

46. GAOR, 3d sess., Annexes, Pt. 2 (1948), p. 6.

47. Lie, *In the Cause of Peace*, p. 287.

48. A brief account is in J. L. Granatstein, "Canada: Peacekeeper; A Survey of Canada's Participation in Peacekeeping Operations," in Canadian Institute of International Affairs, *Peacekeeping*, pp. 118–19.

CHAPTER 5

1. *United Nations Emergency Force: Summary Study of the Experience Derived From the Establishment and Operation of the Force*, UN Doc. A/3943, Oct. 9, 1958.

2. Joseph P. Lash, *Dag Hammarskjold: Custodian of the Brushfire Peace* (Doubleday, 1961), pp. 178–79.

3. Leon Gordenker, *The UN Secretary General and the Maintenance of Peace* (Columbia University Press, 1967), Chap. 4.

4. Wilder Foote (ed.), *Servant of Peace: A Selection of the Speeches and Statements of Dag Hammarskjold, 1953–1961* (Harper & Row, 1962), p. 94.

5. UN General Assembly, *Official Records* (GAOR), 12th sess., Suppl. 1A (1957), reprinted in *United Nations Review*, Vol. 4 (October 1957), p. 15.

6. "Force for the U.N.," *Foreign Affairs*, Vol. 35 (April 1957), pp. 402, 401.

7. This dual readiness was clearly the expectation evident in the *Summary Study:* "The approach indicated," Hammarskjöld wrote, "suggests a way in which the United Nations, within the limits of the Charter, may seek the most practical method of mustering and using, as necessary, the resources—both of nations and its own—required for operations involving military personnel which may be conceived in response to the needs of specific conflict situations" (p. 75).

8. In 1957 Hammarskjöld used the phrase "should *the Organization* wish to build an agreed standby plan" (emphasis added); GAOR, 12th sess., Suppl. 1A (1957), reprinted in *United Nations Review*, Vol. 4 (October 1957), p. 15. In 1958 he said that he hoped the *Summary Study* would "prove useful to any consideration that may ensue of the feasibility of standby arrangements for a United Nations Force" (GAOR, 13th sess., Suppl. 1A [1958], p. 2).

9. He noted that "the arrangements discussed in this report do not cover the type of force envisaged under Chapter VII of the Charter" (*Summary Study*, pp. 62–63).

10. Ibid.

11. Ibid., pp. 68–69, 72–73. This assertion that a military staff in the secretariat would have to be specifically authorized by the Assembly was later regretted by those who were resigned to Assembly inaction and therefore encouraged the establishment

of a unit simply by virtue of a secretary-general's ordinary discretion over internal staff matters.

12. The fate of the Study is traced in Ruth B. Russell, "United Nations Experience with Military Forces: Political and Legal Aspects" (Brookings Institution, 1964; processed), pp. 79–86; Lash, *Dag Hammarskjold*, pp. 177–82.

13. GAOR, 13th sess., Special Political Committee, 100th Mtg. (Nov. 5, 1968), pp. 63–64.

14. Lash, *Dag Hammarskjold*, pp. 181–82.

15. The twenty-three recipients were Afghanistan, Argentina, Brazil, Burma, Canada, Ceylon, Chile, Colombia, Denmark, Ecuador, Finland, India, Indonesia, Ireland, Italy, Nepal, the Netherlands, Norway, Peru, Portugal, Sweden, Thailand, and Yugoslavia. *U.S. Participation in the UN: Report by the President to the Congress for the year 1959*, U.S. Department of State Publication 7016 (1960), p. 26. Singling out these twenty-three was not as arbitrary as it might at first appear. Given the absence of any formal authority and the controversial subject matter, Hammarskjöld would have been on even thinner ice had he sent this communication to all member states. By tying the request to a natural or logical group of suppliers who had already performed this service, he was protecting himself at least partially.

16. John W. Holmes, "Is There a Future for Middlepowermanship?" in J. King Gordon (ed.), *Canada's Role as a Middle Power* (Toronto: Canadian Institute of International Affairs, 1966), p. 24.

17. *The Economist* (Great Britain), March 16, 1957.

18. The sentiment was Lord Salisbury's and is recounted in Gordon A. Craig, *War, Politics, and Diplomacy* (Praeger, 1966), p. 249.

19. Erik Lonnroth, "Sweden: The Diplomacy of Östen Undén," in Gordon A, Craig and Felix Gilbert (eds.), *The Diplomats: 1919–1939* (Atheneum, 1967), Vol. 1. p. 90.

20. A concise comparison of the respective powers' roles during the formative periods of the League and the UN is found in Inis L. Claude, Jr., *Swords into Plowshares* (3d ed., rev., Random House, 1964), Chaps. 3 and 4. See also the essays in Norman J. Padelford and Leland Goodrich (eds.), *The United Nations in the Balance* (Praeger, 1965), especially Pt. 3.

21. Quoted by Blair Fraser, "Canada: Mediator or Busybody?" in Gordon (ed.), *Canada's Role as a Middle Power*, p. 7.

22. F. H. Hinsley, *Power and the Pursuit of Peace* (Cambridge University Press, 1967), pp. 319–20.

23. Paul E. Zinner, "Czechoslovakia: The Diplomacy of Edward Beneš," in Craig and Gilbert (eds.), *The Diplomats: 1919–1939*, Vol. 1, p. 117.

24. Ruth B. Russell, *A History of the United Nations Charter* (Brookings Institution, 1958), p. 652.

25. Quoted in Marina S. Finkelstein and Lawrence S. Finkelstein (eds.), *Collective Security* (Chandler, 1966), p. 147.

26. Quoted in K. Brodin, K. Goldmann, and C. Lange, "The Policy of Neutrality: Official Doctrines of Finland and Sweden," *Cooperation and Conflict*, No. 1 (1968), p. 26.

27. Annette Baker Fox, "The Small States of Western Europe in the United Nations," in Padelford and Goodrich (eds.), *The United Nations in the Balance*, pp. 410–22.

28. The phrase is attributed to the Finns. Ibid., p. 418.

29. Foote (ed.), *Servant of Peace*, p. 111.

30. Fox, "The Small States of Western Europe in the United Nations," p. 419.

31. An interesting attempt has been made by the military sociologist Morris Janowitz to develop some preliminary connections between UN peacekeeping and his concept of modern military establishments as "constabulary" forces, which are devoted less to victory-oriented fighting roles than to violence-reduction functions, including arms control and disarmament, that minimize the instabilities threatening international order. See Morris Janowitz, "Armed Forces and Society: A World Perspective," in Jacques van Doorn (ed.), *Armed Forces and Society: Sociological Essays* (The Hague: Mouton, 1968), pp. 15–38. See also J. A. Jackson, "The Irish Army and the Development of the Constabulary Concept," in ibid., pp. 109–26.

32. Address to the Third Banff Conference on World Development, Banff, Alberta, August 27, 1965; reprinted in Gordon (ed.), *Canada's Role as a Middle Power*, pp. 195–209.

33. "Scandinavia's Peace-Keeping Forces for UN," *Foreign Affairs*, Vol. 42 (July 1964), pp. 675–76. This article is generally regarded as a semiofficial position paper on the Scandinavian forces.

34. This was Thant's official position in 1964 after the Nordic offers had been publicly announced: "I have welcomed the offers, but have been in no position to do much more than this, in the absence of any authorizing action by an appropriate organ of the United Nations." GAOR, 19th sess., Suppl. 1A (1964), p. 9.

35. Brian E. Urquhart, "Problems of the Secretariat," in Richard N. Swift (ed.), *Annual Review of United Nations Affairs, 1963–64* (Oceana Publications, 1965), p. 112.

36. GAOR, 15th sess., Suppl. 1A (1960), p. 4.

37. During this UN preparatory period there were, in addition to discussions through the UN missions, a series of visits to New York by Scandinavian planners. Close contact with the Scandinavians was maintained especially by the small military adviser's staff in the secretariat, which at one point prepared, at the request of the Swedish General Staff, blueprints for the entire Scandinavian force.

38. U Thant, "United Nations Peace Force, An Address to the Harvard Alumni Association . . . June 13, 1963 . . .," in Lincoln P. Bloomfield and others, *International Military Forces: The Question of Peacekeeping in an Armed and Disarming World* (Little, Brown, 1964), p. 259.

39. Haekkerup, "Scandinavia's Peace-Keeping Forces for UN," pp. 676–78.

40. "Recruitment for the UN Standby Force," Papers of the Conference on Ear-

marked Units for United Nations—The 2nd Oslo Conference (1965; processed), p. 5.

41. J. B. Goth and others, "The Status of Nordic Standby Forces for UN Duty," Papers of the Conference on Earmarked Units for United Nations—The 2nd Oslo Conference (1965; processed), p. 4; and Per Frydenberg, *Peace-Keeping: Experience and Evaluation* (Oslo: Norwegian Institute of International Affairs, 1964), p. 321.

42. Frydenberg, *Peace-Keeping*, pp. 314–15.

43. L. M. K. Skern, "United Nations Peace-Keeping Operations from a Danish Viewpoint," reprinted in *IPKO Documentation*, No. 2 (February 1967), p. 10.

44. Basic data are found in Institute for Strategic Studies, *The Military Balance 1968– 1969* (London: ISS, 1968), p. 155.

45. See, for example, Ole Karup Pederson, "Scandinavia and the UN Stand-by Forces," *Cooperation and Conflict*, No. 1 (1967), p. 38.

46. Job-protection legislation has long been part of the scene in Scandinavia because the mobilization armies undergo frequent refresher training after compulsory service, usually every few years or so. Such legislation is clearly needed. Therefore the Norwegians did not have to write new law in 1964, but merely amended one already on the books.

47. Frydenberg, *Peace-Keeping*, p. 321.

48. Ibid., pp. 321, 327. The defense minister's caution may be read into his acknowledgment that in some undefined circumstances "it might not be considered justifiable to recruit ordered personnel" (p. 325).

49. What the military were proposing would not have required amendment of the constitution, but only a legislative exception permitted by the constitution's Article 25, which says that the territorial army "may never, without the consent of the Storting, be employed beyond the borders of the Kingdom."

50. These revisions of the original January legislative proposal were reported by the military committee in *Innst. S. nr. 248 (1963–64)*, May 28, 1964. (Translated for the author.)

51. Ole Espersen, *FN-Styrker I Retlig Belysning* (Köbenhavn: Juristforbundets Forlag, 1965), pp. 194–95. (Translated for the author.)

52. UN mobilization for a standby would be even more troublesome than ordinary national service remobilizations for refresher training, which are regularly scheduled in advance.

53. Cary E. Landis,"Blue Bonnets for Doctor Bunche: Some Aspects of Earmarked Military Forces for United Nations Duty," study prepared in the U.S. Department of State Seventh Senior Seminar in Foreign Policy, Foreign Service Institute (June 11, 1965; processed), p. 56.

54. Ibid., p. 44.

55. Seventy-eight signed three-year contracts and 124 made the more reasonable one-year commitment. *IPKO Documentation*, No. 14 (June 1967), p. 16.

56. In the air force, however, there was some difficulty getting officers for a seventy-three-man, four-aircraft, medium-range transport unit, and the incident uncovered one unexpected effect of the disparate financial and contractual conditions in Scandinavia. By 1965 staff and observer standby positions for air force officers had been filled. Recruiting for a helicopter unit had not been started. An initial drive to get transport unit volunteers had failed because the potential signatories, all members of Norway's only regular air transport squadron, knew very well that they were getting less favorable contract terms, especially insurance and overseas allowances, than their counterparts elsewhere in Scandinavia. The officers forwarded their complaints via their union, the Air Defense Officers' Association. It was known at the time (1965) that Norway was negotiating with Sweden and Denmark about standardizing some of the contract conditions, and the Norwegian officer then in direct charge informed the Ministry of Defense that unless contract conditions were changed a volunteer transport unit would not be set up. As of early 1967 the situation remained unchanged, though it was acknowledged by those concerned that the officers were objecting "in principle" and that if they were needed in a UN emergency they would be speedily available, as they had been in the past. In later years the army, perhaps with an eye on this air force experience, raised its overseas allowances for UN soldiers, bringing them in line with Denmark's. St. Prp. Nr. 1 (1967–68), Forsvarsdepartementet Forsvars Budgjettet For Terminen (1968), Chap. 1789, pp. 75–76. (Translated for the author.)

57. Odd F. Klein, "Course for Officers at the Norwegian UN Peace-Keeping Battalion," Papers of the Conference on Earmarked Units for United Nations—The 2nd Oslo Conference (1965; processed), p. 1.

58. In June, Norwegian voters ended thirty years of Social Democratic Labor Party rule by installing in power a nonsocialist coalition.

59. The rather complicated details of the new procedures as well as the slight differences between the suggestions of the minister of defense and the chief of the army are described in *IPKO Documentation*, No. 14 (June 1967), pp. 14–19. The new legislation is reprinted in ibid., pp. 24–31.

60. As of January 1969, contracts actually in force numbered: 149 officers, 110 of them regulars; 45 sergeants, 33 of them regulars; and 948 other ranks.

61. Some may want to revolunteer, but most will not, if only because marriage sharply reduces the inclination to risk overseas duty. Most other ranks are now recruited in their twentieth or twenty-first year, and in the initial wave of volunteers only about 5 percent were married.

62. UN Doc. A/AC.121/14, March 20, 1968, p. 2.

63. From planners in the army command, suggestions were heard again during the 1965–66 reevaluation that one of the regular mobilization units be identified as a standby unit. Even if politically and legally acceptable, this would involve greater expense. Most of the members are married and in Norway receive correspondingly higher allowances while abroad. These are eventually charged to the UN, which assumes responsibility for most costs incurred after a standby unit begins actual service.

64. This was in response to Resolution 2134 (XX) of the General Assembly calling for national measures to enable rapid assistance in cases of natural disaster. UN Doc. E/4413, July 26, 1967.

65. The unit's readiness was tested in a mock exercise in 1965, and again in 1966. In the second, on signal, all personnel and equipment were moved to a staging area, transported elsewhere in Norway, and four hours after arrival at the destination were set up completely. Independent medical experts observed and evaluated the maneuver. The entire affair was given a great deal of press coverage, partly as propaganda for the new UN recruiting drive already under way in the army.

66. Goth and others, "The Status of Nordic Standby Forces for UN Duty," p. 8. Danish legislation in April 1964 stressed, however, that "the plans for the proposed force do not make the discontinuation of present UN commitments a precondition. Thus the establishment of the force could possibly take place concomitant with the withdrawal of forces presently serving under the UN" (Frydenberg, *Peace-Keeping*, p. 314).

67. Landis, "Blue Bonnets for Doctor Bunche," p. 44. Job protection is not available even for ordinary Danish army reserve officers, who can arrange for their reserve call-up periods only with some difficulty, or loss of vacation time. The laws do not completely eliminate the problem either. In Norway, and probably elsewhere, some employers have refused to give jobs to UN contractees—a step that does not violate the law, which only precludes dismissal from positions already held.

68. Goth and others, "The Status of Nordic Standby Forces for UN Duty," p. 10. The routine administrative servicing of the UN forces—personnel, finance, and the like—are taken care of within the ordinary channels of the Danish Ministry of Defense. Each Nordic practice varies in this regard. Matters handled in one country by a UN training unit are covered in another by a specially designated regular army regimental staff or elsewhere in the usual military bureaucracy.

69. Frydenberg, *Peace-Keeping*, p. 314.

70. Cited in *Ombudsman's Report—Addressed to the Department of Defense to Consider Whether It Was Necessary to Order Soldiers to Serve the UN Abroad* (J. No. 599/66). (Translated for the author.)

71. Formally, regular officers who do not volunteer are said to "be seconded" to UN forces. UN Doc. A/AC.121/12, March 20, 1968, p. 5.

72. The facts and disposition of this case, as described, are based largely on the *Ombudsman's Report.*

73. Letter to the author from Major E. M. Veisig, Danish Ministry of Defense, Nov. 12, 1969. The new authority was approved on June 18 and came into force on January 1, 1970.

74. A single legislative enactment provided continuing authorization for the use of conscripts in this unit, which contained 4,000 men until the early 1950s, when it was reduced to a commando detachment of 1,500 which remained until early 1958.

75. The same party had earlier insisted that any Danish combat troops going to

Korea (none went) must be volunteers. Aside from military tradition, the use of volunteers for Korea was urged because it was felt by some that direct national security interests were not at stake there—apparently the same reasoning that prompted the French and the Turks to send only volunteers to Korea. Brief coverage of this period of Danish debates on the Uniting for Peace Resolution is in Max Sorensen and Niels J. Haagerup, *Denmark and the United Nations*, National Studies on International Organization, prepared for the Carnegie Endowment for International Peace (Manhattan Publishing Co., 1956), pp. 21–32.

76. One suggestion considered in Denmark as early as 1964 was to ask conscripts to volunteer for standby duty and to give them in return reduction of their regular twelve- to fourteen-month service obligation. This was rejected because it would mean that the UN gets soldiers with incomplete training by Danish standards, or that standbys who are not called up during their contract period would get off with less military obligation than those who did not sign contracts and instead served the usual full time.

77. The Riksdag received these proposals on March 6, two days after the Security Council had authorized UNFICYP.

78. Permanent Mission of Sweden to the UN, press release, April 9, 1964.

79. Permanent Mission of Sweden to the UN, press release, July 16, 1964. Several things are confusing. "Provisionally organized" is vague, and the Mission's announcement did not indicate that this would be an ordinary replacement unit. In fact it implied the contrary by annexing "further information" reviewing the original general standby plans. The Mission may have been hinting at the government's intent by explaining that the unit would have "the same composition and equipment as the Swedish Battalion now serving in Cyprus." However, one observer who soon after this went to Sweden got the impression that the unit would not be similar to the Swedish Cyprus unit but would instead be an abbreviated version of the 1,600-man blueprint, consisting of 1,043 men organized as one battalion and the technical contingent. Landis, "Blue Bonnets for Doctor Bunche," p. 46.

80. This was the description used by Nils Stenqvist, then head of the Swedish UN Army Department, when, in April 1967, 1,212 Swedes were in the field. *The Swedish UN Stand-By Force and Experience*, IPKO Monograph 4 (August 1967), p. 2.

81. For instance, important supplementary legislation of 1967 states only that the standby force "shall be organized . . . in not more than three contingents, namely, two battalions and one technical contingent." Proclamation of the King in Council, No. 18, Jan. 13, 1967, Swedish Code of Statutes, No. 18/67.

82. This was true of the unit actually rotated to Cyprus in the spring of 1967, and it would have been true of the one going to UNEF that autumn if the operation had not been terminated in May. This information on training, rotation, and applications is drawn from an official recruiting notice dated April 10, 1967, and an application printed in 1966. (Translated for the author.)

83. A Swedish memorandum says only that "one of the [standby] battalions is

serving with UNFICYP," and does not mention the status of the other. UN Doc·
A/AC.121/11, March 20, 1968, p. 7.

84. The Service Act is quoted in Hidejiro Kotani, "Peace-Keeping; Problems for
Smaller Countries," *International Journal*, Vol. 19 (Summer 1964), p. 310; and the
legislation is in Frydenberg, *Peace-Keeping*, p. 330.

85. This is a small planning and coordinating unit of army headquarters. One section is responsible for general policy guidance, organization, and training; a second for
recruitment of infantry battalions; a third for handling all matters pertaining to observers and the technical contingent.

86. Landis, "Blue Bonnets for Doctor Bunche," p. 57.

87. Stenqvist, *The Swedish UN Stand-By Force and Experience*, p. 11.

88. Referring in 1965 to Denmark and Sweden, Landis noticed that "volunteers
are selective and Cyprus duty has not been as popular as duty in Gaza where the UN
has operated for over ten years. Adequate living facilities, recreation and well developed rotation programs are provided for the troop personnel, while in Cyprus duty
is taxing, military personnel are under considerable strain, housing accommodations are
not as good as those in Gaza and operations are often long and tiresome. These facts
are well known and have had their effects on recruiting" ("Blue Bonnets for Doctor
Bunche," p. 57).

89. Stenqvist, *The Swedish UN Stand-By Force and Experience*, p. 11.

90. Reserve officers serve an initial two and a half years and undergo annual service
every year. Conscript officers have an eighteen-month initial obligation and periodic
refresher training every second year. The Swedish unit rotated to Cyprus in spring
1967, for example, contained fifteen regular officers, eighteen reserve officers, and
thirteen conscript officers.

91. UN Doc. A/AC.121/11, March 20, 1968, p. 12.

92. GAOR, 5th sess., 1st Cttee, 361st Mtg. (Oct. 12, 1950), p. 108.

93. Swedish Institute of International affairs, Special Study Group, *Sweden and the
United Nations: Report . . .*, National Studies on International Organization, prepared
for the Carnegie Endowment for International Peace (Manhattan Publishing Co.,
1956), pp. 115–16. See also pp. 116–21.

94. The commander in chief had made an earlier investigation of standby possibilities, but in view of the then-heavy Congo and UNEF involvements, a decision was
postponed. However, new legislation was enacted for the voluntary training program
designed to meet current needs. Frydenberg, *Peace-Keeping*, pp. 328–29.

95. A semiofficial Finnish declaration on this point reads: "Should . . . UNFICYP
forces be reduced and the Finnish surveillance force disbanded, then preparations will
begin for the establishment of a permanent standby force under the law for a Finnish
peacekeeping force." See *IPKO Documentation*, No. 8 (June 1967), p. 5.

96. This ceiling was a tactical concession to the Finnish Communist party, which
not only tries to reduce overall defense expenditures but also harbors a special fear of a
potential Finnish "invisible" army like the one created in the 1930s and responsible for

the stubborn resistance against the Soviet invaders in the 1939 "winter war." The other tactical concession in 1964 was to the Social Democrats, who insisted on strong parliamentary controls over the government's participation in UN operations. The government accepted an obligation to "consult" with the committee on foreign relations before deciding on Finnish involvement.

97. Each branch is separately restricted, the army to 34,400, the navy to 4,500, and the air force to 3,000. Men who have completed their conscript service and are on reserve number half a million. Ninety percent of every adult age group liable for military duty can be trained within the framework of the treaty.

98. See UN Doc. A/AC.121/13, March 20, 1968.

99. The defense costs for 1968 are taken from Institute for Strategic Studies, *The Military Balance 1968–1969*, pp. 41–42. UN financial data are from unpublished national sources.

100. UN Doc. A/AC.121/13, March 20, 1968, p. 5.

101. UN Doc. S/5679, May 2, 1964.

102. When New Zealand withdrew in 1967 for administrative and financial reasons, the four remaining participants all increased their contributions to fill the gap. In December 1968, the roster read: Australia 50, Austria 45, Denmark 40, Sweden 40. But before the withdrawal, Denmark and Sweden, along with Australia, were the heaviest contributors.

103. This was less critical for the Danish police, who, like their military, were latecomers to UNFICYP.

104. UN Doc. S/5593, March 12, 1964.

105. UN Doc. S/5671, April 29, 1964, Annex 1; and UN Doc. S/5679, May 2, 1964.

106. Johs. K. Möller-Jensen, "DANCIVPOL—The Danish Civilian Police Contingent of UNFICYP," *IPKO Documentation*, No. 27 (October 1967), p. 17. This translated reprint from the Danish professional journal *The Police* (February 1967) is one of the best available descriptions of the day-to-day operations of UNCIVPOL.

107. Nils Andren, "Nordic Integration," *Cooperation and Conflict*, No. 1 (1967), p. 11.

108. Quoted in Pederson, "Scandinavia and the UN Stand-By Forces," p. 41.

109. A good description is by Dick Lago-Lengquist in "The UN Course for Observers," Papers of the Conference on Earmarked Units for United Nations—The 2nd Oslo Conference (1965; processed). The author has been the chief administrator of the Nordic courses.

110. The organizers of the course have proceeded slowly with membership expansion. They preferred to say for a time that the Austrians and Swiss had "asked" to participate and were not technically "invited." This, it was thought, avoided the need to explain a principle of selection about who could attend and who could not.

CHAPTER 6

1. Malta has offered the services of a "small armed unit," largely a symbolic gesture since the island has neither armed forces nor defense budgets, and only a small police

force. UN General Assembly, *Official Records* (GAOR), 19th sess., 1297th Plenary Mtg. (Dec. 9, 1964), p. 2.

2. Quoted in George F. G. Stanley, *Canada's Soldiers, 1604–1954* (Toronto: Macmillan, 1954), p. 272.

3. J. L. Granatstein, "Canada: Peacekeeper; A Survey of Canada's Participation in Peacekeeping Operations," in Canadian Institute of International Affairs, *Peacekeeping: International Challenge and Canadian Response* (Toronto: CIIA, 1968), pp. 101–02. This is an excellent, richly informative review of Canada's entire peacekeeping record.

4. Lester B. Pearson, "Force for the UN," *Foreign Affairs*, Vol. 35 (April 1957). He did not say, however, that the Canadian unit had been set up at the time.

5. Former External Affairs Minister Paul Martin recalls that the unit has existed "since 1957." Canadian Department of External Affairs, Information Division, *Statements and Speeches*, No. 67/12, p. 4. (Cited hereafter as *Statements and Speeches*.) One expert's "guess" is that earmarking began "early in 1958" (Granatstein, "Canada: Peacekeeper," p. 148). For general information, see R. B. Tackaberry, "Organizing and Training Peace-keeping Forces: The Canadian View," *International Journal* (Canada), Vol. 22 (Spring 1967).

6. Canada and Denmark had exceptionally long head starts in mobilizing for Cyprus. Canada apparently had been asked to take part in either the NATO or the Commonwealth "peace forces" unsuccessfully advocated in the early months of 1964. Granatstein, "Canada: Peacekeeper," pp. 170–72. Danish officials acknowledge that they also were approached during this period for a contribution to the proposed NATO force.

7. Paul Hellyer and Lucien Cardin, *White Paper on Defence* (Ottawa: Queen's Printer, 1964). Cited hereafter as *White Paper*.

8. Leonard Beaton, "The Canadian White Paper on Defence," *International Journal* (Canada), Vol. 19 (Summer 1964), p. 364.

9. Michael E. Sherman, *A Single Service for Canada*, Adelphi Paper 39 (London: Institute for Strategic Studies, 1967), p. 1.

10. Statement to the House of Commons, *Debates* (June 22, 1967), p. 1816.

11. Craig Powell, "The Canadian Armed Forces: Peace-Keeper of the Seventies?" *Armed Forces Management*, Vol. 13 (June 1967), p. 36.

12. After admitting that it is "impossible to state in categorical terms exactly where and how our forces will be required and allocated in the decades ahead" (p. 21), the *White Paper* outlines these requirements (p. 24):

1. Forces for the direct protection of Canada . . .
2. Forces-in-being as part of the deterrent in the European theatre.
3. Maritime forces-in-being as a contribution to the deterrent.
4. Forces-in-being for UN peace-keeping operations which would be included also in (1) above.
5. Reserve forces and mobilization potential.

13. *White Paper*, pp. 16, 21.

14. It occurred over several years in three phases: first the integration of service headquarters, next the integration of commands, and finally the merger of the three services, or unification, which formally became effective in February 1968. A good description of the progressive changes, written by the lieutenant general who was second in command of the unified service, is F. R. Sharp, "Reorganization of the Canadian Armed Forces," *Air University Review,* Vol. 18 (July–August 1967), pp. 17–28.

15. National Defence Committee, *Defence Committee Hearings,* quoted in David Cox, "Canadian Defence Policy: The Dilemmas of a Middle Power," *Behind the Headlines* (Canada), Vol. 27 (November 1968), p. 32.

16. *New York Times,* April 4, 1969, and May 29, 1969.

17. Cox, "Canadian Defence Policy," p. 32.

18. Ibid. As of 1968 Canada's emergency strategic transport capabilities are restricted to operations about the size of the 1966 NATO exercise "Winter Express," in which Canada, with some strain, moved 1,000 men, 197 vehicles, and 100,000 pounds of supplies to Norway in five days. Ibid., pp. 33–34.

19. UN Doc. A/AC.121/17, June 18, 1968, pp. 10–17, passim. This is perhaps the first official description of Canada's preparedness beyond the standby battalion, the first UN preparedness inventory released by the Trudeau government, and in general the first comprehensive description of UN preparedness policy within the post-1964 framework. Much of the paper, nonetheless, is not new, though never before made public and collected in one place. Part 1 on Canadian readiness contains numerous adaptations of earlier papers on the standby battalion, excerpts from old speeches by Lester Pearson, and fragments from the *White Paper* and its subsequent refinements. Part 2 is a Canadian version of a general UN standing operating procedure for peacekeeping and observer missions, much of which has been privately circulated for some time or has been condensed from Canadian papers presented at the peacekeeping conference in Ottawa in 1964. Part 3 is a proposed Status of Forces Agreement that had been drafted and circulated in 1967 by Canadian legal experts.

20. GAOR, 18th sess., 1208th Plenary Mtg. (Sept. 19, 1963), p. 10.

21. Granatstein, "Canada: Peacekeeper," p. 179.

22. Lester B. Pearson, "A New Kind of Force," *Maclean's* (Canada), Vol. 77 (May 2, 1964), p. 11.

23. Lester B. Pearson, "Keeping the Peace," in Andrew W. Cordier and Wilder Foote (eds.), *The Quest for Peace* (Columbia University Press, 1965), pp. 108–12.

24. Attending were Brazil, Canada, Colombia, Denmark, Finland, Ghana, India, Ireland, Italy, Liberia, Malaysia, Morocco, the Netherlands, New Zealand, Nigeria, Norway, Pakistan, Senegal, Sierra Leone, Sweden, Tunisia, the UAR, and, as an observer, the secretary-general's military adviser.

25. Three working groups divided the agenda, one dealing with command and control, training, and operations; another with logistics; a third with administrative accounting, public relations, and legal problems. A useful summary of the discussions

is Bjørn Egge, "Report on the Ottawa Conference on U.N. Peace-Keeping," *Disarmament* (Paris), No. 8 (December 1965), pp. 21–24.

26. Granatstein, "Canada: Peacekeeper," p. 180; and *Washington Post*, Nov. 7, 1964.

27. For example, see the report on British attitudes toward Pearson's proposal in *The Economist* (Great Britain: May 16, 1964), p. 694. In the *Izvestia* article the Russians attacked an early 1964 speech by Harlan Cleveland, the U.S. assistant secretary for international organization affairs, as proof of Washington's collusion.

28. *Statements and Speeches*, No. 67/12, p. 9.

29. Parts 2 and 3 of UN Doc. A/AC.121/17, June 18, 1968, are examples. A few years before the UN requested certain national information on preparedness in 1968, Canada made available in New York numerous copies of a paper describing its national standby program, reprinted as *IPKO Documentation*, No. 12. External Affairs Minister Martin offered in 1967 "to produce guide-books and training manuals based on our own experience, and after consultation with other governments concerned, to make them available for the use of the United Nations or of any of its member states" (*Statements and Speeches*, No. 67/12, p. 9).

30. Granatstein, "Canada: Peacekeeper," pp. 155, 176; and R. B. Tackaberry, "Keeping the Peace," *Behind the Headlines*, Vol. 26 (September 1966), p. 13.

31. Granatstein, "Canada: Peacekeeper," pp. 183–86.

32. Wiebe Wierda, "The Armed Forces of the Netherlands," *Military Review*, Vol. 44 (September 1964), p. 63.

33. Among suppliers relying on active-duty soldiers, practice has varied on this point. Ireland and Brazil use regulars too, but these are men who leave their normal national units to constitute a brand-new, one-time-only UN contingent.

34. GAOR, 18th sess., 1213th Plenary Mtg. (Sept. 24, 1963), pp. 11–12.

35. Cary E. Landis, who visited this marine unit in 1965, came away believing that "unquestionably the political decision in the Netherlands had the support of the military leaders." For the repatriated marines, a substitute mission "would counter the usual incentive to reduce the overall military forces." The Royal Marines were not part of the Netherlands' commitment to NATO. It can be argued that, without such a mission, maintenance of this contingent would have constituted an unjustifiable financial drain. Landis, "Blue Bonnets for Doctor Bunche: Some Aspects of Earmarked Military Forces for United Nations Duty," study prepared in the U.S. Department of State Seventh Senior Seminar in Foreign Policy, Foreign Service Institute (June 11, 1965; processed), p. 22; also p. 13.

36. GAOR, 20th sess., 1348th Plenary Mtg. (Oct. 5, 1965), p. 11.

37. UN Doc. A/AC.121/18, June 21, 1968, p. 5.

38. Ibid., p. 10. The Dutch did not spell out the implications of this for the actual composition of army standby units. In their essentials, the army contingents, like those of the marines, are intended to be regular, already existing units. But obviously, to the extent that the wishes of conscripts who "prefer" not to serve the UN are honored, the composition of units will have to change if they are called up for UN duty.

39. The marine unit on standby in 1967 contained 40 percent conscripts and 60 percent regulars. The army battalion had 70 percent conscripts and 30 percent regulars: everyone from platoon leaders on down was a conscript; all above this rank were regulars.

40. All Dutch marine officers are exposed to at least a brief UN orientation, and some marine planners are hopeful that the overall amount can be increased. The expectation is that promotion examinations will contain some coverage of peacekeeping. A UN handbook containing relevant public UN documents on the subject has been prepared for marine officers.

41. Alfred Verdross, "Austria's Permanent Neutrality and the United Nations Organization," *American Journal of International Law*, Vol. 50 (January 1956), p. 61.

42. Austrian policy in international organizations is traced in Nalini Rewadikar, "The Role of a Neutral State in the United Nations: The Austrian Case," *International Studies* (New Delhi: Indian School of International Studies), Vol. 7 (October 1965).

43. Quoted in Karl Zemanek, "Neutral Austria in the United Nations," *International Organization*, Vol. 15 (Summer 1961), p. 417.

44. Wolfgang Strasser, *Österreich und die Vereinten Nationen* (Wien: Wilhelm Braumuller, Universitäts—Verlagsbuchhandlung G.m.b.H., 1967), p. 109. A general survey of Austrian peacekeeping policies is found in ibid., pp. 107–25.

45. "Austrian Federal Constitution Act of 30 June 1965 Regarding the Dispatch of Austrian Units on Missions of Assistance Abroad at the Request of International Organizations, Section I," reprinted in *IPKO Documentation*, No. 1 (February 1967), p. 1.

46. An illustrative statistical pattern, based on responses of the first-year enlistments, is: 70 percent signed for a full three years, 92 percent said they would go anywhere, and only 8 percent restricted their service to one continent. When the total had reached 2,016, 69 percent were regulars, 15 percent were conscripts, and 16 percent were in the reserve.

47. UN Doc. A/AC.121/19, July 9, 1968, p. 12.

48. Altogether, approximately 650 army personnel had had UN experience by mid-1968, in ONUC, UNFICYP, and UNTSO (United Nations Truce Supervision Organization).

49. UN Doc. A/AC.121/19, July 9, 1968, p. 16.

50. An account is in the *New York Times*, June 10, 1964.

51. The statement is reprinted in *External Affairs Review* (New Zealand), Vol. 14 (October 1964), pp. 30–31.

52. Usually in groups of twenty at a time, these policemen remained in UNCIVPOL until 1967, when they were withdrawn because of "continuing staffing difficulties" (*External Affairs Review*, Vol. 17 [April 1967], p. 20). One of the countries taking up the slack after their departure was neighboring Australia, which has provided UNCIVPOL with numerous contingents as well as two police advisers, as the senior UN policeman in the force is called.

53. In reply, the foreign minister reminded his audience that selection of force personnel, "of course, is entirely undertaken by the Army Command and there is no interference with them and there should not be" (*Parliamentary Debates*, April 7, 1964, cols. 1081 and 1094).

54. "Service of Irish Army Personnel with the United Nations," *IPKO Documentation*, No. 15 (July 1967), pp. 17–18. Because many soldiers have served in both major operations, the total number of individual UN veterans is only about 8,000, a little over 1,000 of them officers.

55. *Parliamentary Debates* (Dail Eireann), Dec. 13, 1960, cols. 980–81. The legislation, *Defence (Amendment) (No. 2) Act, 1960*, permitted men already in service to refuse UN duty if they wished. In essence, the terms of service and liability in this act were an extension and refinement of legislation enacted in July 1960 when ONUC began, which was valid for six months only.

56. *Parliamentary Debates* (Dail Eireann), Dec. 15, 1960, col. 406, and April 7, 1964, col. 1063.

57. One such special program, advocated by Lt. Col. P. T. P. Ua Caoinde Albhain in the Irish professional military journal, *An Cosantoir*, of January 1966, is described in the article "Training for Military Service with the United Nations," reprinted in *IPKO Documentation*, No. 33 (February 1968), pp. 4–5.

58. *Parliamentary Debates* (Dail Eireann), April 7, 1964, col. 116.

59. Ibid., col. 1063.

60. Small numbers of Indians have done observer duty and a reconnaissance unit of 114 men was transferred in 1963 from UNEF to Yemen.

61. Swadesh Mehta, "The Organization of an International Force: The Indian View," *International Studies* (New Delhi: Indian School of International Studies), Vol. 7 (October 1965), p. 227.

62. In minor ways, having such a thoroughly professional unit intact can be a mixed blessing for the secretariat. It is difficult to break up such battalions and send portions back home for the sake of economy and force-level reductions, and the UN may have to foot the bill for the continuation of normal training routines, which require, for example, a higher than ordinary ammunition scale for drills at the firing range, and so on. In addition, the use of regular national units that have to be replaced back home can cost the UN extra money, as happened during India's ONUC participation: "While not paying the salaries of Indians in the Congo, the United Nations was required to reimburse the Indian Government for the salaries and equipment of reserve units called up in India to replace some of the regular Indian troops in the Congo" (Ernest W. Lefever and Wynfred Joshua, *United Nations Peacekeeping in the Congo: 1960–1964; An Analysis of Political, Executive and Military Control*, prepared for the U.S. Arms Control and Disarmament Agency [Brookings Institution, 1966], Vol. 2, p. 382). It is not known that India ever expected the UN to follow this procedure for UNEF.

63. "Speech by Finnish Foreign Minister Jaakko Hallama During the 1964 Supple-

mentary Budget Debate," *IPKO Documentation*, No. 8 (June 1967), p. 12. The foreign minister stated: "Brazil announced its willingness to send a naval force of 260 men and 10 officers for United Nations use."

64. UN Doc. S/5593, March 12, 1964.

65. *Keesing's Contemporary Archives* (1963–64), p. 20299.

66. Statement to the House of Commons of Foreign Secretary Michael Stewart, Feb. 23, 1965, reprinted in *IPKO Documentation*, No. 16 (July 1967), p. 5. The prime minister himself would have announced the offer in a major speech to the General Assembly earlier in the month, but his visit to New York was canceled.

67. Ibid., p. 7. Subsequently, the government said even more vaguely that "the final arrangements with regard to training depend on the offer being taken up. That, in turn, depends upon the Peace-keeping Committee's operations in the coming months being as successful as we hope they will be" ("United Nations and Peace-Keeping Operations, House of Lords, February 23, 1965," *IPKO Documentation*, No. 16 [July 1967], p. 16).

68. UN Doc. A/AC.121/16, May 27, 1968, p. 1. The rest of the paper is an annex setting forth British views on some of the important preparedness problems.

69. *The Economist* (June 18, 1966), p. 1281.

70. *Hansard's* (Great Britain), Vol. 692 (March 26, 1964), col. 24.

71. *Hansard's*, Vol. 695 (May 12, 1964), col. 219.

72. *Keesing's Contemporary Archives* (1963–64), p. 20196.

73. "Reorganization of the Army Reserves," Cmnd. 2855 (London: Her Majesty's Stationery Office, December 1965), p. 5. Annex B lists the normal reserve support units that might be drawn upon.

74. Feb. 27, 1965, p. 875.

75. Britain's only other UN involvements were in the early Indonesian and Greek missions in the 1940s.

76. *Hansard's*, Vol. 693 (April 13, 1964), col. 19.

77. U.S. money was equally critical in UNEF's early life. During its first two years the United States paid nearly 50 percent of the total costs. *United Nations Emergency Force*, Hearings before the Subcommittee on International Organizations and Movements of the House Committee on Foreign Affairs, 85 Cong. 2 sess. (1958), p. 67.

78. *To Amend the United Nations Participation Act of 1945*, Hearings before the House Committee on Foreign Affairs, 81 Cong. 1 sess. (1949); *Amendment of the United Nations Participation Act of 1945*, H. Rept. 591, 81 Cong. 1 sess. (1949).

79. *United Nations Participation Act of 1945, as Amended*, 63 Stat. 734. Other portions of the act dealt with U.S. relations to Chapter VII military arrangements.

80. Washington Center of Foreign Policy Research, School of Advanced International Studies, Johns Hopkins University, *National Support of International Peacekeeping and Peace Observation Operations*, prepared for the U.S. Arms Control and Disarmament Agency, ACDA/IR-161 (February 1970), Vol. 2, Chap. 3, especially pp. 83–98. Cited hereafter as Hopkins Report.

81. Remarks of Harlan Cleveland, assistant secretary of state for international organization affairs. *Foreign Assistance Act of 1964,* Hearings before the House Committee on Foreign Affairs, 88 Cong. 2 sess. (1964), p. 465; also p. 461.

82. On the surface, the presence of Americans in UNTSO has caused few ripples, but recently there have been some troublesome moments. After the 1967 war Sy ria reportedly refused to allow certain nationalities to participate in renewed observat¹on on its borders. These may well have been American officers, who were also inelig¹ble for duty in the Suez Canal sector.

83. Hopkins Report, Vols. 1–5. Case by case, this lengthy analysis examines in minute detail the magnitude, nature, organization, and procedures of U.S. logistical support for all UN operations.

84. Dag Hammarskjöld, *United Nations Emergency Force: Summary Study of the Experience Derived From the Establishment and Operation of the Force,* UN Doc. A/3943, Oct. 9, 1958, p. 72.

85. *United Nations Emergency Force,* Hearings, p. 52.

86. William R. Frye, *A United Nations Peace Force* (Oceana Publications, 1957), pp. 59–60.

87. GAOR, 15th sess., 868th Plenary Mtg. (Sept. 22, 1960), Vol. 1, p. 47.

88. GAOR, 16th sess., 1013th Plenary Mtg. (Sept. 25, 1961), p. 57.

89. GAOR, 18th sess., 1209th Plenary Mtg. (Sept. 20, 1963), p. 7.

90. *Department of Defense Appropriations for 1969,* Hearings before a Subcommittee of the House Committee on Appropriations, 90 Cong. 2 sess. (1968), p. 136.

91. The proposal was inserted into the *Congressional Record,* Vol. 111, Pt. 10, 89 Cong. 1 sess. (1965), pp. 13826–27. Curiously, the statement did not recall Eisenhower's U.S. earmarking proposal, though it did list him as one of the main proponents of the standby concept.

92. A year or so later, the sponsors of the plan inserted it into a congressional resolution urging a permanent UN peacekeeping force. Now the authors opted for an "unqualified" offer from the United States. See *Congressional Record,* Vol. 112, Pt. 10, 89 Cong. 2 sess. (1966), pp. 12895–97.

93. "The United Nations," report presented by the Task Force on the Conduct of Foreign Relations on June 11, 1966, and adopted by the Republican Coordinating Committee on June 28, 1966. The Republican National Committee issued a summary press release on July 11.

94. The *New York Times* editorialized that the Republican "statement on the United Nations is less important for its specific proposals or election-year criticism of the Democrats than for its resounding support for the world organization" (July 16, 1966).

95. *United Nations Peacekeeping,* Hearings before a Subcommittee of the Senate Committee on Foreign Relations, 90 Cong. 2 sess. (1968), pp. 105–06, 124.

96. UN Doc. A/AC.121/15, May 17, 1968, p. 2.

97. Much of the congressional emphasis grew from the panoply of suggestions made during the UN's first ten years for standing armies, with or without accompany-

ing world government. A number of these are discussed in Francis O. Wilcox and Carl M. Marcy, *Proposals for Changes in the United Nations* (Brookings Institution, 1955), pp. 57–81, 166–72.

98. Address to San Francisco Commonwealth Club, reprinted in the *Washington Post*, Sept. 27, 1968.

99. *Congressional Record*, Vol. 104, Pt. 2, 85 Cong. 2 sess. (1958), p. 14747. See also the remarks of Senator Mike Mansfield, *Congressional Record*, Vol. 104, Pt. 9, 85 Cong. 2 sess. (1958), p. 11454.

100. S. Res. 15, Jan. 7, 1957. It was adopted without roll call on August 8 of that year. A House version had been introduced in May. See *Congressional Record*, Vol. 103, Pt. 5, 85 Cong. 1 sess. (1957), p. 6316.

101. S. Res. 359, Aug. 11, 1960, 86 Cong. 2 sess. (1960).

102. Alfred O. Hero, Jr., "The American Public and the UN, 1954–1966," *Journal of Conflict Resolution*, Vol. 10 (December 1966), pp. 442–48.

103. *United Nations Emergency Force*, Hearings; *United Nations Peacekeeping*, Hearings.

104. *United Nations Emergency Force*, Hearings, p. 98. The resolution is H. Con. Res. 373, 85 Cong. 2 sess. (1958).

105. S. Con. Res. 47, 90 Cong. 1 sess. (1967).

106. H. Con. Res. 130, 90 Cong. 1 sess. (1967).

107. It was given in a July 28 letter from the assistant secretary of state for congressional relations, William B. Macomber, Jr., to the chairman of the House Committee on Foreign Affairs, Thomas E. Morgan.

108. *United Nations Peacekeeping*, Hearings, p. 103.

109. Other resolutions pending at the time advocated both. See *United Nations Peacekeeping*, Hearings, p. 3. Congressman Richard Schweiker (R.-Pa.), one of the original co-sponsors of the 1967 House resolution, H. Con. Res. 130, however, seemed personally to support U.S. earmarking. In introducing the bill he recalled Eisenhower's earmarking pledge and added, "It is tragic that in 1967 we are still without action on a step that our President could announce with such certainty in 1960" (*Congressional Record*, Vol. 113, Pt. 3, 90 Cong. 1 sess. [1967], p. 3057).

110. Foreign Assistance Act of 1967, Sec. 304, 81 Stat. 454. When introduced on the floor this section provoked a brief, lively debate that revealed just how confusing the Charter and UN constitutional questions can be—one strong supporter of the language confidently answered a conservative critic by saying the section was really nothing to get all excited about because provision for these forces is already made in Article 43! *Congressional Record*, Vol. 113, Pt. 18, 89 Cong. 1 sess. (1967), p. 23949.

111. The criticism is in *United Nations Peacekeeping*, Hearings, p. 168. This report is unpublished and remains in the files of the Senate Foreign Relations Committe.

112. UN Doc. A/AC.121/SR.29, March 6, 1968, p. 14.

113. GAOR, 15th sess., 868th Plenary Mtg. (Sept. 22, 1960), pp. 46–47.

114. Section 501 of the Foreign Assistance Act of 1961, as amended, permits use of

assistance "to permit the recipient country to participate in regional or collective arrangements or measures consistent with the Charter . . . or . . . to participate in collective measures requested by the United Nations for the purpose of maintaining or restoring international peace and security."

115. Mutual Defense Assistance Act of 1949, 63 Stat. 714.

116. Mutual Security Act of 1951, Sec. 525, 65 Stat. 385. See *Mutual Security Act*, H. Rept. 872, 82 Cong. 1 sess. (1958), p. 53.

117. The Mutual Security Act of 1954, 68 Stat. 832, altered it slightly and it was again changed in 1961. See *The International Development and Security Act*, Hearings before the House Committee on Foreign Affairs, 87 Cong. 1 sess. (1961), pp. 500–01. Discussion during these hearings shows that the changes in 1961 were not intended, as sometimes thought, to implement the Eisenhower offer at the Assembly in 1960. They were basically legislative drafting clarifications, and nothing more.

118. The earliest published recommendation seems to be by Lincoln P. Bloomfield, *The United Nations and U.S. Foreign Policy: A New Look at the National Interest* (Little, Brown, 1960), pp. 73–74. He argued that the approach would not only benefit the UN but also infuse the military aid program with a new rationale and perhaps even a slightly more acceptable image. See also Lincoln P. Bloomfield and others, *International Military Forces: The Question of Peacekeeping in an Armed and Disarming World* (Little, Brown, 1964), pp. 85–86.

119. UN Doc. A/SPC/SR.465, Nov. 24, 1965.

120. For example, statement by the U.S. representative in the UN Special Political Committee, Nov. 28, 1967; reprinted in press release USUN-214 (Nov. 28, 1967), p. 7.

121. "Report of the Committee on Peacekeeping Operations," in Richard N. Gardner (ed.), *Blueprint for Peace* (McGraw-Hill, 1966), p. 69.

122. The exchange in the legislature is in *Foreign Assistance Act of 1965*, Hearings before the House Committee on Foreign Affairs, 89 Cong. 1 sess. (1965), pp. 749–50. The address, "Time for Decision at the United Nations," was by Richard N. Gardner, deputy assistant secretary for international organization affairs, at International House, New York, Nov. 1, 1964; reprinted in a U.S. Department of State press release of the same date. He said: "The United States will respond to requests to support" earmarking. Gardner, as a private citizen, was an adviser to the U.S. delegation to the UN when Goldberg's formulation was prepared, and he later supported the idea in his introduction to *Blueprint for Peace*, p. 12.

123. *Department of Defense Appropriations for 1968*, Hearings before the Senate Committee on Appropriations, 90 Cong. 1 sess. (1967), Pt. 1, p. 35.

124. *Department of Defense Appropriations for 1969*, Hearings before the House Committee on Appropriations, 90 Cong. 2 sess. (1968), Pt. 1, p. 136.

125. *United Nations Peacekeeping*, Hearings, p. 105.

126. Ibid., p. 125.

127. *Foreign Assistance Act of 1965*, Hearings, pp. 749–50; *Foreign Assistance Act of*

1966, Hearings before the House Committee on Foreign Affairs, 89 Cong. 2 sess. (1966), pp. 601–02.

128. These are presented every year during consideration of the Foreign Assistance Act. See, for example, *Foreign Assistance Act of 1967*, Hearings before the House Committee on Foreign Affairs, 90 Cong. 1 sess. (1967), pp.149–57.

129. *Foreign Assistance Act of 1966*, Hearings, p. 602

CHAPTER 7

1. Interview, reprinted in *Congressional Record*, Vol. 104, Pt. 5, 85 Cong. 2 sess. (1958), p. 5902.

2. Quoted in Alexander Dallin, *The Soviet Union at the United Nations* (Praeger, 1962), p. 127.

3. UN General Assembly, *Official Records* (GAOR), 13th sess., 750th Plenary Mtg. (Sept. 18, 1958), p. 27.

4. Efforts to resolve constitutional and financial problems are traced in Ruth B. Russell, *The United Nations and United States Security Policy* (Brookings Institution, 1968), pp. 198–209, 333–54.

5. *United Nations Peacekeeping*, Hearings before a Subcommittee of the Senate Committee on Foreign Relations, 90 Cong. 2 sess. (1968), p. 105. The Swedish ambassador to the UN had used similar language a month or so earlier; UN Doc. A/AC.121/SR.31, March 20, 1968, p. 34.

6. Some Canadians say that Prime Minister Trudeau's sour remarks about peacekeeping soon after his election in 1967 were precipitated in large part by events at the 1966 Assembly, during which he was an observer in the Canadian delegation.

7. UN Doc. A/6654, May 17, 1967, p. 60.

8. GAOR, 19th sess., Suppl. 1A (1964), p. 9.

9. GAOR, 19th sess., Annex 21 (1964–65), p. 2.

10. Ibid., p. 21.

11. UN Doc. A/AC.121/SR.23, March 14, 1967; UN Doc. S/7841, April 5, 1967.

12. UN Doc. A/6959, Dec. 9, 1967.

13. *UN Monthly Chronicle*, Vol. 5 (January 1968), pp. 41–47.

14. UN Doc. A/AC.121/SR.28, March 4, 1968, p. 7.

15. Ibid.

16. The design for the first phase and progress to the end of 1968 are outlined in GAOR, 23d sess., Annexes, Agenda item 32 (1968).

17. Remarks in the Special Political Committee, press release USUN-253 (Dec. 16, 1968).

18. UN Doc. A/AC.121/SR.32, March 27, 1968, p. 48; see also UN Doc. A/AC.121/SR.36, Feb. 19, 1969, p. 8.

19. UN Doc. A/AC.121/SR.22, Sept. 29, 1966, p. 5, in UN Doc. A/6414, Sept. 30, 1966.

20. UN Doc. A/6603, Dec. 15, 1966, p. 18.

21. See UN Doc. A/7742, Nov. 3, 1969.

22. UN Doc. A/AC.121/SR.36, Feb. 19, 1969, p. 5.

23. UN Doc. A/AC.121/SR.35, Aug. 6, 1968, p. 5.

24. The U.S. statement is UN Doc. A/AC.121/WG.B/SR.2, May 2, 1967, p. 5. For the Soviet remarks, see UN Doc. A/AC.121/SR.28, March 4, 1968, p. 8, and UN Doc. A/AC.121/SR.32, March 27, 1968, p. 44.

25. *United Nations Emergency Force: Summary Study of the Experience Derived From the Establishment and Operation of the Force,* UN Doc. A/3943, Oct. 9, 1958.

26. GAOR, 15th sess., Suppl. 1A (1960), pp. 3–4.

27. "Introduction to the Annual Report of the Secretary General on the Work of the Organization," *UN Monthly Chronicle,* Vol. 4 (October 1967), p. 102.

28. Brian E. Urquhart, "Problems of the Secretariat," in Richard N. Swift (ed.), *Annual Review of United Nations Affairs, 1963-64* (Oceana Publications, 1965), p. 110.

29. Vladimir F. Petrovsky, "The Soviet Union and the United Nations," *Vista,* Vol. 4 (May–June 1969), p. 35.

30. The Council incident is reported in the *Washington Post,* June 15, 1967; the Assembly incident in the *Washington Post,* Dec. 1, 1967.

31. UN Doc. S/7841, April 5, 1967, p. 6.

32. Leon Gordenker, *The UN Secretary-General and the Maintenance of Peace* (Columbia University Press, 1967), p. 103. From this analysis (especially Chap. 5, "Internal Administration") a coherent picture of secretariat organizational evolution over twenty-five years emerges.

33. Sydney D. Bailey, *The Secretariat of the United Nations* (rev. ed., Praeger, 1964), p. 60.

34. L. M. K. Skern, *Military Staffing at UN Headquarters for Peace-Keeping Operations: A Proposal,* IPKO Monograph 3 (Paris: International Information Center on Peace-Keeping Operations, 1967).

35. Even Field Service has nonpeacekeeping responsibilities, supporting economic commissions and various ad hoc bodies often set up by the UN.

36. GAOR, 21st sess., Suppl. 5 (1967), p. 114. By this rationale the limit would not have applied to ONUC either.

37. The 31 in UNFICYP and the 56 in UNEF that year brought the figure almost to 350 for field missions. More were serving with the UN development program.

38. In 1968 and 1969, changes in the form of budget presentation made it more difficult to distinguish categories of lower-level support personnel. Previous practice had been to budget and identify "field service" people as such. With the change, there is now listed for each mission only a group titled "administrative and technical services personnel." See GAOR, 23d sess., Suppl. 5 (1969), Pt. 6. The nationalities of the 327 members of the Field Service in 1966, the last published list, are given in GAOR, 21st sess., Suppl. 7 (1966), p. 48.

39. GAOR, 23d sess., Suppl. 5 (1969), p. 175; GAOR, 23d sess., Suppl. 7 (1969), p. 44.

40. Near the end of his career at the UN, General Rikhye reflected briefly but interestingly on the job he had held since 1960. I. J. Rikhye, *United Nations Peace-Keeping Operations: Higher Conduct*, IPKO Monograph 1 (Paris: International Information Center on Peace-Keeping Operations, 1967). Military thinking in the secretariat during the early 1960s was hinted at in a modest output of unofficial, published articles by the general. See, for example, I. J. Rikhye, *Preparation and Training of United Nations Peace-keeping Forces*, Adelphi Paper 9 (London: Institute for Strategic Studies, 1964).

41. P. S. Gyani, *Characteristics and Some Aspects of Launching UN Peace-Keeping Forces*, IPKO Monograph 6 (Paris: International Information Center on Peace-Keeping Operations, 1968).

42. GAOR, 19th sess., Suppl. 1A (1964), p. 9.

43. These letters have communicated the substance of a press release that was distributed by the secretary-general's office on Oct. 1, 1963 (SG/1588), which is reprinted in D. W. Bowett, *United Nations Forces* (Praeger, 1964), p. 333, note 6g. The links between the standbys and the secretary-general are reinforced in symbolic ways when occasion permits. When standby programs were reported to the Special Committee in 1968 the Nordic countries pointedly visited his office to "discuss the question" (*New York Times*, March 21, 1968).

44. GAOR, 15th sess., Annexes, Agenda item (1950), p. 50.

45. "Introduction to the Annual Report of the Secretary-General on the Work of the Organization," *UN Monthly Chronicle*, Vol. 4 (October 1967), p. 102.

46. Rikhye had been commander of UNEF when the force was dismantled in 1967. He returned to New York, was given no significant responsibilities during 1968, and offered his resignation at the end of the year, saying that peacekeeping is "going through a phase of re-examination and restricted activity" (*New York Times*, Dec. 19, 1968).

47. The conference records are classified "For official use only," but a good survey by a participant is Bjorn Egge, "Report on the Ottawa Conference on U.N. Peacekeeping," *Disarmament* (Paris), No. 8 (December 1965), pp. 21–24.

48. Few of these conference records and documents have been given security classifications, yet some of those unclassified were not circulated widely and are considered "private" materials. One exception, the result of the first Oslo conference in 1964, was published: Per Frydenberg, *Peace-Keeping: Experience and Evaluation* (Oslo: Norwegian Institute of International Affairs, 1964). The records of the second Oslo meeting, also sponsored by the Norwegian Institute of International Affairs, are unpublished: "Conference on Earmarked Units for United Nations." The most important British convocation is summarized in Royal Institute of International Affairs, Institute for Strategic Studies, *Résumé of the Joint Conference on United Nations Security Operations* (Ditchley Park, Oxfordshire: RIIA, 1965). A Canadian meeting is summarized in Canadian Institute of International Affairs, *Peacekeeping: International Challenge and Canadian Response* (Toronto: CIIA, 1968). One recent American session produced Browne and Shaw

International Studies Division, "The United States and UN Peacekeeping: A View Toward the 1970s," prepared for the Office of the Assistant Secretary of Defense, International Security Affairs (1968; processed).

49. One of the most useful and digestible examinations of technical and organizational issues is Browne and Shaw International Studies Division, "The United States and UN Peacekeeping," Chap. 3. An enormously detailed study of logistics and administrative problems is Washington Center of Foreign Policy Research, School of Advanced International Studies, Johns Hopkins University, *National Support of International Peacekeeping and Peace Observation Operations*, prepared for the U.S. Arms Control and Disarmament Agency, ACDA/IR-161 (February 1970), Vols. 1–5. Also, Edward H. Bowman and James E. Fanning, "Logistics—Experience and Requirements," in Lincoln P. Bloomfield and others, *International Military Forces: The Question of Peacekeeping in an Armed and Disarming World* (Little, Brown, 1964).

50. UN Doc. A/AC.121/15, May 21, 1968 (United States); UN Doc. A/AC.-121/16, May 29, 1968 (United Kingdom); UN Doc. A/AC.121/17, June 19, 1968 (Canada).

51. See William R. Frye, *A United Nations Peace Force* (Oceana Publications, 1957), pp. 74–80; Bloomfield and others, *International Military Forces*, Chap. 7.

52. James E. Knott, *Final Report, Analysis and Recommendations* (Paris: International Information Center on Peace-Keeping Operations, 1968).

53. The former secretary of state's recently published memoirs give some interesting indications of the overall American foreign policy context of the Uniting for Peace proposal. See Dean Acheson, *Present at the Creation* (Norton, 1969), Chaps. 46 and 47, passim. He recounts his approach to Latin American states on pp. 497–98.

54. A brief survey of changing Soviet behavior toward the UN during this period is Dallin, *The Soviet Union at the United Nations*, pp. 37–41.

55. See K. Brodin, K. Goldmann, and C. Lange, "The Policy of Neutrality: Official Doctrines of Finland and Sweden," *Cooperation and Conflict*, No. 1 (1968), pp. 20–24, 26.

56. The language about Lie is Andrei Vishinsky's, quoted in Stephen M. Schwebel, *The Secretary-General of the United Nations* (Harvard University Press, 1952), p. 187; about Hammarskjöld, Nikita Khrushchev's, quoted in Gordenker, *The UN Secretary-General and the Maintenance of Peace*, pp. 49–50.

57. Lawrence S. Finkelstein, "International Cooperation in a Changing World: A Challenge to United States Foreign Policy," in Finkelstein (ed.), *The United States and International Organization: The Changing Setting* (M.I.T. Press, 1969), p. 3.

58. See Gordenker, *The UN Secretary-General and the Maintenance of Peace*, p. 48; and Dallin, *The Soviet Union at the United Nations*, p. 160, note.

59. "Do We Need the United Nations?" address before the Students Association, Copenhagen, Denmark, May 2, 1959; reprinted in Wilder Foote (ed.), *Servant of Peace* (Harper and Row, 1962), pp. 200–11.

CHAPTER 8

1. Inis L. Claude, Jr., "The Containment and Resolution of Disputes," in Francis O. Wilcox and H. Field Haviland (eds.), *The United States and the United Nations* (Johns Hopkins Press, 1961), p. 126.

2. UN General Assembly, *Official Records* (GAOR), 15th sess., 868th Plenary Mtg. (Sept. 22, 1960), p. 46.

3. Arnold Wolfers and others, *The United States in a Disarmed World* (Johns Hopkins Press, 1966).

4. GAOR, 19th sess., Annex 21 (1964–65), pp. 2–4.

5. Ibid., pp. 21–24.

6. Ibid., p. 43.

7. See, for example, UN Doc. A/6652, May 3, 1967.

8. GAOR, 19th sess., Annex 21 (1964–65), pp. 33–34, 59–62.

9. Ibid., p. 34.

10. For example, a rather definite and businesslike statement is: "States providing troops for the United Nations force, as well as the permanent members of the Security Council, should be invited to participate in the work of the Military Staff Committee. They should also be entitled to participate in the general strategic direction of the force" (UN Doc. A/AC.121/SR.23, March 14, 1967, p. 9). Compare the far more sweeping promise: "The newly independent States should be invited to participate to the greatest possible extent in the Security Council's work on the preparation and conduct of United Nations peace-keeping operations." This "would make it possible for a large number of these States to participate in the work of the Security Council's Military Staff Committee, in the general strategic direction of a United Nations force created for a given purpose, and in the operational command of this force" (UN Doc. S/7841, April 5, 1967, pp. 7–8).

11. GAOR, 19th sess., Annex 21 (1964–65), p. 34.

12. To give one sample, shortly after the United States first employed this tactic the USSR charged that "the United States and certain other States were unfortunately trying to create the impression that efforts to realize the possibilities offered by the Charter, as in Article 43 . . . were of secondary importance; the main effort in their view should be directed towards violating the Charter, although they lacked the courage to admit the fact" (UN Doc. A/AC.121/WG.A/SR.6, June 19, 1967, pp. 4–5).

13. See, for example, U.S. statements in UN Doc. A/AC.121/WG.B/SR.2, May 2, 1967; UN Doc. A/AC.121/SR.29, March 6, 1968, pp. 23–24.

14. John Ehrman, *Grand Strategy: History of the Second World War*, ed. by J. R. M. Butler (London: Her Majesty's Stationery Office, 1956), Vol. 5, pp. 15–24; Vol. 6, pp. xiii–xvi, 338–51.

15. Specialists were not at the time very sanguine about how this five-headed structure would meet a real test. On the basis of the difficult and sometimes disastrous experiences of pre-1945 military coalitions, the military historian B. H. Liddell Hart

wrote that the UN Military Staff repeated the major "faults of the past with some fresh ones added" (*Defence of the West* [Morrow, 1950], p. 290).

16. Statements in the Special Political Committee, press release USUN-214 (Nov. 28, 1967), p. 7.

17. *To Amend the United Nations Participation Act of 1945*, Hearings before the House Committee on Foreign Affairs, 81 Cong. 1 sess. (1949), p. 50. On the same page, Ernest Gross, another assistant secretary, says cryptically that this interpretation "is in the record of the hearings on this measure," apparently meaning congressional hearings on ratification of the UN Charter or on the act itself.

18. Relevant remarks of the governments listed can be found in the following: for Canada, UN Doc. A/AC.121/WG.B/SR.1, May 2, 1967, p. 10, and *UN Monthly Chronicle*, Vol. 6 (January 1969), p. 91; for the Netherlands, UN Doc. A/AC.121/WG.B/SR.3, May 2, 1967, p. 5; for Mexico, UN Doc. A/AC.121/SR.29, March 6, 1968, p. 18; for Japan, UN Doc. A/AC.121/SR.33, March 29, 1968, p. 54; for France, UN Doc. A/AC.121/SR.30, March 13, 1968, p. 29; for Sweden, UN Doc. A/AC.121/SR.31, March 20, 1968, p. 34.

19. GAOR, 21st sess., Annexes, Agenda Item 33 (1966), p. 18. Official records do not indicate who was in which category, but presumably the twelve were mostly communist delegations that of course favored the step but cast a negative vote for tactical reasons having to do with the paragraph's sponsorship.

20. GAOR, 19th sess., Annex 21 (1964–65), p. 4.

21. Ibid., p. 61.

22. UN Doc. A/AC.121/SR.29, March 6, 1968, p. 25.

23. UN Doc. A/6652, May 3, 1967, p. 3.

24. A review of these practices is in *Repertory of Practice of United Nations Organs*, Vol. 2 (1955), pp. 113–31; Vol. 2 (1964), pp. 319–21.

25. *Repertory of Practice of United Nations Organs*, Vol. 2 (1955), p. 122.

26. Ibid., p. 419.

27. The Russians have suggested that the main draft provisions of these agreements be prepared by the Military Staff Committee. To emphasize the politico-military nature of such agreements, the Mexican representative has urged that they be drawn up by a political subcommittee of the Security Council, with assistance by the Military Staff Committee. UN Doc. A/AC.121/WG.B/SR.1, May 2, 1967, p. 13.

28. UN Security Council, *Official Records* (SCOR), 2d year, Special Suppl. 1 (1947), pp. 3, 14–17.

29. Ibid., p. iii.

30. *Repertory of Practice of United Nations Organs*, Vol. 2 (1955), p. 418.

31. A recent report on UNITAR programs, in existence and planned, is UN Doc. A/7263, Oct. 14, 1968. An expert panel of consultants to UNITAR has already urged this course on the executive director; see ibid., pp. 17–18.

32. United Nations Institute for Training and Research, *Manual of United Nations Technical Assistance*, UN Doc. UNITAR/EX/11, February 1968.

33. United Nations, *Organization of the Secretariat* (rev. ed., New York, 1966).

34. L. M. K. Skern, *Military Staffing at UN Headquarters for Peace-Keeping Operations: A Proposal*, IPKO Monograph 3 (Paris: International Information Center on Peace-Keeping Operations, 1967), p. 6.

35. Even halfway suggestions for part internationalized, part national forces are unlikely to be realized in the foreseeable future. One such recent proposal has been for a 2,000-man standing corps controlled exclusively by the secretary-general, which "could be rushed to the scene of trouble and keep order until the Secretary General has had an opportunity to select the earmarked contingents and get them on the spot" (Commission to Study the Organization of Peace, *New Dimensions for the United Nations: The Problems of the Next Decade*, Seventeenth Report . . . [New York, 1966], p. 33).

36. Clarity will also make somewhat easier the job of unofficial observers who try to decipher precisely what it is that standbys are really doing. As an example of how misleading the present state of affairs is, even to those close to UN activities, consider the factual errors in the recent expert panel study, United Nations Association of the United States of America, National Policy Panel on Multilateral Alternatives to Unilateral Intervention, *Controlling Conflicts in the 1970's* (UNA-USA, 1969). The panel assumes that its proposal for "20,000 to 25,000 men on standby" represents "a doubling of the presently available units" numbering 11,000 from ten member countries (pp. 42, 38). Aside from certain internal inconsistencies in the report's use of the terms "standby" and "earmarked," the facts on present capabilities are plainly incorrect. There are not, and have never been, anywhere near 11,000 soldiers on advance call for the UN in any significant sense of the word "available." Numerous other examples of similar misinformation could be cited.

37. See Chapter 5. The two systems are not entirely alike, however, in that the Norwegians use volunteers for both phases.

38. Prime Minister Sato and other government spokesmen in recent years have disavowed any intention of even considering the possibility of offering Japanese soldiers for peacekeeping. See, for instance, *New York Times*, Aug. 7, 1968; and New York *Herald Tribune* (International), Dec. 19, 1967. The constitutional arguments turn on peacekeeping's noncoercive and impartial character, which are said to distinguish it from war-related activities that are universally admitted to be proscribed by the constitution. Shigeru Kozai, "Japanese Participation in United Nations Forces: Possibilities and Limitations," *IPKO Documentation*, No. 34 (February 1968); also Philip W. Quigg, "Japan in Neutral," *Foreign Affairs*, Vol. 44 (January 1967), p. 253.

39. See the statement of the Japanese representative in the Committee of Thirty-three, UN Doc. A/AC.121/SR.33, March 29, 1968, p. 55.

40. *Washington Post*, June 14, 1969.

41. *The Economist* (Great Britain), March 5, 1966.

42. The U.S. language was indirect: after noting that both Washington and London had "indicated a willingness" to continue giving logistical assistance, a U.S. memoran-

dum added that "others, particularly the permanent members of the Security Council, might indicate their willingness to supply logistic support for future operations" (UN Doc. A/AC.121/15, May 21, 1968).

43. An excellent analysis of the level and rationale of military aid during the 1960s is Harry J. Shaw, "The Military Assistance Program: A Study of Interdepartmental Relationships and Influences" (Ph.D. thesis, University of Virginia, 1967), Chaps. 3–5.

44. In country programs for fiscal 1969, 85 percent of the requested authorization of $420 million was intended for the five so-called forward defense countries: Taiwan, South Korea, Greece, Turkey, and Iran; approximately 5 percent apiece was scheduled for the entire African and Latin American regions. It was spread thin: twenty-five countries receive equipment and training; twenty-three others receive training only. Along with Iran, though at much lower levels, other potential peacekeepers that are prime recipients are countries like Brazil, Argentina, and Ethiopia. *Foreign Assistance and Related Agencies Appropriations for 1969*, Hearings before a Subcommittee of the House Committee on Appropriations, 90 Cong. 2 sess. (1968), Pt. 1, pp. 421, 440–47.

45. See Alistair Buchan, "Commonwealth Military Relations," in W. B. Hamilton and Kenneth Robinson (eds.), *A Decade of the Commonwealth, 1955–1964* (Duke University Press, 1966).

Index

Acheson, Dean, 20, 63–64, 121, 217
Acheson Plan. *See* Uniting for Peace Resolution
Administration of UN peacekeeping, 34, 72, 75, 198–210, 213, 241, 247. *See also* Secretariat; Secretary-general
African states, 15, 84, 237
Aiken, Frank, 157, 159–61
Air force units, standby, 110, 124, 137, 146
Albania, 56
Antilles (Netherlands), 146
Arbitration, League of Nations efforts in, 59
Argentina, 162
Armed forces: Austria, 151–52; Canada, 133–37; Commonwealth proposal, 167; Great Britain, 168–69; India, 161–62; Ireland, 158–59; Netherlands, 144–48; New Zealand, 155; United States, 170–71, 175. *See also* Military service
Armed forces, international, 13–14, 42, 84, 232; Nordic program, 98–105, 108–10, 116–24; for peacekeeping, 4–5, 28, 33, 35–36, 55, 61, 172, 177; in Saar plebiscite, 45, 50; transit rights for, 48, 58. *See also* Infantry; Standby forces
Armed force, UN, 1, 58–62, 200–01, 213; Guard proposal, 74–75, 215–16; performance standards, 251, 253–54; proposed call-up arrangements, 251–53; Soviet position on, 60, 74–75, 84, 185, 215, 220, 235–39, 242; U.S. position on, 60–61, 75–76, 84, 177–79, 215, 232. *See also* Charter, UN: Article 43
Article 43. *See* UN Special Committee on Peacekeeping Operations; Military Staff Committee
Assessment for peacekeeping, 160, 162, 227–28
Attlee, Clement, 167
Australia, 71, 124, 191n
Austria: admission to UN, 150, 218–19; as middle power, 88; peacekeeping role (League of Nations), 48; peacekeeping role (UN), 52–53, 90, 92, 123–24, 130, 149–54,

257; standby offer, 33; training for peacekeeping, 128; use of volunteers, 254
Authority issues in peacekeeping, 37, 192–93, 207–09, 230–31, 235–37, 247. *See also under* General Assembly; Security Council
Avenol, Joseph, 55

Belgium, 25, 45–46, 70
Bellers, John, 40
Beneš, Eduard, 89
Bernadotte, Folke, 70, 73
Bidault, Georges, 77
Big Five, 1, 5–6, 58, 61, 215, 239
Big Four, 14, 150, 195, 244n, 257
Bourgeois, Léon, 46, 59
Brazil, 34, 130, 156–57, 162–64, 253
Brind, J., 49, 51, 53–55
Bulgaria, 56, 236
Bunche, Ralph, 73, 200–02, 213
Burma, 64
Burns, E. L. M., 138

Call-up system for UN forces, 61, 251–55
Cambodia, 77
Canada: on Committee of 33, 191n, 195–96, 241; and Cyprus mission, 124, 158; interest in IPKO, 212; in Korean mission, 27; as middle power, 86–92; participation in UN peacekeeping, 25–26, 99, 130–44, 266–68; peacekeeping proposals, 192–93, 196, 209, 211, 223; preparedness program, 11, 33, 52, 129, 147, 173, 253; as source of peacekeeping information, 149, 154; training for peacekeeping, 128, 134–35, 138, 142; in UNEF, 47. *See also* Ottawa conference; Pearson, Lester
Caradon, Hugh M. F., 169
Cease-fires, UN monitoring of, 17–18, 67
Charter, UN, 1–2, 40, 87–90, 139, 162, 181; Article 19, 140–41, 156, 160, 176, 191, 193, 217, 223, 250 (*see also* Financing UN peacekeeping); Article 43, 58–63, 74, 83, 98, 120–21, 147, 194, 217, 232–51, 255–59; Article 47, 58 (*see also* Military Staff Committee);